Regulating Women

Regulating Women

Policymaking and Practice in the UK

Sarah Cooper

ROWMAN & LITTLEFIELD
INTERNATIONAL
London • New York

Published by Rowman & Littlefield International, Ltd.
Unit A, Whitacre Mews, 26-34 Stannary Street, London SE11 4AB
www.rowmaninternational.com

Rowman & Littlefield International, Ltd. is an affiliate of Rowman & Littlefield
4501 Forbes Boulevard, Suite 200, Lanham, Maryland 20706, USA
With additional offices in Boulder, New York, Toronto (Canada), and London (UK)
www.rowman.com

British Library Cataloguing in Publication Information Available
A catalogue record for this book is available from the British Library

ISBN: HB 978-1-78348-184-2
ISBN: PB 978-1-78348-185-9

Library of Congress Cataloging-in-Publication Data

Names: Cooper, Sarah Geraldine Louise, author.
Title: Regulating women : policymaking and practice in the UK / Sarah Cooper.
Description: London ; New York : Rowman & Littlefield International, [2016] |
Includes bibliographical references and index.
Identifiers: LCCN 2015033053| ISBN 9781783481842 (cloth : alk. paper) | ISBN
9781783481859 (pbk.) | ISBN 9781783481866 (electronic)
Subjects: LCSH: Women--Government policy--Great Britain. | Women's
rights--Great Britain. | Women--Great Britain--Social conditions.
Classification: LCC HQ1236.5.G7 C66 2016 | DDC 305.420941--dc23 LC record available at http://
lccn.loc.gov/2015033053

Printed in the United States of America

Contents

Acknowledgements

This book is the product of a series of research ideas that have been encouraged by several important people. Undeniably my original interest to produce such a project was sparked by my PhD thesis, and I must express my gratitude to my supervisor Claire Dunlop for her support and guidance throughout those years. Thanks are also due to Andrew Massey, Dorte Martinsen, Claudio Radaelli, Karen Johnston and Fiona Mackay for their feedback along the way. In addition, an early version of this project was presented at the IPSA 23rd World Congress of Political Science, and I appreciate the comments received on my work at that event.

I have also been very fortunate to begin my academic career with incredibly supportive peers and, in particular, I must thank Helen Turton, Helena Cook and Owen Thomas for acting as my sounding boards over many cups of coffee. My colleagues, along with fantastic friends and family, have really helped this project come to fruition. In that vein, credit similarly needs to be afforded to Anna Reeve at Rowman & Littlefield International, whose enthusiasm for the book has been encouraging from the outset.

Finally, this project went beyond my work life, becoming a labour of love, and I feel compelled to note that it was in many ways inspired and increasingly driven by the strong women in my life, who provide me with support, guidance and friendship. Although not explicitly gendered in its approach, I hope this goes some way towards strengthening the understanding of why issues with an inequitable burden upon us are regulated in the manner evidenced in the UK. What became increasingly clear during the course of writing this account is that these matters are not limited to the most extreme, and sometimes harrowing of circumstances, but can also affect what we sometimes perceive as the mundane aspect of our everyday lives, and thus are topics of incredible importance that we all have a responsibility to engage with.

List of Abbreviations

APT	Act to Prevent Trafficking
BPAS	British Pregnancy Advisory Service
CARE	Christian Action Research and Education
CPS	Crown Prosecution Service
DoH	Department of Health
ECHR	European Convention on Human Rights
ECtHR	European Court of Human Rights
EMA	early medical abortion
EU	European Union
GP	General Practitioner(s)
HFEA	Human Fertilisation and Embryology Act
HoC	House of Commons
HoL	House of Lords
IPCC	Independent Police Complaints Commission
ISP	internet service provider
LGBT	Lesbian, gay, bisexual and transgender
MoJ	Ministry of Justice

MP	Member of Parliament
NGO	non-governmental organization
NHS	National Health Service
NI	new institutionalism
NIMBY	'not in my backyard'
ONS	Office for National Statistics
PM	Prime Minister
PMB	private members' bill
RCOG	Royal College of Obstetrics and Gynecology
SLB	street-level bureaucrat
SPUC	Society for the Protection of Unborn Children
STD	sexually transmitted disease
UK	United Kingdom
UN	United Nations
WHO	World Health Organization

Chapter One

Analysing the Status of Women in UK Policymaking: How Do Institutions Matter?

Aspects of female conduct in the United Kingdom (UK) oscillate between the legal and the illegal across an array of matters. A woman will commit an offence if she solicits sex on the street, for example, yet can offer escort services from her own home. Abortion is a treatment offered on the National Health Service (NHS), but a potential patient is deemed a criminal in her request for a termination until two doctors state otherwise. In a further instance, the law bans female porn stars from producing certain material that may inflict harm or threaten life, yet excluded from that list are a range of gender-biased and arguably dangerous subordinate acts (Burnett 2014). Repeatedly butting heads with the popular assertion centered on the empowerment and forwarding of the gender, therefore, in which claims of smashing through the 'glass ceiling' are audible, it glumly appears that the mutual thread that runs throughout decision making in female-dominated issues is the incessant balancing act faced by policymakers between regulation that indicts, and regulation that protects. A continual dance between the labels of 'criminal' and 'victim' thus appears to be performed in the overlapping domains, with little regard given to how these fields intersect. True, previous work has attempted to address such inconsistencies, and feminist scholars in particular have long attributed these arbitrary distinctions over good or bad conduct to a Madonna/whore duality; a binary that is largely predicated on biblical recantations of Mary, the eternal virgin who allows for honourable reproduction, and the contrasting Eve, the inventor of dangerous female sexuality (Tumanov 2011). Certainly not a new construct, this simple two-fold distinction of women's behaviour has since become prevalent in the field of psychology and occupied centre stage in Freud's infamous complex in which men afflicted by the syndrome perceive women to be either saintly or debased (Hartmann 2009). Adopting a pessimistic view of the erotic life of civilized people, he claimed that male impotence, as stemming from a neurotic fixation, resulted in the splitting of the tender and sensual dimensions of sexuality along these dimensions of stereotypical female imagery (Hartmann 2009). The worrying encroachment of the dichotomy into the operation of the criminal justice system is covered copiously by Feinman (1994), and discussed further in terms of 'fair and virginal' women, and 'dark and sensual' evil women, by McDermott and Blackstone (2002). Although undoubtedly this bi-fold typology has a discernible role in how issues of an inequitable level of female bias are perceived, either consciously or unconsciously at both the formal and systemic level of the political system, it is suggested that this dual categorization alone fails to satisfactorily explain the reasons why these determinations are made by policymakers irrespective of the commonalities that may lie between the issues.

As a result, a myriad of inconsistent and conflicting policy positions exist in the UK in regard to the aggregate regulation of women. Rape legislation, for example, whether unwittingly or not, places a significant burden of responsibility on the woman to prove a criminal act has taken place, yet once this has been approved legal recognition, and a guilty verdict delivered, no explicit access to abortion on these grounds alone is recognized in statute. Additional examples go beyond this black letter of the law and include more subtle competing stances, such as the recourse to appropriate forms of justice for the prostitute who has been violently attacked, herself a criminal. Although it is appreciated that the very observation of stereotypical images of women in varying roles is not particularly groundbreaking or especially shocking, the seemingly isolated creation of policy across these domains creates an important point of interest. Initially spurred on by this inherent contradiction and perceived absence of a joined-up approach, therefore, the necessity of further research into the matters of an inequitable level of female bias becomes pressing. Granted, authors have previously addressed a range of feminist policies from a comparative perspective, both at the global level (Mazur 2002) and in a British context (Lovenduski and Randall 1993), but these have sought to inquire into gender-based inequalities, explicitly engaging with patriarchal values, as opposed to affording primacy to the contradictory status of the woman across disparate fields. This is to some extent understandable, as each issue grouped under this title of 'women' invites a very specific collection of actors to assume a key position at the policymaking table, from the medical profession in abortion, police force in terms of rape, and the media in regard to pornography, thereby suggesting that the corresponding policy should be logically studied in isolation. In this sense, 'women's issues' is perceived by many to be a misleading title that requires substantial unpacking, and can be more fruitfully divided along alternative lines. Even typologies such as Htun and Weldon's (2010) distinction between matters that improve the status of women, or those that challenge religious doctrine or major cultural groups, however, thereby separating gender-based violence and reproductive matters, are not entirely helpful in this respect, as they still overlook the problematic nature of disjointed regulation and arguably contribute to this oversight. In this sense, it is with the ambitions of Harrison (1989) several decades earlier, and her account of women's issues in the United States, in which she distinctively stipulates that the study takes policymaking on all women as its core subject matter, that this endeavour garners much inspiration.

When analysing the management of the issues that fall within this umbrella term, however, it appears short sighted to focus attention solely upon the aggregate consequences of personal utilitarianism (Bentham 2005) and moral individualism (Hobbes and MacPherson 1982), thereby excluding any causal exogenous influences. Granted, figureheads throughout history are considered monumental in the regulation of specific issues, such as Lord David Steel in the 1967 Abortion Act, and Prime Minister David Cameron's recent tough line on pornography, but these actions are not conducted in a moral or political vacuum. Rather the policymaking process is unquestionably shaped by a number of structural constraints that shroud the individual agent, from religious values to conventions in lawmaking, from the desire to succeed in an organization, to the want to fit in with work colleagues, and thus regulation must logically be shaped in varying degrees by these wider forces. Indeed, in a similar vein to the blinkered approach to women's issues uncovered above, studies that focus solely on the individual have often been subject to the criticism of being 'undersocialized' (Lowndes and Roberts 2013, 40) and obscure much of the complexity of the manner in which people, regardless of gender, are governed across the globe. Thus outcomes in this field of women's issues are much more likely to be attributed to a wider shaping of collective behaviour through organizational structures, and rules of appropriate behaviour, perpetuated by a range of formal and informal bodies (March and Olsen 1984), than a single-level operation on the part of a number of lone agents. To move beyond the emotive examples listed above, therefore, the constraints on a holistic approach to the regulation of women in the UK requires a solid theoretical framework, and it is consequently towards the rules, practices and narratives (Lowndes and Roberts 2013) deeply embedded in an array of institutions that collectively shape the actions of agents that this project turns.

In the course of this book, a series of inquiries into the regulation of abortion, prostitution, rape and pornography in the UK will be undertaken. Performed in a comparative manner, through the lenses of historical, rational choice, normative and discursive institutionalism respectively, it is intended that the culmination of these studies will uncover the structural constraints that shape these enduring stereotypes and ensuing contradictions, and hinder an integrated approach to the regulation of women. To begin such an undertaking, however, this introductory chapter first outlines the existing scholarship in the field of new institutionalism (NI) studies, charting the chronological development of the literature from its traditional normative roots to the contemporary range of multi-dimensional conceptualizations we now recognize. Although disposing of alternative theoretical frames in favour of the rich causal insight proffered by NI, the recent converge of its multiple strands, posited as a significant benefit to this empirical study, is still a bone of contention among scholars and is a critique that is addressed in the second sub-section. Acknowledging the common core at the heart of NI that permits their multiple and overlapping use, however, the final section tackles the methodology, and operationalizes the collective use of the four selected strains of NI. The cumulative effect of these disparate policy fields undeniably has harmful consequences not only for the woman that straddles one or more of these policy domains, but for women in the UK more generally, and the lessons that can be drawn from uncovering these institutional constraints is a worthy pursuit.

1.1. INSTITUTIONAL LEGACIES AND POLICYMAKING

The organization of political life matters (March and Olsen 1984), this much we have heard contended across a vast array of literature and in multiple different formulations, and it is difficult to now rebut the contention that understandings of governance across a variety of matters are deeply enriched by an analytical focus on institutions. Attempts have spanned early political philosophers' endeavours to capture the success of institutions in governing the masses (see Aristotle 1996, as quoted in Peters 2011), through March and Olsen's (1984) refocusing of political science on older concerns with institutions in the wake of behaviouralism, up to modern debate pitting suggestions of a fragmentation of the theory (e.g., Crouch 2005) against claims of a convergence and consolidation of a common core of concepts (e.g., Lowndes and Roberts 2013). Across these theoretical periods, the role of institutions has undeniably fluctuated in popularity, only really assuming the heart of analysis from the 1980s onwards, and still with some critics to this day. The path to such prominence for the theory was therefore not without its obstacles, and significant challenges to its utility have been mounted across the ages, the most notable emanating from the behavioural revolution in the 1950s. When reviewing the contemporary scholarly work on NI, however, the varying schools of thought that have set up camp under the umbrella of 'new institutionalism' demonstrate a valuable theoretical field, with new and exciting formulations constantly added to its repertoire. That said, this ongoing proliferation is not immune from critique, and alarm bells have been sounded by other scholars of the risk of concept stretching (Pierson 2000) that has come to characterize the term 'institution', and its continued theoretical utility in the context of contemporary trends of an increasingly decentralised state has been questioned (Ingram and Clay 2000). Strongly asserting that a return to a position of methodological individualism (Elster 1982) is far from satisfactory, however, it is submitted that NI boasts an innovative academic field that is in fact rejuvenated by its new and expanding variants, such as the recently added feminist institutionalism (Krook and Mackay 2011). In particular, the evolution of the literature to the current state of convergence and consolidation embodied in the so-called third phase institutionalism, and the important appreciation of boundary-spanning institutional constraints (Lowndes and Roberts 2013, 40), provides an advantageous and appropriate setting for this project.

Having largely been replaced by the behavioural movement in the mid-twentieth century, old institutionalism failed to offer much more than an empirical and descriptive account of such bodies, and largely evaded any causal hypotheses. Indeed, although NI has now come to occupy a vast array of political science literature, the theory around this class of actor has not always been so helpful or indeed fashionable (March and Olsen 1984). Much of what was instead written in early works could be classified as atheoretical, largely concerned with the normative values (Peters 2011, 3) of a valuable society, such as the radically egalitarian institutions of an ideal world that were the key theme of Aristotle's work (Kraut 2002), or the need for balance in political structures in Montesquieu's (1989). Even recantations from the early twentieth century, anchored as they were within the study of history, retained such narrative, and political science was, for the most part, happy with this approach, perceiving no great need to challenge for further analytical richness. Prior to the 1950s, therefore, studies of this nature easily assumed a dominant role in political inquiry, avoiding any form of sustained criticism (Lowndes 2002). As time went by, however, the narrative hold on the field, and emotive stipulations of what constituted a 'good' institution, could not fully mitigate the absence of the sorts of theoretical aspirations and motivations now synonymous with social sciences (Peters 2011). With the study of political science radically transformed by the behaviourial revolution of the mid-twentieth century, therefore, an explicit concern for theory development arose (Peters 2011, 12), and the observations housed within the old institutional approach failed to provide a causal account of how these governing bodies could be of consequence in political life. Certainly, one-dimensional accounts of various bodies, attempting little explanation as to the mechanisms for creating and running a political system, were no longer considered robust, and the status of this underdeveloped scholarship was

usurped by detailed empirical investigations into who really governs in different contexts, and a focus upon individualistic assumptions arose (Eulau
1963). Moving into the 1970s, this methodological approach became the
focus of concern for political scientists, and the rational calculation of personal utility dominated the analysis of autonomous individuals, creating their
series of preferences exogenous to the political system (Riker and Ordeshook
1973).

Importantly, however, this did not spell the end for the study of institutions, and as sophisticated and nuanced as these individualistic theories became, the shadow cast by institutions upon the political arena could not be
readily dispelled. It was thus with much warmth and clamour that March and
Olsen's statement that 'organizations of political life makes a difference'
(1984) was met in the 1980s, and the updated agenda quickly attracted an
abundance of followers and theoretical activists. Looking to reignite the line
of inquiry with deep explanations on how institutions actually matter in
political organization, and learning from past mistakes, the principle that
both formal and informal interactions should be incorporated was enthusias-
tically extolled. Although heavily criticized as providing limited theoretical
insight, and failing to answer the pertinent question of 'how', the sentiments
of even traditional institutionalism that a number of seemingly insignificant
details can have a pervasive impact on the actions of institutions, and thereby
the individuals within them, found truth and causal reasoning in this new
endeavour (Peters 1996). Furthermore, these innovative strands termed NI
expanded their perception of institutions, taking into account both formal and
informal bodies, and stating that the strategies and goals of actors in the
policy process could be shaped by a spectrum of beliefs, paradigms, codes,
culture and knowledge embedded in institutions (March and Olsen 1984). In
response came various strains that added to this institutionalist turn in the
literature (Jessop 2000), favouring a deductive approach, tackling head-on
the proto-theoretical criticism levied at old institutionalism, and taking as
their starting point conceptual propositions about the way institutions work
(Lowndes 2002).

By 1996, a tidal wave of researchers had set up camp under the broad
heading, and the favour of the approach was well and truly entrenched in
political science literature. Sociologists, concerned primarily with a 'logic of
appropriateness', brought insights around the legitimization of roles within
originations (DiMaggio and Powell 1991), whereas historians advocated the
notion of 'path dependency' (Krasner 1988). The study of economics, on the
other hand, retained an individualistic basis, but sought to infer how these
agent-centric incentives operated within a wider institutional context (Tsebelis 1990). There was also further cross-pollination with the intuitionalist turn
infiltrating further spheres of political science research, such as Europeanization. Indeed, Scharpf's criticism of supranational integration theory as limit-

ed in its attention to the impact of decision-making rules in the process coincided with the publication of March and Olsen's (1984) seminal work, and firmly brought institutions back into the academic field. Inevitably running alongside this ever-expanding literature, however, was the strengthening of the critique of concept stretching (Satori 1970); a pitfall common of an array of theoretical approaches, it was claimed that with expansion came dilution of the term. Although the definition of an institution should not be treated lightly, therefore, and a just rationale underpinning the identification of such will feature in the succeeding methodological section, the red flags around analytical fuzziness held by the likes of Pierson (2011, 21) are not enough to discourage the important insights that can be uncovered through such innovations. Holding back these frontiers, and advocating a return to methodological individualism in this sense, would not be helpful.

Turning to the utility of the approach to the study at hand, therefore, and already mindful of the idea that a process of learning can arise from the study of institutionalisms generally, it again must be noted that this is not often done in the form of comparative empirical analysis in a specific policy field such as women's issues. Consequently, initially inspired by this concern around the contradictory status of women in public policy unveiled above, and the gap around empirical investigation into women being treated in different manners, this project was theoretically 'spurred on' by two key developments in NI in recent years. The first can arguably been seen as an ongoing response to the demands set by seminal leaders of the approach Hall and Taylor (1996), who, highlighting the infancy of the field, and characterizing the research as 'burgeoning', invited further steps in the research agenda. Thus enticing new and innovative formulations, NI itself has multiplied in its strains, welcoming developments such as the appreciation for policy change housed in the discursive approach (Schmidt 2000, 2008, 2010) and, more recently, a feminist branch positing gender itself as an institution and concerning itself with the 'mobilisation of masculine bias' (Krook and Mackay 2011). Adding to the conceptual strains originally suggested by March and Olsen (1984) is certainly not a new action, therefore, but the work carried out by this latter example helpfully summarizes a fruitful turn in the literature. By their own admission, the authors draw together the traditional approaches to NI and apply a gendered lens to analysis of contemporary scholarship in the field, the result of which is to highlight an increasing trend towards investigating women as key actors in the political process, and a growing preponderance to study the interplay between gender and the working of political institutions. Acting on the assumption that there is an embedded idea of neutrality in institutions that make it difficult for women to make claims of bias, feminist institutionalism sees constructions of masculinity and femininity as the 'logic' of the institution (Krook and Mackay 2011). In the very simplest of interpretations, the approach is concerned with gender inequality, and how the presence of women in politics may, or may not, affect policy outcomes to benefit other women.

Certainly a welcome addition to the literature, and a development from which this study has drawn much inspiration, it is contended that to further highlight the need for this to continue, however, the role of key institutions broadly, regardless of gender, need first to be applied to core 'women's issues' in a more sustained manner. This will provide a rigorous espousal of how regulation of these policy domains is actually constructed in the real world, and will address the question of whether the traditional arms of NI are indeed insufficient in explaining this. To reiterate an aforementioned point, the project seeks to provide a rich empirical analysis of the image of women in different settings. As feminist studies in political science have advanced, undeniably a more complex understanding of women has emerged, with institutionalized advantages and disadvantages highlighted, and exclusionary practices brought to the fore, all of which are worthy and fruitful endeavors. Yet again, however, it must be stressed that this is not the sole preoccupation of this piece of work, and gender, in this sense, is not used as an analytical category; rather it is the subject of investigation, and it is here that the project diverges from feminist scholars. Although 'to level the playing field' is necessary, this broad-stroke approach does not suffice for this piece of work, and it is instead the need to address the micro-level dichotomies mentioned above that drives the research conducted in the subsequent chapters.

Marking the second notable theoretical development of impetus to this project, the convergence of NI around a common core has been identified by leading texts in the field. Peters (2011), for example, deliberates the various approaches, and their subtle facets, throughout the course of his copious book, finally arriving at the conclusion that there is indeed a sufficient core to justify consideration of these variants as one (184). Much more exacting, however, are the claims of Lowndes and Roberts (2013) that the living body of NI is now experiencing a process of assimilation around key concepts, a process to which they afford the title 'third phase'. By adopting a more holistic approach to rules, norms and practices, as advocated by the authors, an array of causal insights into the influence of institutions can be garnered across a disparate field of governance such as women's issues, and it is thus with this development that the theoretical framework of this project progresses.

Today, the innovative field of NI scholarship has come to represent a multi-faceted collection of claims, housing a proliferation of strains and variants, and diverging theoretical emphasis. It is, however, with inspiration from two key developments in this field—third phase institutionalism and the newly formed feminist institutionalism—that this project can bolster the future of these broad research agendas. Undoubtedly, both have significant merits for the study of women, but a key stepping-stone first requires attention. Before the empirical benefits of convergence extolled by third phase institutionalists can be fully supported, the necessity of a rigorous espousal of each variant within the same, broad policy setting, such as women's issues, is contended. Conversely, prior to engaging the gendered approach of Krook and Mackay (2011) in a study of women's issues generally, a comparative analysis without such a lens, taking full advantage of all the broad conceptualizations of institutions and structural forces provided by a multi-variant approach, is necessary. It is within this study, therefore, that four longstanding strains of NI will be engaged in a comparative manner. Despite this contemporary popularity of consolidating strains, however, it would be foolhardy to embark upon such a study without first positing a range of queries around its practical utility, and what can be gained from extrapolating a common core of NI. Indeed, to address the old adage, are we inappropriately comparing apples to oranges (e.g., Jackson 2010)? To this end, the succeeding sections will fully explore the comparative ambitions of the project.

1.2. ADDRESSING THE THEORETICAL CORE: COMPARING APPLES AND ORANGES?

A convoluted array of rules, practices and narratives are located within the analysis of political institutions (Lowndes and Roberts 2013). When drawing together an expansive field such as women's issues, that cover topics as broad as reproductive technologies, pornography and sexual assault, and that are frequently subject to division and typologies that try to break them down into palatable units of study, a broad conceptual framework is essential to tackle such a huge task. The popularity of third phase institutionalism (Lowndes and Roberts 2013) is mounting in this regard, and it is now plausibly contended that despite the proliferation of multiple strains, the assimilation of these variants provides a fruitful conceptual approach. With any fashionable trend, however, doubt must be raised as to whether an en vogue status is enough to drive on a project such as this, and its popularity should not be taken for granted. It is here, therefore, that this book looks to both borrow from these advances and bolster the work that has gone before. Prior to engaging this comparative approach, however, the variants of NI pertinent to this study need to be outlined, and it is suggested that both their similarities and differences, when assimilated under the umbrella terms of rules, practices and narratives (Lowndes and Roberts 2013) will provide a rich insight into the regulation of women. In this sense, comparing apples and oranges is a worthy endeavour in the study of fruit more generally.

According to Hall and Taylor (1996), the three traditional strains of NI comprise the historical, rational choice and sociological takes on the debate. Beginning with the simple notion that history matters, a notion of 'path dependency' (Krasner 1984) is said to guide an institution, strongly predicated on the choice that is made when the policy is first initiated (Skocpol 2002). Thus providing strict identifiable examples, such as government structures or legal institutions (Thelen and Steinmo 1992), they often perceive institutions to be somewhat of an intermediary between the state and actors (Peters 2011). Rational choice institutionalism, on the other hand, having its roots in economics and the individualistic traditions of the 1950s, retains the strong notion of utility-maximizing individuals, but places the assumption within the context of political institutions (Tsebelis 1990). As such, these bodies are the rules and incentives that establish the parameters of behaviour within them (Duquech 2001). Largely as a reaction to this overly formulistic approach, however, a concern for a cultural approach (Hall and Taylor 1996), hereinafter referred to as normative institutionalism, arose with a mission to assign importance to the role of values in complex collective relationship within institutions (Garnovetter 1985). Arriving from the sociological school of thought, a 'logic of appropriateness' (March and Olsen 2008) strongly underpins the actions of agents according to this strain, in which an array of cultural and sub-conscious factors can have a discernible impact on the individual. Finally, adding to Hall and Taylor's (1996) original list and the newest of all the selected strains, discursive institutionalism concerns itself with the role of ideas (Schmidt 2008) but, unlike previous schools of thought, it views such entities as forming an interactive process through dialogue, and following a 'logic of communication' from which policy change can be incited. On the surface, therefore, it may appear that a mismatched bunch of causal claims have been heaped together, and the cries of 'concept stretching' (Pierson 2000) again come into earshot. Indeed, such a conceptual approach does, at this stage, run the risk of drawing in attributions from many a far-reaching sphere under the broad domain of women's issues. Beyond the term 'institutionalism', however, these diverging formulations actually share at their core a series of commonalities that bond, and are beneficial to, a process of iterative comparison such as this.

When March and Olsen (1984, 1989) so helpfully shone light on the resurgence of institutionalism in political science studies, they were quick to refute that the term alone constituted a theory, and instead favoured the notion that it simply constituted the search for alternative ideas (1984, 747). Throughout their collating exercise, however, the core approach of observing a set of phenomena in regard to the casual position of institutions tied all of their references together. Although seemingly a very loose familiar bond, it is with this first step that this project is guided, and specifically the call from the authors for more rigorous empirical application of such conceptual work. Granted, this has been undertaken in a multitude of ways over the last three decades, but the marriage of aggregate variants of NI with a convoluted and multifaceted policy domain is limited. Helpfully, points of convergence across the traditional strains (Lowndes and Roberts 2013) are now far from taxing to locate, and although starting their life as separate entities (Hall and Taylor 1996), under separate branches of scholarship (Immergut 1998), the array of tenants of this approach have since arguably converged to the dominant conceptual approach we now acknowledge in three discernible ways. Huddled around the idea of institutions as both formal and informal, and stable and dynamic, the strains in varying degrees address power without fear of critiquing it. Furthermore, the variants take a broad approach that observes convoluted institutions that can be a determining factor in policy outcomes, but also can be contingent on the action of agents. Finally, the enduring debate of structure and agency clearly ties all the strains together, and demands deliberation of the respective freedom of individual actors (Lowndes and Roberts 2013, 44). This is not to say, however, that the images presented of the political are identical within these groupings; rather it is the synthesis that can be extracted across its major tenants that is commendable and allows for comparative analysis. Indeed, the drawing together of how institutions are of consequence under the overarching categories of rules, practices and narratives (Lowndes and Roberts 2013) will allow for an overview of the manner in which women are regulated in the UK in the concluding chapter.

Not only the sum of all their parts, however, the strength of these four strains also lies in their disparity. Drawing analogy with Etzioni's mixed scanning model of decision making (1967), in which the author details the benefit of both a broad-angle camera, that would cover all aspects of the sky, and a second one that would zoom in on details discovered by the first, the differences between the macro level and micro level of policy formulation demand sensitive approaches that can be offered by separate variants. Rational choice analyses institutions at the micro level, for example, but is concerned with the effect of institutions on macro-level political outcomes (Weingast 2002). Normative, on the other hand, concerns the links between micro and macro level (DiMaggio and Powell 1991), whereas discursive emphasizes change from within (Schmidt 2008, 2010). Thus appreciating that the policy domains grouped under women's issues will not all represent the same structured design, but rather will harbour unique idiosyncrasies ripe for research, the variation in focus in this manner is a welcomed addition to the conceptual framework. Take prostitution policy, for example. The legislative inertia that typifies this field is coupled with limited political discourse, suggesting a link between the work of the individual MP and the context of the legislature. In comparison, the management of rape in the UK appears to permit significant degrees of victim-blaming at the grassroots level. In robust institutional arrangements, therefore, historical, regulatory, normative and discursive arrangements will all work together to shape behaviour and can contribute to a collection of insights in a comparative field, but the real agenda for institutionalism is to better understand how these distinctive

modes of constraint interrelate in practice, and detailed application of a specific strain to a clear case study allows this direction to flourish. Thereby
addressing a potential criticism for this project in terms of the cumulative
effect of institutions, as opposed to their interrelated influence, it must be
asserted that this distinction is overly theoretical. The use of the strains in
tandem is more effectively engaged at the macro level of women's issues to
determine how the gender is governed, rather than shifting focus throughout
the course of the book to how abortion in isolation is regulated, or rape policy
alone implemented.

The analysis of how rules, practices and narratives (Lowndes and Roberts
2013) shape the governance of the four policy domains will only be of
significance, however, and allow for the drawing of lessons for practitioners,
if a rigorous and well-justified scheme is adhered to. The next sub-section
therefore details the methodological demands of the project, and outlines
three main components from which causal insights into the cumulative regulation of women can be drawn.

1.3. OPERATIONALIZING THE MULTI-VARIANT APPROACH

Acceptance of this multi-variant study is accompanied by a range of methodological demands, and despite the field's move towards a more synthesised
approach, the precise details of how this will be achieved need to be mapped.
Beginning at the individual policy domain, the application of a specific strain
of NI will address the stereotyping inherent in that field, suggesting the
institutional constraints that attribute to this position. This in turn will create
a body of rules, practices and narratives (Lowndes and Roberts 2013) that
foster apparent contradictions across women's issues, and from which important lessons for practitioners can be learned. Unpacking these requirements
here will allow for the creation of a blueprint to be followed throughout the
course of this book, and it is in this section that the application of specific
variants and the demands of data collection require consideration in turn.

Utilizing third phase institutionalism for a comparative analysis of wom-
en's issues poses two intertwined dilemmas. Not only does this approach
question how it will be achieved theoretically, as was the focus of the above
sub-section, but the empirical practicalities are also pressing. As has been
contended from the outset, the broad nature of these two aspects dictates that
they are both broken down into iterative stages, comprising single variants of
NI that are applied to individual policy domains. It is here, however, that it is
additionally suggested that if completed in a structured and focused manner,
it is the sum total of these findings that will create a valuable comparative
analysis of the regulation of women, in addition to avoiding criticism of
fragmentation and departmentalization. Indeed, the separate methodological

demands of each variant cannot be overlooked, and in fact engaging one strain after another, rather than in tandem, actually allows for these divergent techniques to flourish. The process of drawing out the commonalities between them is therefore excluded from this process, and is conducted only upon receiving the final output of institutional causation. The third phase of institutionalism compounded by Lowndes and Roberts (2013) vehemently encourages the observation of how these distinctive modes of constraint interrelate in practice (Lowndes and Roberts 2013, 50). It is contended, however, that this is not overlooked throughout the course of this book by applying an individual stain of NI in turn; rather each chapter is the first stage in a process, which will conclude how rules, practices and narratives (Lowndes and Roberts 2013) coincide to regulate women more generally in the conclusion. It is here, therefore, that the grouping of policy domains, and their subsequent study through a branch of NI, must be attended to.

First, the grouping of 'women's issues', referring not only to the matters of abortion, prostitution, rape and pornography, all of central concern in this book, but additionally more peripheral domains such as contraception and further health-based matters, incorporates hugely diverging actions and behaviour in the UK that serve to create novel problems requiring creative, and sometimes unique, regulatory and legal responses. It must therefore be considered that the subtleties and nuances across this sector are so vast in number and effect that a blanket approach will arguably not suffice, and full appreciation must be given to the fact that it is perhaps naive to question why such an elaborate web of rules and sanctions is weaved; a lack of uniformity within this broad communal heading could, in this sense, be seen as unsurprising and doubt raised as to whether stipulating sexual characteristics as a unifying theme is both appropriate and conceptually useful. The issue of climate change, for example, houses within it a host of different regulatory proposals and decisions, from the European Union's directive phasing out of incandescent lightbulbs, to the Kyoto Protocol's binding obligations to reduce emissions of carbon dioxide.[1] It would be foolhardy, and lack any form of critical eye, to suggest that these positions all symbolize the same reasoned calculation, or attract identical sanctions. To a discernible degree, however, the foundations of decision making remains constant and transparent throughout, with considerations of how exogenous interference with the environment can be halted, and better practice promoted, providing a framework for good governance (the United Nations [UN] Framework Convention on Climate Change, 2005, Article 2). Policy proposals are consequently viewed in the context of their ramification for this programme more generally, and it is important to view them in their totality. The same logic applies here, and assessment of how the whole woman is regulated is deemed a worthy pursuit in this regard. Difficulties around researching the status of the woman in particular, however, and the demand for sensitivity for the distinctive interplay between ranging variables, has certainly been cited previously in the literature (Mason 1986), and this critique looms even larger when the project in question, as in the case of this book, does not seek to explicitly engage a gendered methodology, but to alternatively explore the reasons for UK policymaking away from such a lens. Although readily assimilated thematically in feminist scholarship, therefore, when considered outside of this remit, the counterfactual is raised as to whether lines should be drawn along alternative distinguishing features such as matters of the criminal law in terms of rape and prostitution, or studies of healthcare administration in regard to abortion. Even this reasoned justification, however, fails to fully appease the inevitability with which these issues overlap and the nagging question of why actions that ostensibly look the same in terms of the potential risk posed to those involved, and the moral dilemmas that accompany them, such as the blend of money and sex in prostitution and pornography, can be viewed so differently in the eyes of the law. Thus, the inescapable fact that the issues covered in the course of the book carry an inequitable level of female bias is of significance, and explanation of the contrasting conclusions of prosecution and protection thus remains the initial rationale for the project's research intentions.

Furthermore, the use of case studies in research projects such as this is widely recognized and growing in confidence across a variety of disciplines and, in particular, in political science (Hartley 2004). The approach is best defined as an intensive study of a single unit with the aim to elucidate features of a chosen phenomenon and to generalize across a larger set of components (Gerring 2004). Indeed not only is the case study method intended to catch the complexity of a single case but, in addition, it can create a valuable platform upon which to make generalizations, and examples that have gone before have successfully provided the means to draw inferences for additional subject matter (Stake 1978). It is thus with inspiration from classic works such as Allison and Zelikow's study (1999) of the Cuban missile crisis that the method was selected in the course of this project, and a consideration of an additional facet that must be addressed at this stage is the parameters of the study set as the increasingly fragmented UK. This region-spanning approach was chosen for the specific reason that divergence in approaches to matters, spurred on by devolution, actually makes for interesting points of consideration, and this is exemplified by the example of Northern Ireland and abortion. Despite a history of continual change in legislative power in the country, moving from devolved back to Westminster rule and back again, some laws have staunchly retained their illegal status in the country, while others have not. In a similar vein, Scotland's newly acquired criminal powers open the door for an array of innovative takes on policy domains, in addition to matters that continue to be approached in the same manner as Westminster. Upon setting the parameters of the case studies, therefore, it is with the consideration of marrying variants with these units of study that the methodology must turn; each case study being informed by a typology and determined by the completion of process analysis.

Taking much inspiration from the work of North and comments that informal institutions are much more likely to be impervious to deliberate policies (North 1990), the aspect of female status under scrutiny in the UK was first categorized and housed under the umbrella term 'deliberate policy' and 'custom, tradition' respectively. In terms of abortion and prostitution, the aspect of feminine behaviour under the spotlight is criminal activity and labour rights respectively. In terms of rape and pornography, it is the notions of 'proper victim' and who needs protecting. Second to be addressed were specific moments or facets of the regulation of each issue that is of concern here, and addressing either institutional change or institutional continuity. In the case of abortion, therefore, it is the convention that appears continually extolled in the UK, both by parliament and the medical profession, that abortion is an offence that is under the spotlight. In contrast to the other fields, individual legislative action, such as private members' bills (PMBs), are scant in prostitution, thus begging the study of individual choice in this scenario. Driven substantially by contemporary attention in the media to the concept of proper victim, it is the organizational field of the police force that entices investigation in regard to rape. Finally, the innovative communication around pornography between David Cameron and his Conservative Party, and the mass media in turn, evidenced over his first term in office is the last field of interest.

Beneath the overarching deficiency of old institutionalism's inability to provide an explanation of how, the movement also displayed an over-reliance on formalism that was to the detriment of a full study of the features of politics (Peters 2011). Assuming institutions to be that which create patterned interactions that are predictable (Peters 2005, 18), and specifically that political institutions are about power, not just government (Held and Leftwitch 1984, 144, as quoted in Lowndes and Roberts 2013). Informal institutions become just as significant when identifying the variables that explain political life (Peters 2005). Certainly, political outcomes are best understood by studying the rules and practices that characterize institutions, and it must be noted at this juncture that core organizations, comprising the legal and criminal justice systems at a national and European level, and organs of the state, namely the government, parliament and the courts, will feature in varying degrees across all the chapters. Additional organizational contexts of particular pertinence to the specific issue in question, however, will also be incorporated and will include the medical profession in the case of abortion, civil society in reference to prostitution, the police force within rape policy and the mass media in the regulation of pornography.

Finally, attention must now be turned to how this comparative analysis within the domains and organisational cultures stipulated can be achieved through data collection. Qualitative methods have much to offer the study of emotive and ethically charged topics such as abortion, prostitution, rape and pornography, all of which, in varying degrees, straddle the lines between the criminal law, health and social policy. Not only do the issues occupy a fractious political position, both domestically and at the supranational level, but all additionally feature heavily in public consciousness and, as such, would not be readily amenable to statistical analysis that would favour the dichotomization of results. It is the objective of this book to provide an informed narrative of the treatment of women, something that can only be effectively achieved through rich and detailed case study analysis regardless of the fact that many factors blend into traditionally science-based disciplines. Certainly, even within healthcare research, a push has begun towards more qualitative methods of analysis (e.g., Lilford and Braunholtz 1996, Pope and Mays 2006). In particular, abortion remains deeply emotive, and socially and politically divisive, and strict numbers therefore have their limits (Kulczyski 2003). Although assuming a causal position for institutions from the outset, exactly why they are of importance is the drive at the heart of this study; to embark upon questions such as 'how big' or 'how many', would have been inappropriate. Although extolling its virtues, however, a series of methodological hurdles did arise in the gathering of qualitative data, the practicalities of which required significant attention. The gathering of empirical evidence thus adopted a broad approach to official documents and considered five principal outlets: parliamentary debates, UK and European Union (EU) jurisprudence, reports of public inquiries, UK-based opinion polls and media searches. These were collated both from archives and contemporary collations.

The book therefore takes four specific approaches to NI—historical institutionalism, rational choice institutionalism, normative institutionalism and discursive institutionalism—and commits to applying these to real-world instances in the form of the regulation of abortion, prostitution, rape and pornography respectively. As previously mentioned, the project is of both empirical and theoretical value for shedding light on the manner in which women are governed in the UK, and a core objective of the project will be the highlighting of similarities and overlap between the theoretical strains, thereby allowing a thorough espousal of how the combined impact of both formal and informal rules, and a range of actors in the political process, can impact upon the status of women in UK policymaking. Each case therefore suggests not an exhaustive list of all factors involved, but a plausible causal explanation of the situation that collectively sheds insight into how the woman, in her entirety, is regulated. In this sense, some moments in decision making, and the institutional account underpinning them, are interchangeable, and the logic of calculation derived from rational choice institutionalism, for example, could explain both the passage of amendments to the Abortion Act in 1967 and recent blocks on prostitution legislation. This is not regarded as a conceptual oversight in the course of this book, however, and at junctures where this occurs it is duly noted; rather, this is seen as providing further corroboration to the utility of adopting a multi-variant approach. Uncovering that the number of veto points constrains change in pieces of legislation infused with morality, for instance, demonstrates the likelihood of policy inertia across many domains of an inequitable level of female bias. This is not to say, therefore, that all women's issues are treated the same, but actually it unveils the need for policymakers to adopt a panorama when it comes to women's issues, to ensure that a joined-up approach is adopted. If both prostitution and rape, for example, exhibit policy inertia, when the two fields are conflated at the base level, and the prostitute is raped, the ability of the regulatory field to combat this situation will be tested. The pursuit of an explanation for this lack of a unified approach to the status of women in female-dominated issues goes beyond academic curiosity. Indeed, in acknowledgement of the potential harm caused by this situation, this account seeks to uncover a range of future lessons for practitioners.

1.4. STRUCTURE OF THE BOOK

It is unashamedly the underlying assumption of this project from the outset that a range of institutional constraints in the form of rules, practices and narratives foster one-dimensional assertions at the individual policy level, and contribute to a disparate collection of women's issues more generally. Learning how to tackle these deficiencies is a worthy endeavour, but importantly first requires a series of interrelated research activities that are applied to the domains of abortion, prostitution, rape and pornography in turn. Thus to address the empirical demands of the study, each of the succeeding chapters will open with an outline of the development of the policy field, tracing its origins at common law through early statutory recantations, and will be directly followed by a statement of the current legislative scheme. These important steps of stipulating the status of the woman in history and in contemporary practice acts as a clear and efficient referencing tool and discusses the arbitrary labelling of good or bad conduct. It must be noted at this point, however, that the protection of women's rights cannot automatically be assimilated with the removal of prohibition. Although undeniably the restriction of female activity can certainly serve to limit gender equality, it can also afford protection to those deemed vulnerable, and rather than focusing purely on decriminalization, it is additionally how these decisions on 'women's issues' are actually reached which becomes of seminal importance throughout this project. Thus marking an obvious and logical progression to the theoretical ambitions of the book, the subsequent sub-section will then address the prevalent debate that features in the domain between policy actors, and will analyse the situation through a stipulated lens of NI, identifying the institutional forces instrumental in shaping the contemporary policy form. Addressing the realities of this reasoning, a fourth endeavour in each chapter will explore the consequences and impact of these constraints on the everyday experiences of women across the three legal jurisdictions of the UK and will be contextualized by a fifth and final section that adopts a European perspective on the matter. Repeating these stages through each policy domain in turn, therefore, the case studies are as follows.

The first concerns the regulation of abortion and the degree of path dependency, and long-standing affiliation to the criminal law, extolled in this field. For over 40 years women living in the UK have been able to access terminations in situations in which their health is at risk; however, this is not an absolute right performed upon request, and fundamentally the termination of pregnancy remains illegal. The 1967 Abortion Act and Offences Against the Person Act 1861 instead run simultaneously and provide a fractious governing scheme for the procedure as both a medical treatment and criminal act. This overlapping legislation attracts much controversy, and curiously not just from the pro-life movement who opposed initial reform. The partial decriminalization of abortion represented an important development in women's healthcare and, by propelling the procedure into the field of health policy, pressure to constantly re-examine and update the provisions of the law is now exerted. In comparison to other areas of medicine, however, in which burgeoning techniques are welcomed in the pursuit of better healthcare, evidence-based policymaking is significantly curtailed in the field and a patient-centred approach is heavily limited by the law's refusal to depart from the criminal status of abortion. Through a process of backward mapping, the reality of medicalization in the 1960s, largely the product of structural legacies, has resulted in a stagnating regulatory field infused with medical hegemony, and the popular perception of the UK as the abortion capital of the EU is thus challenged.

Following on from this clinical field, chapter 3 addresses the rationality of policy inertia that typifies prostitution legislation in the UK. Although the issue has witnessed diverging amendments in alternative EU states, such as Germany's regulation of labour rights contrasted with Sweden's neo-abolitionist approach, the UK retains its basic principles against the provision and facilitation of sexual acts for money, and the concurrent Sexual Offences and Street Offences Acts have long housed warring stances on protection and prosecution. The incentive structure for parliamentarians legislating in this domain is heavily constrained both by the costly nature of morality politics generally, and by the dominant Victorian perception of the matter as one of social order and decency, rather than the recognition of individual damage evidenced in Northern Ireland's move to criminalizing the purchase of sex. Although displaying a similar dependency on history uncovered previously, therefore, the continued divide between acts in the legislation are arguably sustained by a 'logic of calculation' (March and Olsen 1984), a process that has only recently been challenged by the expanding recognition of the risks involved in street solicitation at the grassroots level—a development that suggests the possibility of a paradigm shift. Considered in the context of the benefits garnered from increased abolitionist measures across Europe in regard to sex trafficking, however, the potential for policy change across England and Wales, and Scotland, nevertheless, remains limited at present due to the associated problems with the typology.

The matter of rape, and the demand for a proper victim, next falls under investigation. Far from a harmonious and evolutionary process, the legislative field on the matter has been shaped by continuous debate around the notions of consent. Despite contemporary regulation now stipulating the burden of proof as falling upon the defendant, a process of attribution of responsibility to the claimant remains prevalent. Focusing on the role of norms and values, therefore, a 'logic of appropriateness' (March and Olsen 2008) can be identified in the range of organizational cultures that shapes the attitude and responses of its individual agents. Of most concern among this revelation is the police force, in which it is suggested that a predetermined set of qualities for a credible victim, driven by a 'cop culture' predicated on an insular, partriarchial brotherhood, significantly impact on the rate at which reported sexual assaults are later recorded as crimes worthy of further investigation. Not only troubling for victims at the point of contact with this street-level bureaucrat (SLB), this further constrains the coming forward of women who have experienced such assault. Challenging the extent to which this body can shoulder the responsibility of creating this category of contestable crime, however, is the legislative disparity that is reflected from a European wide perspective, demanding diverging levels of proof from alleged victims. Indeed, an array of member states fail to reach UN minimum standards of regulation, adding further fuel to the fire that it is instead poorly defined legislative intentions that permit such behaviour at the implementation stage.

The fourth and final case study proffers a more optimistic take on the possibility of policy change and concerns the regulation of pornography in light of burgeoning open debate. Up until fairly recently, the regulation of such material largely revolved around obscenity legislation, and reflected the rate of liberalization in the UK. The last decade, however, has witnessed the introduction of tighter measures around hardcore material, particularly in regard to the Internet. Far from the product of anti-porn radical feminists, however, the success of these changes can be attributed to a long-standing agenda centred on child protection forwarded by David Cameron from his time as leader of the party, to his current position as prime minister. Utilizing the process of coordinative and communicative discourse, as exemplified in the debates surrounding the death of Baby P, and later applied to the cases of April Jones and Tia Sharp, the single agent has extended these cognitive ideas through a 'logic of communication' (Schmidt 2008) and garnered support for the tightening controls to protect this vulnerable grouping. Thereby suggesting a blueprint for future challenge to this regulatory field, and indeed neighbouring domains, it is deliberated if the marriage of violent crime statistics with pornography could incite legislative amendments in regard to the protection of women more generally. This potential for change, however, is heavily shaped by values concerning freedom of speech, and must inevitably be considered in the context of the comparatively liberal approach of neighbouring EU states, and deliberations of supranational law around the safeguarding of rights and the open Internet.

Drawing together these rules, practices and narratives, the concluding chapter will address the consequences of disaggregate policymaking across women's issues. Revisiting the stereotypes asserted by each policy domain, the combined institutional constraints on an integrated approach to women's issues are asserted and the damaging impact this can have on those that fall between the gaps explored. It is at this point, however, that additional consideration will be afforded to a key counterfactual addressed in each individual study: How do we know that institutions matter? Might people have acted in that way even if the rules weren't there (Przewoski 2004)? The book comes to close with a consideration of the lessons that can be drawn from these insights for practitioners in the field, and three improvements to policymaking around joined-up governance, evidence-based policymaking and descriptive representation suggested. Filling an apparent hole in the surrounding literature, the book slowly reveals the blinkered fashion in which issues sharing the common denomination of female effect are regulated. Varying degrees of institutional stronghold, manifesting from a range of sources and prescribing a series of 'logics' to which their agents pledge, are uncovered through utilizing the recent convergence in NI studies. As a result, the harmful stereotyping of the subjects in individual matters, in which labels such as 'criminal' and 'victim' are replete, are further to the detriment of the woman in her totality, and problems quickly arise when she dares to straddle two policy fields. Uncovering this problematic approach to abortion, prostitution, rape and pornography in the UK therefore, lacking as it does a unified approach, suggests the need or further study in regard to the gendered construction of female roles.

NOTE

1. The EU ban on incandescent lightbulbs was introduced via Directive 2005/32/EC of the European parliament, also referred to as the Ecodesign Directive ; the Kyoto Protocol imple-

ments the United Nations' 1992 Framework Convention on Climate Change and was committed to by the UK in 1995.

Chapter Two

Hanging on to the Old: Path Dependency in UK Abortion Regulation

Women living in the UK are potentially able to access medical abortions in situations in which their health is considered to be at risk; however, this is not an absolute right performed upon request and is only available in limited circumstances. The illegal status of the procedure can instead be traced back at least as far as the eighteenth century under the jurisdiction of the Royal Courts, and the criminality of the procedure has been enshrined at common law since Lord Ellenborough's Act of 1803. Current prohibition is by virtue of the Offences Against the Person Act 1861, a statute that continues to prescribe sanctions for the unlawful procurement and administration of abortion, and under which prosecutions are still sought to this day. The legal situation for parts of the UK did experience a transformation in the 1960s, however, and an additional Act of Parliament was introduced, partially decriminalizing the procedure and providing a series of health-based mitigations for the harsh line of the 1861 scheme. As a result, the 1967 Abortion Act and Offences Against the Person statute now run simultaneously in England, Wales and, according to Department of Health (DoH) statistics, a total number of 184,571 lawful abortions were carried out in the UK in 2014 (DoH 2015), the jurisdiction of Northern Ireland displaying a slightly different study. Despite the large numbers of women now accessing the procedure on medically justified grounds, and the limited policy change over the last forty years, however, the overlapping statutes and fractious management of abortion by both the criminal law and health profession remain vulnerable to attack. Curiously, the source of this dissent does not exclusively emanate from the pro-life movement who opposed the initial reform, but abortion policy in the UK is under constant scrutiny from pro-choice groups alike.

Running contrary to the perception of a liberal scheme in the UK, therefore, legislative preservation of the offence of abortion in statute created a halfway house in which medical control of a crime was assumed and is a situation that remains in place to this day. In consideration of why the termination of pregnancy continues to be tied to the law in this manner, however, it is with several works of historical institutionalism, and the causal narrative the approach can offer, that this chapter is concerned. First engaging the concept of 'path dependency' (Krasner 1988) as an evolutionary term for a route informed by the history of a policy (Hall 1986) that is likely to be followed in the absence of competing pressures (Huber and Stephens 2001), the legacy of misconduct, so deeply entrenched in abortion, can be observed as the key common feature across statutory amendments regardless of the introduction of new measures. Indeed, although marking a period of significant statutory overhaul, the 1967 act fails to remove the critical merits of this mechanism, and can be further analysed in terms of acceptance by a number of scholars that historical events are said to be characterized by long periods of continuity punctuated by 'critical junctures' (Thelan 1999). In addition, and continuing with, as Peters (2011) declares, the deceptively simple notion that the choice made when a policy is being initiated will have a largely determinate influence on its future trajectory (Skocpol 2002), the lack of clarity over a woman's bodily autonomy, and messy body of rights created in the 1960s, has had a significant impact upon clinical developments in the UK. Indeed, as institutions can be seen to be located in a complicated causal chain (Hall and Taylor 1996), this historical context has further influenced the decisions of healthcare providers. It is therefore suggested that the crime of abortion has become a convention in the UK, substantially restricting evidence-based policymaking and contributing to a sub-optimal regulatory scheme. Although a mismatch between the reality of a policy field and the preservation of archaic legislation is not a new revelation, and literature has previously highlighted the disparity between optimal and actual outcomes (Cammack 1992, 401), the important lack of full acceptance of abortion as a medical treatment evokes problems in regard to patient-centered care in the region, and challenges the dominant assumption of the region as Europe's 'abortion capital' (Doughty 2005).

The chapter is organized in the following manner. The development of the law surrounding abortion is first presented, providing historical context of the procedure in the UK, and its strict retention as part of the criminal law, particularly in Northern Ireland. This is then followed by an outline of the contemporary legislative arrangements that determine the level of access for women living in England, Wales and Scotland today, and the range of health-based mitigations that are provided in statute. Thus mapping out the legal landscape in these first two sub-sections, the chapter then addresses the friction created by this overlapping legislation, and the controversy that surrounds the principal status of the procedure. It is here that the lenses of historical NI are utilized to determine exactly why the policy domain has so far been characterized by limited change, and to explore the organizational contexts that have been instrumental in preserving this path. The ramifications of this stagnating regulatory field are pertinently examined through the case study of approved methods of legal termination, and the institutional barriers to optimal care for British women is demonstrated through the contrasting administration of the abortion pill here and in the United States. Thereby questioning the perception of the UK as the European capital for abortion, the international context addressed in the final section instead engages the realities of the region's medical hegemony over the matter. Ironically, however, this academic challenge is not mirrored in grassroots activism, and society appears increasingly disengaged with elite debates. A conclusion therefore submits that the sentiment of 'no absolute right' to abortion is deeply entrenched across both the legal system and service providers in the UK, dictating that the full acceptance of the procedure as a medical issue in the near future is unlikely without a sharp exogenous shock to the system.

2.1. A BRIEF HISTORY: CRIMES AGAINST THE UNBORN 1200–1900

The termination of pregnancy is undoubtedly a frequently practiced procedure across the contemporary world and has become a significant feature of modern reproductive healthcare for women. Interestingly, however, the action has also been a regularly occurring phenomenon throughout recorded history, and studies claim that techniques of terminating an unwanted foetus were widely available in antiquity. Certainly classical and medieval documents have uncovered specific reference to such methods and detail countless women transferring their knowledge, and a 'pharmacopoeia' of effective herbal abortifacients, down through the generations (Alston 2001, Riddle 1992). Whereas the dangers of physically induced abortion in the ancient world were considerable (Caldwell 2004), the innovation in the discipline over the centuries has been extensive, and clinical evidence now suggests that the variety of modern techniques are among the safest medical treatments in industrialized countries, with only a negligible risk of morbidity having long been accepted by the healthcare sector (e.g., Högberg and Joelsson 1985). Despite such advances, however, abortion continues to occupy a significant position in political discourse across the world and is a policy domain infused with a myriad of ethical considerations. The fundamental status of the procedure in the UK as a criminal activity, in particular, has long been entrenched in common and statutory law, guided heavily by early moral teachings. Since this time, only incremental changes to the policy field have been evidenced, and the principal status of the procedure has, for the most part, been left untouched.

Although appearing of limited significance in an increasingly securalized contemporary state, Christian literature was undeniably of crucial significance in the early formation of Western sexual ethos across an array of matters (Brundage 2009, 1), often with lasting effects to this day. Consequently, although the Bible itself makes scant reference to the specific act of abortion, with curiously no specific commandment referring to the practice (Ward 1993), religious teachings in antiquity have nevertheless importantly addressed the issue. Sources such as *The Didcahe* and the *Epistle of Barnabus*, for example, base much of their writing around three propositions; that the foetus is the creation of God, abortion is in fact murder, and that the judgement of God falls on those guilty of abortion (Gorman 1998). Although there is some debate among historians on the success of prosecutions, in addition to contestation over the underlying legislative purpose of outlawing abortion (e.g., Means 1971, Keown 1988), common law deliberations in England appear, at least in part, to corroborate this position. In the colloquially termed '*Twinslayer's Case*' of 1327, for example, a writ was issued to the Sheriff of Gloucestershire to apprehend the defendant who had allegedly beaten a heavily pregnant woman bearing twins, both of which subsequently died. Similarly, the '*Abortionist Case*' concerned an indictment for killing a child still in the mother's womb and was latterly heard in 1348 (Means 1971). Furthermore, in the case of *R v. Turner*, a weaver was accused of persuading a woman to take and swallow a quantity of arsenic mixed with honey in order to destroy her child (Means 1971). And sanctions were also enforced for the deliberate termination of a foetus, as exemplified in the 1732 instance of Elizabeth Beare, in which the defendant was charged and convicted for procuring the abortion of another by use of an instrument (Keown 2006). Granted, much historical interest has been galvanized around interpreting the precise meaning of these cases, but, regardless of the successful prosecution rate prior to statutory law, the association of the act with the notion of wrongdoing is arguably demonstrated by such jurisprudence and lays the foundations of the status of abortion as an unlawful activity to this day.

Moving behond this early common law, however, infused as it was with moral scripture and biblical teachings, the period of statutory prohibition over abortion, and official recognition of the offence in the criminal law, further entrenched this illegality, beginning in the nineteenth century with Lord Ellenborough's 1803 Act. Enshrining the concept of misconduct, and prescribing absolute prohibition was section 1 of the legislation that stipulated that any person with intent to procure a miscarriage would be declared a felon and suffer death (43 Geo. III c. 58 as quoted in Keown 1988, 3). Thus extolling the punishment for abortion after quickening—an archaic term used to define the first maternal perception of movement (Keown 1988, 3)—to that of a capital offence, the situation at common law in the years previously was not significantly altered and, despite several amending statutes enacted since, the principle of abortion as a crime has remained throughout. Indeed, subsequent instruments such as Lord Landsdowne's Act of 1828, which in turn was replaced by the Offences Against the Person Act 1837 (Kennedy and Grubb 2000), have all shared this sentiment of liability, although the latter importantly disbanded with the death penalty. Currently the offence of terminating a pregnancy is provided for by the Offences Against the Person Act 1861, section 58 of which stipulates that the intention of a woman to deliberately induce her own miscarriage is a crime and will face the sanction of life imprisonment. In addition, the provision addresses those administering abortions and states that they too will be guilty and liable to punishment if they unlawfully administer a poison or use any instrument or other means with intent to cause miscarriage, and will be kept in penal servitude for life. Section 59 adds liability for up to five years for the supply of any instrument or substance in the knowledge that it will be used to procure a miscarriage.

Despite creating little change to the domestic situation, and resulting largely from a legislative oversight, of additional consequence in this time-line, as noted in leading studies of the development of the law in this domain (e.g., Lee and Morgan 2001), is the implementation of the Infant Life (Preservation) Act in 1929. In the case of *R v. Poulton*, attention was alerted to a lacuna in the law failing to provide protection for a foetus 'killed' during the course of birth. As a result of the wording of the 1861 Act, if a child was aborted in the course of delivery, it would not be covered by the statutory crime of abortion, as there would be no artificial facilitation, or 'procure', of a miscarriage. In the same vein, no criminal sanctions would be imposed under the law of homicide, as the provisions for both manslaughter and murder require the victim to be 'living' (section 1-3). This was made clear by a direction to the jury by Littledale, J., in which it was stipulated 'with respect to birth, the being born must mean that the whole body is brought into the world; it is not sufficient that the child respores in birth' (quoted in Lee and Morgan 2001, 242). As the 1861 Act was not intentionally designed to remove liability in such cases, and the effect appears to be merely an over-sight at the time of drafting, the Infant Life (Preservation) Act 1929 was therefore enacted to create the offence of 'child destruction', section 1 of which stated that any person, by willful act, who causes a child capable of being born alive to die shall again face penal servitude for life. Importantly, and arguably setting the tone for medical interjection discussed in due course, the caveat was added that no person would be found guilty of such an offence if it were done in good faith for the purpose of preserving the life of the mother (section 1, 1).

Domestic prohibition and sanctions in regards to the procedure is certainly not a nineteenth-century construct, therefore, with reference to its outlawed status rooted in biblical text and appearing in the courts at least as far back as the fourteenth century. Formal statutory restriction has thus long enshrined the fundamental idea of wrongdoing in abortion, and incremental amendments to the law during this time have repeatedly towed this line. Clearly extolled in the Offences Against the Person Act 1861, this latter statute importantly continues to prescribe sanctions for the unlawful procurement and administration of abortion in the UK's current regulatory system. Of more than merely historical interest, however, the next section illustrates that this aged tie to the criminal law oddly persists in today's legislative scheme, despite the procedure's widely reported, but inaccurately interpreted, decriminalization in 1967. As a result, it is these antiquated roots that have arguably set the tone for the element of path dependency (Krasner 1988) to be discussed later, creating problematic attrition with the healthcare domain.

2.2. THE 1967 ABORTION ACT

Reproductive healthcare in the UK experienced radical transformation in the latter half of the twentieth century when abortion was legalized for the first time in the country, and a list of health-based defences for the crime of terminating a pregnancy under the Offences Against the Person statute were implemented by the 1967 Abortion Act. In practice the law now ensures the procedure is treated solely as a public health matter, creating no *de jure* choice for women, and providing strict health-based mitigations that serve only to protect the well-being of mothers and foetuses in cases of potentially harmful pregnancies. An examination of the terms of the 1967 Act exemplifies this very point.

Having enshrined the crime of terminating a pregnancy within the Offences Against the Person Act 1861, the Abortion Act introduces circumstances under which the procedure would not attract prosecution. Section 1(1) stipulates that a person shall not be guilty of an offence when abortion is carried out by a registered medical physician, based on the opinion formed by two clinical practitioners in good faith, that the continuation of pregnancy would involve risk to the health of the woman or the foetus. Such risks are detailed in four paragraphs that cover the physical and mental health of the woman, that of her existing children, and the substantial risk that the foetus born would suffer from serious physical or mental abnormalities. The original wording of the Act failed to provide an upper time limit for these clauses, however, and demanded only the stipulation of two doctors' approval. The gestational restriction was therefore applied from section 1(1) of the Infant Life (Preservation) Act that stated liability for the crime of child destruction was effective when an abortion involved the destruction of a child 'capable of being born alive'; section 1(2) further deliberated that the presumption for this was 28 weeks (Dunn and Stirrat 1984). This position was later altered by section 37 of the Human Fertilisation and Embryology Act (HFEA) 1990, however, which introduced into the first paragraph a time limit of 24 weeks for situations in which the continuation of pregnancy would involve a *risk* of injury to the mother. No such cap was put on the three remaining paragraphs relating to grave permanent injury or risk to the life of the mother, and foetal abnormality.

The second provision of the 1967 Act elaborates that when evaluating the risk of injury, account can be taken of the woman's actual or reasonably foreseeable environment. The original intentions of this caveat were for it to be used in the course of assessing the risk of injury to the mother or threat to her life only. Due to a further amendment by the HFEA, however, this now additionally applies to the future physical or mental health of the woman. On the contrary, the requirement in the act for two doctors' signatures to permit treatment has lasted since the original enactment of the legislation and is an important regulatory feature to be discussed in greater detail later in the chapter. In a similar vein, and further adding to this aggrandized role for the clinician, section 4(1), excusing the conscientious objector from participating in treatment other than in circumstances where the procedure is necessary to save the life of the mother, has also loyally retained its original wording from the 1967 text. It has been mooted in surrounding debates, however, that the circumstances it evokes are far from uncomplicated (Mason and Graeme 2002), and although it is important to note that refusal to participate does not extend to a complete withdrawal from the process, and a practitioner is still under a duty of care to advise and make the appropriate referrals, this can cause delays for the woman receiving treatment (Warden 1990). In a study conducted in the North East of England in 2006, for example, of the 107 women referred by General Practitioners (GPs) for an induced abortion, 16 (15 percent) had to make a second appointment with another practitioner willing to refer them, and 34 (32 percent) waited 2 to 3 more days to receive a date for their hospital appointment. The national standard waiting time of 3 weeks from first appointment to the procedure was therefore achieved in only 56 of the 127 (44 percent) total cases (Finnie et al 2006). Furthermore, a wide regional variation in the number of procedures actually administered across the UK has become a widely accepted fact and is similarly revealed from studies conducted in 2010. The rate per 1,000 women aged 15 to 44 receiving NHS-funded terminations ranged from 25.7 in London to just 13.9 in the East Midlands and 13.8 in the North East (DoH 2010). It is submitted that social and healthcare factors, such as a higher level of teen pregnancy or treatment required on mental health grounds, could not alone provide explanation for this level of disparity, and must in large part be attributed to the extent of medical discretion to what essentially remains a criminal matter.

In a similar vein, the design of the provisions of the statute, as seemingly appreciative of the expertise provided by the medical profession, causes further difficulties in terms of equality of access. Paragraph (d), for example, stipulating foetal abnormalities as criminal mitigation for termination, is sufficiently broad to cover those considered by doctors to result in physical or mental disabilities if the baby is born, rather than providing an arbitrary and exhaustive list of conditions. This clause of the 1967 Act establishes that in such circumstances, an abortion can be performed after the 24-week upper time limit has lapsed and, on the surface, it is reasonably expected that decisions made in this context will largely rest upon objective evidence at the disposal of practitioners. Returning to inconsistencies across treatment, therefore, these are thus likely to be further compounded in terms of terminations sought in such instances.

It is of importance to note at this juncture, however, that although the statute does apply in Scotland, it has not been extended to cover Northern Ireland, where the termination of a foetus remains a crime. This situation in the region has since been mitigated by the application of the judgement in *R v. Bourne* [1939] 1 KB 687, which stipulated no liability would be incurred if a termination of pregnancy was conducted for the purpose of saving the life of the mother. Although the facts of this case will be discussed further in the next sub-section, the judgement was instrumental for the country in the case of *Re K (a minor), Northern Health and Social Services Board v. F and G* (1991) 2 Med L R 371 in which the termination of a 13-week pregnancy of a severely handicapped ward of court was authorized. Similarly, in Re A *(Northern Health and Social Services Boards v. AMNH)* (1991) 2 Med L R 274 the court engaged the reasoning of *Bourne* and acted in a handicapped woman's 'best interests'. Evidencing the same cultural sensitivities that ensure abortion remains a crime in the Republic of Ireland, therefore, deeply embedded in core religious values and a strong coalition between Church and state, Northern Ireland chose to preserve the crime in its entirety under the Offences Against the Person Act 1861.

Regardless of the partial decriminalization of the crime of abortion in the mid-twentieth century, therefore, the status of medically terminating a pregnancy in the UK since that time has indeed remained largely untouched. The introduction of the 1967 Act staunchly refused to fully remove abortion from the criminal law, instead following a path of medicalization—a term largely borrowed from sociology and applied to the matter by a number of scholars (e.g., Lee 2003, Sheldon 1997)— and enshrining an ongoing debate to determine the fundamental status of abortion as either a healthcare treatment or a criminal act.

2.3. A HEALTHCARE TREATMENT OR CRIMINAL ACT?

The perception of a comparatively unregulated system in the UK fails to acknowledge the fractious management of abortion by both the criminal law and health domain, and an idle regulatory situation extols the notion that the choice made when a policy is being initiated will have a determinate influence long into the future (Skocpol 2002).

Looking back over the legislative debates on the status and function of terminating a pregnancy over the centuries certainly illustrates a continual perception of abortion as a criminal act. Thus despite partial decriminalization permitting women to access the procedure if they meet certain health-based criteria, and its now frequent use in clinical settings in the UK, the heavily value-laden procedure is simultaneously shrouded in a regulatory field largely concerned with the adjudication of rights, which far from achieves the same levels of acceptance experienced by other healthcare treatments such as heart transplants or even elective cosmetic surgery. It thus becomes pressing in this comparative context to question the rationale underpinning the creation of a halfway house in the 1960s, and why severely limited change, and a largely stagnating field, has since come to characterize the policy domain. Engaging the lens of historical institutionalism, therefore, a strong path dependency (Krasner 1988) on an established institution of wrongdoing around the termination of pregnancy can readily be extrapolated from this chronology. Interestingly, however, this section further questions why such an uncharacteristic change to the statutory field therefore occurred in the form of the 1967 Abortion Act. Far from disbanding with the utility of the historical approach to NI, it is the welcoming of Kingdon's policy streams model (1995) into this bank of research that provides valuable insight at this point. Identifying an opportune moment for change—or policy window—in the 1960s, a break from the norm is claimed to have come to fruition due to the conflation of three important factors, which have since failed to coalesce in such a manner. Certainly, the entrenched value of wrongdoing, not entirely replaced by the 1967 Act, has reassumed the default position underpinning the legislation and, in the absence of any real pressure for change, this pathway remains.

As part of agenda-setting literature more generally, the multiple streams approach proffered by Kingdon (1984) certainly has its flaws. Appreciated throughout this chapter as lacking in prescriptive power, the schema nevertheless sets forth details that in order for a policy window to open, and a moment for change to be actualized, three facets must combine. These are namely the problem stream, in which much recognition is given to the temporal and cognitive constraints placed on the attention of policymakers and the requirement of a certain level of magnitude surrounding an issue. Second is the policy stream, which constitutes a sort of primeval soup, in which ideas float around awaiting to be attached to a problem. Finally, the political stream demands a salient national mood, organized political forces and events within government to further drive change (Kingdon 1995). In summation, therefore, the policy stream at a larger macro level can be characterized as a series of problems seeking plausible solutions (Mason and Levitt 1998, 128), and it is changes to either the problem or political streams that can create a 'window of opportunity' (Kingdom 1995). The insights garnered by this approach should not be diminished, and this explanatory power in mapping policy change has already been acknowledged (John 2003, Laraway and Jennings 2002). Thus adopting this regressive tool to explore the policy decision around abortion that occurred in the 1960s allows much critical insight to be garnered, and reasons for the 'medicalization' of abortion suggested. Bound by the strong historical and normative ties (March and Olsen 1984) to the criminal law, it can be revealed that the liberalization of abortion was not driven by a human rights schema determining the fundamental status of abortion, but a reasoned willingness to pass political control to the clinical field.

Providing the first need for reform and highlighting the problem stream of abortion policy, therefore, an exploration of the approach to the treatment among certain sections of the medical profession reveals a divergence from the 1861 legislation, and appeals for the statutory recognition of therapeutic abortion were frequent. In reality, by the early twentieth century, the procedure was often endorsed by clinicians if performed for health-based reasons, and a questionnaire sent out to London doctors in 1965 provides colour to this assertion. Receiving 751 replies, 69 percent of respondents stipulated that they approved of reforms to the law set out in the survey, with a further 84 percent indicating belief in the safety of the operation and 75 percent supported its availability on the NHS (Hindell and Simms 1968). By adhering rigidly to the time-honoured principles on the issue of abortion, the existing statutory regime was therefore largely believed not only to compromise the status of women, but to prevent doctors from acting in the best interest of their patients, and clinicians consequently demanded appropriate protection from criminal liability. The earlier case of *R v. Bourne* [1939] 1 KB 687, concerning a practitioner who openly performed an abortion at St Mary's Hospital on a girl of age fourteen who was raped by two soldiers in the Guards' Barracks, further highlights these trends. On 1 July, the doctor was charged at Marylebone Police Court for his actions under section 58 of the Offenses Against the Person Act 1861, for using an instrument with the intent to procure a miscarriage. At trial, three leading medical professionals, a gynaecologist, a psychiatrist and a physician, independently gave evidence supporting Bourne's decision that the continuation of pregnancy would have affected the girl's mental health. In summing up, J. McNaghten highlighted that section 1(1) of the Infant Life (Preservation) Act 1929 prescribed the unlawfulness of destroying the life of a child capable of being born alive. Thus inferred from his conclusion was that the prescription of the unlawfulness of an act necessarily indicates there are situations in which the act is lawful. If Bourne had acted in good faith 'for the purpose of preserving the life of the mother' he was legally performing the duties of a doctor.

Although *Bourne* was sufficiently determined in this desire to highlight the need for reform, many doctors feared the legal backlash and damage to their reputation performing an abortion might incite, and demanded the government provide clarification of the law and afford them the appropriate protection (Grear 2004). Although access to safe abortion, even to this day, depends upon the capacity and willingness of physicians to provide such services, society more generally was not fully engaged with the need for reform, and the pressure on the government was alone insufficient to negate the risks involved in overturning an ethically infused topic such as abortion (Faúndes and Hardy 1997). In practice, therefore, the problem was instead sidestepped by limiting the number of prosecutions (Keown 1988), and medical practitioners had nevertheless long been able to find room to regulate access to abortion for therapeutic reasons. In this sense, logic can be borrowed from the study of economics, and the government, as the ultimate risk manager, required additional motivation to abscond from the entrenched arrangement (Moss 2004).

In addition to the demand for change from the medical profession, however, the pathway for the act also reveals that parliamentary action was significantly driven by the recognition of the procedure within the policy stream as a vital healthcare treatment. Indeed, a departure from the long-standing criminal law on abortion would require more than a liberal climate among clinicians for the contemporary government to risk further legislating on the matter, and campaigns for an ideological closure on the issue were instead strengthened by a growing public health epidemic. Building upon the successful framing of contraception in scientific terms by the family planning pioneer Marie Stopes in the 1920s, the push for reform represented much more than a decline in moral standards among practitioners and was instead perceived by many as a vital step in the development of healthcare (Cohen 1993). The number of women dying from backstreet abortions, or indeed attempts to self-abort, contributed substantially to female ill health, and the need to reduce the incidence of criminal activity through the creation of a legal framework of services in which the procedure could be conducted in clinically safer conditions became pressing and was at the centre of advocacy work conducted by the Abortion Law Reform Association (ALRA) (Isaac

1994). According to figures collated from Reports on Confidential Enquiries into Maternal Deaths in England and Wales by the Royal College of Obstetricians and Gynaecologists between 1958 and 1963, for example, of 50 fatal cases of abortion each year, approximately 60 percent were presumed to be in circumstances where the abortion was criminally induced. As a result, the College unanimously voted in the report that, irrespective of the debates surrounding concrete numbers, it was clearly desirable to eliminate them if possible (BMJ 1966).

Acknowledging that these dangerous methods had long been flourishing in the UK, however, it was actually the much-publicized thalidomide tragedy that performed a key catalysing role in the 1960s, drawing society's attention to the inadequacies of the existing statute and galvanizing public support for a change to the law. The epidemic concerned a sedative drug popularly used in the late 1950s to cure morning sickness, but by 1962 was widely known to cause severe deformities in many children (Dally 1998). Victims of the tragedy inevitably argued their right to abort the potentially disabled foetuses and, aware of the increasingly liberal climate, the government feared that any refusal to do so would gain negative publicity (Lovenduski and Outshoorn 1986). The experience of the American actress Sherri Finkbine, in particular, who was administered the drug during her fifth pregnancy, caused widespread controversy. When she was made aware of the possible damage that had been done to the foetus she was carrying, she sought an abortion and, on refusal, was eventually forced to fly to Sweden and received much sympathy for her situation (Francome 1986). Such events clearly aided the introduction of Lord David Steel's PMB in the mid-1960s; in the fifteen years prior to the disaster, no fewer than five parliamentary initiatives with the aim of reform were unsuccessfully introduced. A large and favourable Labour majority, however, supported the proposal, and the Abortion Act was carried at the third reading by 167 votes to 83 (Buxton 1973), thus indicative of the additional need for an accepting political climate that will be explored in greater detail below. Suffice to say at this juncture, however, that this stream alone does not provide the whole story, and it is next to the policy stream that the account turns to explore the available solutions to the government of the day, and locate more pressure for change.

The solution of an appropriate healthcare scheme was clearly a principal driver in the introduction of legalized abortion, and the government was mindful in the drafting of the legislation that this fact would be the overriding sentiment. Indeed, despite a favourable climate of opinion for introducing legal abortion, the risks of embarking upon a 'moral law' for the contemporary government in the 1960s were substantial, and the healthcare frame helpfully avoided such costly debates while still addressing the immediate problems posed by maternal mortality and the thalidomide crisis. Departing from the original intentions of the ALRA, a woman's reproductive choice was therefore not unfettered in the statute, and the British Medical Association (BMA) quickly assumed moral and scientific authority over the procedure (Gleeson 2007). As such, the new statute did not allow room for women to have reproductive choice, but instead perpetuated the 'public health frame'. Although action was required to improve healthcare, the morality of the topic continued to polarize opinion, and vote-maximizing politicians avoided costly ethical debates by legislating only for therapeutic abortion. Indeed, although significant temporal factors demanded government attention, liberalization of the law was largely substituted for medical control over the statutory scheme in order to preserve this historical stance. It is within this context that the legalization of abortion should be considered, as no new rights were created by the Act, despite terminations becoming a legitimate aspect of health policy, and the dual personality of the procedure within the UK was instead born.

Turning attention to Kingdon's final, political stream, however, pressure on parliament to partially remove the sanctions attached to abortion additionally exploited the tolerant atmosphere of the 1960s. Occurring at a time when gender inequality was being successfully challenged and Britain was experiencing wide cultural change, the introduction of legal abortion in the UK is often attributed to the recognition of women's rights and a growing trend of secularization (Wleisien 1995). Although clearly riding the wave of permissive reforms that swept Britain during the 1960s, and certainly aided in its arrival on the government's agenda by the feminist movement, restricting the decriminalization of abortion to the context of a general liberalization of attitudes towards women and sexual relationships, and an overall decline in the influence of the Church, fails to fully capture the complexities of the situation. The latter half of the twentieth century indeed witnessed major social developments and, in sharp contrast to the strict Victorian values of pre-war Britain, two consecutive world wars served to break down the archetypal roles within the family. The status of the woman in the intervening years had already been strengthened by the growth of the suffrage movement, and by 1928, the Representation of the People Act granted women the vote on equal terms as men. Due in large part to the shortage of manpower in Britain during World War II, by the 1960s women had established their role in the workplace, and the government was being bombarded with demands for employment equality, ultimately culminating in the introduction of the Equal Pay Act in 1970, the Sex Discrimination Act in 1975 and the creation of the Equal Opportunities Commission in the same year. Furthermore, such vociferous campaigning was not exclusive to the equal treatment of women and, as part of what Theodore Roszak described as a 'growing social revolution', society rejected the government's position on many issues (1970). In 1957, for example, the Campaign for Nuclear Disarmament was formed and organized annual marches from the Atomic Weapons Research Establishment at Aldermaston to London until the international test ban treaty was signed in 1963. Attitudes towards sex and sexuality were also shifting, and those laws perceived as overly conservative were similarly challenged. The introduction of the Wolfenden Report in 1957 recommended the decriminalization of homosexuality, and the statutory prohibition was lifted in 1967 for men over the age of 21. Court rulings placed further pressure on the government to recognize this new outlook and in the infamous case involving the banned publication of D. H. Lawrence's 'Lady Chatterley's Lover', Penguin Books were unsuccessfully prosecuted under the Obscene Publications Act 1959, and the novel instead gained widespread popularity, a noteworthy case that will be returned to in the discussions on pornography in chapter 5. Realizing it must cater to contemporary demands, by the 1960s the government was beginning to yield to this new permissive society, and the contraceptive pill was made available to all women for free on the NHS. A steady decline in the influence of the Church could also be observed, and many of the laws previously entrenched in religious values were reformed; the provisions for divorce under the Matrimonial Offences Act were adapted to acknowledge the irretrievable breakdown of marriage and removed the emphasis placed on specific offences, effectively making it easier and simpler for couples to separate. A climate ripe for change was thus clearly evident during this time and provided much impetus for reform of the matter of abortion.

In summation of these three streams, therefore, the growing problem posed by maternal mortality and demand for appreciation of the dilemmas faced by clinicians, further catalysed by an acute medial crisis, fruitfully combined with the pre-existing public health frame proffered by contraception. Further coalescence was provided by a liberal climate of opinion, resulting in a window of opportunity (Kingdon 1995) in the 1960s to successfully introduce a new piece of legislation. Returning again to the power of historical legacies, however, and the notion posited at the start of this section that the criminality of abortion has become convention in UK society, this is still exemplified by two key facets of the regulation. First, and as deliberated in the previous sub-section, it retained its strong links to the criminal law. Second, and important to the ensuing analysis, in the time since the passing of the 'necessary' 1967 Act, the policy inertia that typifies ideological matters has been happily endorsed by successive governments. Indeed, the entrenched nature of abortion has severely limited the possibility of institutional change, and this is illustrated by a range of parliamentary trends.

Certainly, prior to the successful Steel bill, five separate legislative initiatives with the aim of reform were ineffectively introduced, and in the years since, several attempts to amend the existing statute have similarly failed. Furthermore, an exploration of the voting figures in these instances indicates no overwhelming majority, and instead points towards fundamental division; the Termination of Pregnancy Bill, for example, was defeated by only 187 votes to 108, and the Pregnancy (Counselling and Miscellaneous) Provisions Bill, by 182 to 107. Thus, in this context, the successful introduction of the 1967 Act was a groundbreaking and innovative measure within parliament and must, to a large extent, be attributed to the exogenous pressure unveiled through a study of Kingdon's (1995) policy streams. Responding to a public health crisis and mounting pressure from society, political action was hastily required at this time, and a number of tactics were employed to ensure that the new legislation was passed and did not fall foul of traditional voting discord. In particular, a recurrent feature of all parliaments is the constant pressure on their time, and this is frequent problem for the passage of PMBs, as the government alone is able to formally decide upon the timetable (Döring 1995). Consequently, as those in power are able to 'get their business through', they will invariably achieve the desired outcome of either thwarting a proposal or, as confirmed by the Video Recordings Bill in 1984 through which the government sought to appease the moral majority (Marsh and Read 1986), assuming a principal role in it success. Returning to abortion, therefore, it has been submitted that the legislation would not have proceeded had the Cabinet not decided to grant extra parliamentary time for debate. The intervention of the then Home Secretary Roy Jenkins in this vein, who expressed his support for reforming what he called the existing harsh and archaic law on abortion, was thus crucial (Potts et al 1977); rather than the issue being simply 'talked out' (Ryle 1966), the strong health justifications for decriminalizing abortion were afforded full attention, encouraging consensus, and were logically granted approval.

Although pointing to a rational choice institutionalism of sorts, Kingdon's policy stream (1995) model still holds veracity in this regard. The original objective of the statute was to reduce the rate of maternal morbidity from unsafe abortive procedures, and, in terms of evaluation, the Lane Committee was briefed to inquire into the workings of the legislation in 1974. The success of the scheme in achieving these ends was indicated through an investigation into the varying workloads of NHS gynaecology departments. In 1966, for example, 72,120 discharges of non-therapeutic abortions (procedures that had either been begun illegally, or were the result of a miscarriage) were made; by 1968, this was reduced to 69,836 (Simms 1971). These statistics, however, were the source of continued debate throughout the 1970s, and Paul Cavadino, in particular, submitted that the legislation had actually failed to decrease the number of abortions carried out in contravention of the law. Across the various indices employed to support his conclusions, of pertinence is the analysis of the number of maternal deaths. He argues that this cannot be attributed solely to the 1967 statute, claiming that cases in Britain were actually falling from the 1930s onwards with the advent of improved antibiotics. Illegal abortions had not necessarily been reduced, but were instead 'clinically safer', thereby accounting for the reduction in fatalities

(1976). Colin Francome strongly refuted these assertions, stating that the major improvements to antibiotics occurred before the introduction of the act; those illegal abortions conducted after 1967 were not necessarily conducted in safer conditions, and it was therefore unlikely that this could account for the drop in deaths (Francome 1976). Regardless of the dissenting academic interpretation, however, the Lane Report offered unanimous support for the Act in its original form, and thus a successful policy initiative was presented to society; one that, on the surface, continues to work for the general public to this day, providing as it does reproductive healthcare and appropriate treatment for those who require it (Committee on the Working of the Abortion Act 1974). Thus, by sufficing the original aims of the statute, successive governments have indeed experienced little rational incentive to further intervene in the legal domain, but more importantly, the element of path dependence has prevailed.

This is not to say, however, that government's behaviour around the law on abortion in the intervening years since the 1967 Act can be characterized as purely apathetic, and this legislative inertia has been threatened. In such circumstances, however, the strong normative and historical values (March and Olsen, 1984) on the misdemeanour of the procedure has meant that tactics have been readily deployed by those in power to protect the status quo. Indeed, the medical control enshrined in the statute has previously been cited as a calculated decision to ward off any ethical backlash, and the maintenance of the public health frame avoids the palpable fear of the moral repercussions that any change to the existing situation could incite (Isaac 1994). On notable occasions, therefore, the government has acted to restrict substantial changes to the legislation; the HFEA debates in 1990 and 2008, in addition to the situation in Northern Ireland, provide two such notable examples. First, tagged on to parliamentary discussion over the regulation of fertility treatments such as in vitro fertilization (IVF), several amendments to the Abortion Act were tabled in the course of the HFEA debates in 1990, and again in 2008 (Montgomery 1991). Government manoeuvring during these two periods, however, limited the number of alterations and, although in the course of the first attack, three successful amendments to the law were made, the extent to which they actually effected change must be questioned. Certainly at first glance they may appear substantial, the effects of which were to restate the grounds for abortion, to institute an upper time limit, and permit the establishment of a wider class of places in which the procedure could be conducted. On closer inspection, however, they are closely related to the original terms of the 1967 Act. Thus, rather than representing a radical departure from the original position, the measures were envisaged as necessary updates to the legislation for reasons of efficacy and to bring it in line with the reality of medical practice in the early 1990s (Stetson 2001). The consolidation of the four grounds for allowing abortion, for example, was born from the ambition to collate the law into one comprehensive statute. As previously deliberated, the original 1967 Act provided two defences to procuring a miscarriage but failed to provide an upper time limit. Consequently, this had no effect on the 1929 Infant Life Preservation Act, which automatically imposed liability for an abortion over 28 weeks of gestation (Davies 1998). This produced the unsatisfactory anomaly that a termination in compliance with the terms of the 1967 Act could still amount to child destruction under the 1929 Act; section 1(1)(b) was therefore introduced, stating that abortion shall be permitted if necessary to prevent grave permanent injury. As guided by the public health frame and the necessity of the procedure, this had little to no effect on the practice of abortion, as doctors already regularly performed terminations in such circumstances.

Furthermore, the reduction in the upper time limit additionally amounted to the codification of established clinical conduct (Montgomery 1991). In *Rance v. Mid-Downs HA and Storr* [1991] 2 WLR 159, it was indicated that the ability to breathe, if only for an hour, would suffice being capable of being born alive, and this was widely considered to indicate a stage of development around 24 weeks of gestation. Having therefore determined that in grave circumstances no upper boundary would be stated, it was deemed appropriate that, for other reasons, this timeframe should be reduced, and section 1(1)(a) was revised accordingly. Finally, the extension to the definition of premises represents a simplification of onerous administrative requirements for the executive. Prior to the drafting of the 1990 Act, the abortion 'pill' mifepristone was introduced and increasingly used for the termination of early pregnancies (Urquhart and Templeton 1990). Around the time of the HFEA debates, it was contemplated that the method could potentially become a primary healthcare service (HC 1990) and thus, in addition to abortion providers such as BPAS and Marie Stopes, be overseen by GPs within their surgeries (Iyengar 2005). As the original wording of section 1(3) demanded, the Secretary of State approved individual premises; however, this would have proved a time-inefficient process to do so for each individual surgery, and thus the provision was altered to incorporate the power to approve a 'class of places' specifically to cover its prescription by GPs. In reality, however, the utilization of this clause has been limited, and this will be more fully discussed in terms of the constraints on evidence-based policy-making in the section below. The amendments in 1990 were therefore necessary measures, with limited associated costs for the government, and were consequently afforded due respect within parliamentary debates.

On the contrary, and returning again to the government's control of the political timetable, further suggestions of modification to the law, representing more than just updates, have contravened the government's strategy of policy inertia and have thus been 'talked out' of parliamentary debates. This includes numerous provisions tabled in the course of updating the HFEA that called for tighter controls over practitioner conduct, such as the requirement of the signature of only one doctor before thirteen weeks to ensure fewer delays. Unlike the necessary updates in 1990, however, these instances marked a move away from the preservation of a simple public health treatment and a step towards arguments of morality. As a result, the Report Stage of the 2008 Bill began with a programme motion to move all new clauses to the end of the proceedings. This in effect pushed the amendments referring to abortion off the agenda, and it was acknowledged by many that there would not be enough time remaining to discuss the issues. Vehemently against the move was the sponsor of one specific amendment, Rt Hon Diane Abbott, who submitted that the behaviour was intended to stop the full and important debate of matters (HC 2008).

Second, referring to the push to extend the 1967 Act to Northern Ireland, and decriminalize the procedure in the region, the government's blocking of substantial debate on this particular matter provides evidence that, in addition to a fear of moral repercussion and wish to maintain policy inertia, the government's strategy represents further political bargaining. Following the outbreak of troubles in the region, the 1973 Northern Ireland Constitution Act abolished the country's parliament and established a new Northern Irish Assembly. The effect of this was to reinstate Westminster rule, with the stipulation that devolution would only occur in the future if a government could be formed that had the support of the community at large. In the meantime, the 1973 Act established a Secretary of State for Northern Ireland, and a list of 'excepted' and 'reserved' matters was drawn up: the Assembly could not legislate on the former, but could upon the latter if the Secretary of State saw fit. The significance of this measure was that criminal law remained under reserved matters throughout this period and, following devolution in 1998, full legislative competence, including authority over abortion, was transferred back to the Northern Ireland Assembly in 2010 (Horgan 2006). Of critical importance to this study is to understand why, when criminal powers were brought back under Westminster Rule in 1972 just five years after the passing of the 1967 Abortion Act, the Northern Ireland situation was not brought in line with the rest of the UK and the country was permitted to retain a level of influence over the matter. Indeed the HFEA discussions represented the last chance to liberalize abortion law in Northern Ireland before Direct Rule came to an end, and criminal powers were devolved back to the region. The vast cultural sensitivity and religious constraints that surround the termination of pregnancy in the country provided a platform for bargaining, however, for the UK government. Investigation into the House of Lords debates as the discussion stage of the Northern Ireland Bill, for example, specifically highlights the government's intention to return all criminal matters, including abortion, back when the time was right. Furthermore, the government made clear that it would not affect the situation in

Northern Ireland relating to the procedure in the intervening period. It is thus argued that the preservation of this position, and prevention of Northern Irish women from accessing an NHS abortion in Great Britain, is indicative of a host of back room deals and, in particular, it is claimed that Gordon Brown assured Democratic Unionist MPs that abortion laws would not be touched in return for them supporting the 42-day detention of terror suspects (BBC News 2008). Within a scheme that for the most part works for its prescribed purposes, therefore, little incentive has arisen for those in power to implement statutory amendments, and the policy field has followed a logical course of evolution (Crouch and Farrell 2004).

As alluded to in the introductory chapter, therefore, the definition of an institution by historical institutionalism (March and Olsen 1984) adopts a far more vague approach than the other strains. Although taken here to represent a convention in the form of the criminal status of abortion, it is of pertinence in this sense to identify the role of ideas (Peters 2012) and the importance of the element of wrongdoing that shrouds abortion. It is here that comparisons can be drawn with the work of Immergut (1990), that analyses government involvement in healthcare. Integral to what determines health policy, she asserts, is what medical practitioners believe to be best practice. By stark contrast, it appears that the convention of abortion as a crime limits this very behaviour, and the critical juncture in 1967 did little to erode this historical legacy. By exploring this path-dependent (Krasner 1988) approach to the termination of pregnancy as underpinning the selection of the 'public health' frame, the section continues to illustrate the impact of these historical constraints on contemporary attempts to amend the Abortion Act. Punctuated by only one critical juncture, and continually extolled by the evolutionary concept that in the absence of other pressures, the established status quo is likely to prevail, medicalization was permitted in the 1960s to appease the pressure for change within the institutional context of criminal activity. The activities of successive governments in the legal domain of abortion thus undeniably demonstrates a lack of incentive for the legislature to amend existing regulation (Tsebelis and Money 1997) and the desire to preserve the status quo and avoid potentially damaging debates over morality. Although these purposeful actions are undeniably important, the decisions taken must continually be viewed in the overarching context of abortion as a crime; the element of misdemeanor has never fully left the legislation, or the ensuing debate, indicating the strong historical institutional constraints (March and Olsen 1984) in place on policy action. As such, the new statute did not allow room for women to have reproductive choice, but instead perpetuated the 'public health frame'. The 'medicalisation' (Nye 2003) of the crime of abortion reflected a strategic action by the government to satisfy the immediate demands for a better level of protection for women (Grubb 1990) but also remain sympathetic to the long historical and normative association abortion

had with the criminal law, and the constraints of this convention have dictated that the legal domain, in the years since, has largely remained untouched.
Within this situation of inertia, however, the ability of the regulation to stay
afoot of advances in health policy is questioned, and merits of medicalization
rightly challenged next.

2.4. HISTORICAL BARRIERS: EVIDENCE-BASED POLICYMAKING AND THE ABORTION PILL

By shifting control over the termination of pregnancy to the medical profession, and ushering the procedure into the neighbouring spheres of health and
social policy, the regulation of lawful abortive treatment in the UK is now a
significant feature of the British welfare state (Shaver 1994) and is thus
accompanied by the inevitable concerns for quality medical care and protection of social inclusion (Lister 1998) this entails. The stagnating legislative
field unveiled above, however, directly impinges upon the status of the woman and her level of care within this healthcare environment. In comparison to
other areas of clinical provision in which burgeoning techniques are welcomed in the pursuit of superior treatment, albeit subject to budgetary constraints, the interface between morality and scientific innovation in areas
such the termination of pregnancy poses a significant problem. Clearly reflected in the regulation of adjacent reproductive methods and contraceptive
technology such as IVF, egg donation and surrogacy, the discovery of new
medical techniques, and the evolutionary nature of clinical practice, places
further demand on the statutory scheme for appropriate amendments. Even at
a cursory glance of the policy field surrounding abortion, however, it is
revealed that legislative acceptance of clinical innovation is, at best, slow,
and the regulatory domain can largely be characterized as in a state of inertia.
Oddly enough, however, by virtue of the 1967 Act, making abortions safe in
the UK became a matter of good public health policy (Berer 2000), and a
fundamental concept for good public health practice is an evidence-based
approach. Indeed making decisions founded upon the best available scientific
facts, using data and information systems systematically, conducting sound
investigation and disseminating what is learned are all key components of
this approach (Brownson et al 2009). Consequently, the domestic constraints
that manifest from what fundamentally remains a crime is a highly contentious issue, constraining the full recognition of the woman as a patient in the
process of a termination; a sub-optimal level of care for those seeking abortions is generated as a result, and the UK is left lagging behind medical
advances in other Western states. This is most readily exemplified by the
comparative use of the abortion pill in the UK, and in the United States, and
indicates that the more appropriate consumer paradigm, so evident in health-

care in the latter region, allows for greater scope of evidence-based approach to policymaking. Unfortunately, the legacies of abortion's past determine that this position is unlikely in the UK.

The term early medical abortion (EMA) refers to the use of medication to induce an abortion within the first trimester of pregnancy and is most commonly associated with the phrase 'abortion pill'. The discovery of the clinically termed RU486—a steroid synthesized by Dr Etienne-Emile in the 1980s—allows for a non-surgical method of inducing abortion at up to 63 days gestation (Costa 2007). Dating back almost three decades, the drug is by no means a new innovation and was actually introduced into the UK back in 1991, and medical abortions now account for almost half the total number of terminations carried out in the country (DoH 2012). In comparison, the United States' relationship with the treatment is far less matured, and the pill was neglected approval by the Food and Drug Administration (FDA) until 2000. Since that time, however, the use of this abortive techniques has become commonplace across the pond and, in 2011, similarly accounted for 36 percent of all abortions performed before nine weeks gestation (Jones and Jerman 2014). The use of medication, as opposed to more evasive, surgical techniques, is thus now seen as common practice in terminations under 9 weeks, or 63 days, gestation across the Western world. For this purpose, three treatment regimens currently exist in the United States: RU486 (also known as mifepristone) with misoprostol, methotrexate combined with misoprostol, and solely misoprostol (Crenin and Aubény 1999). This first technique of combining the a dose of mifepristone with a second misoprostol tablet is mirrored in the UK and is highly effective at ending early pregnancies; in a study conducted in 1993, 96.9 percent of 505 women under 50 days gestation, and receiving misoprostol 48 hours after mifepristone, had their pregnancy terminated. Furthermore, abortion occurred in 2.9 percent of the women within 48 hours of administration of mifepristone, and 60.9 percent within 4 hours of the misoprostol (Peyron et al 1993). According to US statistics, the method similarly carries a low associated death rate that is comparable to surgical abortion, and less than pregnancy to full term with delivery (Crenin and Aubény 1999).

The colloquially termed 'abortion pill' is thus widely viewed as a clinically safe method of terminating an unwanted or harmful pregnancy and, to the uninitiated, it would appear that little controversy surrounds its use. Indeed, if used within the parameters of the law in terms of gestational limits and conditions for granting an abortion, it could easily be assumed that the therapeutic process would only be of professional interest to practitioners in charge of its use. Contrary to initial assumptions of a largely liberal UK, and an internally conflicted United States, however, examination of the use of the abortion pill in both regions uncovers a new angle to the debate and unveils a somewhat surprising twist in the abortion narrative; challenging the seemingly lenient approach housed in the UK's law, it appears that women in the United States actually receive a more comprehensive level of treatment, and an empathetic patient-centered approach, to this specific aspect of reproductive technology. Far from merely an issue of prescription in the UK, the pill is in fact at the heart of medical and societal debate for two reasons: its close association with contraception and the possibility of its use in settings other than medical facilities.

In recent years, a specific clash between the 1967 statute and the development of the abortion 'pill' has indeed arisen that clearly illustrates the statutory constraints of evidence-based policymaking. In addition to the four grounds upon which two registered practitioners can grant a termination of pregnancy, the text of the 1967 Act stipulates where these 'lawful' procedures can be administered, detailing a hospital, or place approved by the Secretary of State for Health. In effect, this clause creates a licensing procedure operated by the Secretary of State, with subsequent monitoring and inspection carried out by medical, nursing and administrative officials from the DoH (Kennedy and Grubb 2000). Several incentives are provided by private-sector development in healthcare generally, such as the complementary expansion of services and redistribution of resources (Bull 2000), and the terms of the act enable the development of collaborative arrangements between the NHS and the abortion providers such as the British Pregnancy Advisory Service (BPAS). In 2010, for example, over half (59 percent) of publicly subsidized abortions took place in the independent sector under NHS contract (DoH 2010). As a further result, however, abortion is consistently one of the most common patient-funded procedures in the UK, with 4 percent (7,583) of the 182,574 total abortions conducted last year administered in this manner (Jackson 2013). In these situations, it is difficult to avoid the fact that private healthcare generally promotes the principle of consumer sovereignty, a notion that runs entirely contrary to the medicalization of the law witnessed above. The government, at least on the surface, is therefore keen to ensure that the legislation is not circumvented, and has thus issued supplementary controls upon the management of private clinics (Bartlett and Phillips 1996). The *Compendium of Guidance*, for example, states that special approval is required for termination after the twentieth week of gestation, and after 24 weeks, is entirely prohibited (DoH 1999). Further direction for the care of women is provided by the Royal College of Obstetrics and Gynaecology (RCOG) and includes aspects such as appropriate services for women with special needs and those who do not speak English, in which verbal advice must be supported by accurate and impartial printed information, and a number of pre-abortion assessments should be conducted (RCOG 2000). Overall, an audit of the management of induced treatment conducted in 2003 demonstrated a good awareness of such recommendations across a range of venues, and this would suggest few problems in the running of this provision of the 1967 Act (Thomas et al 2003). It has been submitted by some abortion providers, however, that there is a growing disparity between law and treatment, and practice is beginning to outpace legislation (Lee 2003).

In this vein, the 'treatment for the termination of pregnancy' under section 1(3) is complicated by the difficult distinction between contraception and abortion. Although many believe there to be a fundamental moral difference between preventing pregnancy and terminating an unwanted foetus, the legitimacy of this boundary is threatened by medical advances, and this has a conspicuous impact upon the concept of 'premises' (Jackson 2001). The drug mifepristone, which blocks the action of the female hormone, causing the membrane of the uterus to be shed, can be used in separate circumstances, with differing effects. When taken a short time after sexual intercourse as an emergency method, it prevents the implantation of a fertilized egg and acts a contragestive. Importantly, when the pill is ingested at this stage, no abortifacient act takes place. Within a time frame of nine weeks of gestation, however, mifepristone can alternatively be taken to act to dislodge a fertilized egg that has been implanted, thus causing the termination of pregnancy (Chung et al 2002). Conversely, this is an abortive process, and concern is rife that it should be viewed as such by patients. Second to this problematic conflation of terms, however, the setting for this treatment is also the source of much contention. As a requirement of the Medicines Act 1968, the accompanying Data Sheet states that this form of medicinal abortion does not require the hospitalization of the pregnant woman as an in-patient. Rather, observation should be conducted for at least two hours, following which she can be discharged home and return between 36 and 48 hours later for the second round of treatment in the form of misoprostol.

In view of these neighboring considerations, RU486's introduction into the pharmaceutical market, from the outset, has attracted much disdain and disapproval to the extent that the company marketing the drug initially wavered on whether to sell it. Rather, owning 36 percent of the French subsidiary of the German company in question—Hoechst—it was the French government's firm order to sell the pill that brought the measure into medical practice in the late 1980s (Ricks 1989). As such, the drug was granted a product license in the UK in 1991 under the brand name 'Mifegyne' and became a feature of clinical practice in 1995. The United States followed with FDA approval in 2000 but, in the years since its arrival, the drug has received different treatment in the two countries. In the United States 59 percent of abortion providers now offer EMAs, and it is standard routine in the majority of these establishments for misoprostol to be given to the woman to take home after her first visit (Jones and Jerman 2014). This is not the case in the UK, and this scientific innovation created two problems for the smooth running of section 1(3) of the 1967 Act and demonstrated the inability of the current regulatory scheme to meet modern scientific demands. Prior to its development, the techniques employed for the termination of pregnancy required a hospital, or approved clinic, because of the facilities and appropriate staff offered. As the use of mifepristone does not demand this level of care, however, questions first arose as to the appropriateness of its administration in alternative venues. Certainly, it had been contemplated that it could be used in GPs' surgeries and, as the individual approval of practices by the Secretary of State would be an onerous task, the HFEA 1990 actually added a new clause to allow for the approval of a 'class' of places in this manner as was discussed in the section above. Second, as aforementioned, the Data Sheet for mifepristone submits that the woman is free to leave the hospital or clinic in between the two stages of medicinal action. Case law states, however, in the instance of *Royal College of Nursing of the UK v. DHSS* [1981] AC 800 that the termination of pregnancy is a process of treatment; therefore, the entire period of time between the two rounds of medication constitutes treatment within the meaning of section 3(1). Within the parameters of the statute, the woman should thus technically stay in hospital for the duration of the procedure, unless the Secretary of State is to approve 'every place under the sun where a woman would go' which, of course, it is not a logical or feasible step (Kennedy and Grubb 2000). Although to retain the patient in hospital would have been the correct interpretation of the act, it would have undermined the advances made by mifepristone, and, in reality, it is not how the system now operates, with the majority of service providers intending that women accessing EMA are discharged after the first round of treatment, but with the significant clause that they return to the clinic to be administered the second round (BPAS 2015).

The supervision of this colloquially termed 'abortion pill' for EMA thus continues to be at the centre of vast clinical debate, largely centering around the contention that the choice should be made available to women whether or not they wish to complete their treatment at home. In such circumstances the patient would be administered the first stage of the abortion (mifepristone) in the clinic and would be provided with the second (misoprostol) to take away with her. Those in favour of permitting this method claim unnecessary time is spent by women in a medical setting, which is especially burdensome for patients who already have children and, according to government statistics, this forms half of the demographic that terminate a pregnancy. In addition, the expense of travel and the risk of miscarrying while returning from the clinic may mean women feel forced to choose a surgical abortion instead (BPAS 2015). Studies have additionally demonstrated that women would welcome being offered the choice of having medical abortion at home or in hospital, with many feeling that the home use of misoprostol is more natural, private and allows for the presence of a partner or friend (Hamoda et al 2004). Indeed in line with the RCOG's recommendation that abortion clinics should ideally offer a choice of methods for abortion, a survey was undertaken by BPAS to obtain the opinions of women in the UK on the matter. The results demonstrated that of the 162 participants, the majority of respondents (86 percent) opted to go home to complete the treatment rather than remain in a clinical setting. To a greater extent, 98 percent believed home management to be very or, at the least somewhat, acceptable, and the results of BPAS's research concluded with a plea for consideration to be given to the updating of section 1(3) (Lohr et al 2010). Adding further corroboration, studies demonstrating the safety of the system have been cited in support of these social factors pushing for change. A trial of self-medication in the woman's own residence using the same drug, but in instances of miscarriage, for example, was conducted by the Early Pregnancy Unit of the Royal Free and University College Medical School in London (Econmides and Sabin 2007).

Spurred on by this positive data haul, BPAS brought legal proceedings against the Secretary of State for Health in 2011 to forward such an argument. The case rested upon a significant interpretation of the law in terms of whether the prescription stage of the medication can be considered to be the termination of pregnancy, rather than the actual consumption, in effect therefore permitting its use in a private environment. In the course of deliberations, Ann Fueredi, Chief Executive of BPAS, reiterated the concerns for social inclusion and consumer welfare held by professionals working in the field, including the time-consuming nature and expense of travel the current scheme demands, and thus submitted that present arrangements were 'suboptimal' (*British Pregnancy Advisory Service v. Secretary of State for Health* [2011] EWHC 235). Although the judgement refused to redefine the ambit of 'treatment for abortion', the conclusion nevertheless placed further pressure upon the stagnating abortion field. A clear division was asserted between the regulatory regime of the termination of pregnancy, and the statutory regime, and by extension the practicalities and moralities of abortion policy, and the power of the Secretary of State to affect a healthcare issue was highlighted by the UK court. As a result, its construction and interpretation staunchly remains a decision for the Secretary of State which, interestingly, has still not been acted upon to this day.

Although there is little evidence against the proliferation of studies in favour of the method, contrary arguments have been submitted on the basis of subjective moral objection. The Pro-Life Alliance, for example, submits that the pro-abortion lobby is 'out of touch' with medical opinion, and cites a survey conducted by a GP newspaper demonstrating that almost two-thirds of primary care nurses would refuse to offer EMAs to patients if legislation were changed to allow them to do so (ProLife 2009). Further to this, the Society for the Protection of Unborn Children (SPUC) claims that GPs similarly demonstrate a high level of personal objection to abortion. Citing the same source as the Pro-Life Alliance, it is submitted that 61 percent of practitioners responding to an opinion poll did not believe that surgeries should be offering the method at all, with more than half stating it would increase the overall abortion rate (Smeaton 2009). In addition, notorious cases in which the use of the drug has been involved in fatalities are focused upon as evidence against the straightforward nature of the system, and it is further stated that the expediency of introducing such methods into places such as GP practices would neglect proper patient care (e.g., *The Daily Mail* 2009).

Indicative of an inhibited regulatory domain more generally, therefore, the contention over EMAs, demonstrated to be safe on numerous occasions and already administered at home in alternative contexts such as miscarriage, therefore illustrates the ethical constraints on evidence-based policymaking in the provision of abortion services, a trend that has previously been observed in areas of morality (Buse et al 2006). Linking back to the stagnating legislative field uncovered in the previous section, the government's actions are significantly shaped by a fear of public backlash, and these competing interpretations would require a potentially harmful moral adjudication. This rationale appears somewhat eroded, however, when the cost-effectiveness of the procedure is considered; in terms of the NHS, it is indeed cheaper and more expedient for women to have abortion earlier in pregnancy, and it therefore appears counterintuitive to oppose them for reasons other than claims of morality (Thong and Baird 2005). Thus logically returning to the constraint of historical legacies, it appears clear in these circumstances that the underlying status of abortion remains a highly influential matter and determines that its regulation continues to be strongly affiliated with the law.

Against the backdrop of reluctance on the part of Congress to fully legislate on the matter of termination of pregnancy, initial assumptions in regard to the introduction of the abortion pill into the United States could easily draw the similar conclusion of federal, and in turn state, resistance to the method. Certainly this was the case in the infancy of the medication and, unlike the UK's adoption in 1995, RU486 did not receive FDA approval until 2000. Operating within a private sphere, however, and unhindered by ties a welfare state such as the UK inevitably fosters, medical practice in the United States continually places customer satisfaction at the heart of its concerns, even when dealing with an essentially criminal activity such as abortion. Here a paradigm shift has been evidenced, and a sharp divide between professionals and the legislature has been drawn; doctors are not politicians, nor vice versa, and therefore, operating alongside the pro-choice/pro-life debate, optimal standards of care when performing legal abortions is of primary importance. Arguably supporting this position further is the demand of a consumer in the private healthcare domain which, although clearly prevalent in the United States, is not a response that is often seen in the UK. Thus despite the greater experience of the UK than the United States in dealing with the medication, the home administration of the second stage of the process through the prostaglandin misoprostol is commonplace in the country. The choice to receive the final tablet at a place of their choosing, other than solely a medical facility, is not a reality for British women, greatly restricting their level of access in comparison to their transatlantic counterparts, 23 percent of whom, in 2011, received nonhospital medical abortions (Jones and Jerman 2014). Thus, despite the United States' late start with the method, on average the statutory scheme now appears to provide women with a wider range of therapeutic choice. Much has been made of this seemingly insignificant detail of accessing EMAs; indeed, at the bottom line, it is available in both countries and therefore should perhaps pose little countenance. Delving below this statutory field to look at the point of service delivery, however, reveals the sub-optimal care received by UK women. This apparent discrepancy in patient autonomy is somewhat surprising, not only for the previously mentioned reason that the UK is largely perceived as a liberal nation on the matter of abortion, but, in addition, an abundance of studies highlighting the safety and efficacy of home administration appear to shed an outdated light on Britain's current situation (Finala et al 2004). Consequently, the regulatory field is plagued with similar controversies in the two countries alike, however, a divide in clinical practice has been witnessed between the two regions, and although the UK prohibits the home administration of the second stage of the process, this has come to be habit in the United States (Finala et al 2004).

In addition to a point of empirical concern, however, this revelation has theoretical implications for the study at hand and again demonstrates the importance of legacies of the past (Peters 2011) dictating the future trajectory of a policy field (Skocpol 2002). Looking towards the development of regulation in the UK, the constrained role of the medical profession raises significant concerns in terms of social inclusion, and both a complete overhaul of the statutory regime and a shift in sociological standing to place patients as consumers at the heart of healthcare appear unlikely in the domestic welfare-based system. Reintroducing the notion of stereotyping referenced in the opening chapter of this book, therefore, it appears that the dominant image in this policy domain, above all others, is the wrongful action of those seeking a termination. Although this may not be readily articulated, and indeed conversation around abortion itself carries somewhat of a stigma at the societal level, it is nevertheless discernible that a women's quest for a termination is characterized by a myriad of regulatory requirements, all working from the same *a priori* basis of a criminal act that can only be mitigated by certain healthcare requirements. The legitimacy of a woman in this domain as a patient is consequently heavily constrained, creating the image of a woman who needs to be closely monitored in her decision to have an abortion, in the sense that she might have made a rash decision and is choosing to terminate lightly. Not only is this inaccurate in its grouping of all female conduct, falling again with the 'Madonna/whore' duality, but it has ramifications in terms of human rights. Although this impacts upon all seeking a termination, this causes particular problems in regard to those that have fallen pregnant as a result of rape, or indeed the prostitute or porn star that requests an abortion. The incidents of those that fall between the gaps of this governance will be returned to in chapter 6.

2.5. THE EUROPEAN CAPITAL FOR ABORTION

A worldwide standard of access to safe abortion is a major concern and is promoted by a number of international bodies such as the UN and the EU; indeed a reduction in the maternal mortality ratio between 1990 and 2010 features in the Millennium Development Goals (MDGs). Despite these measures, attitudes towards the deliberate ending of pregnancy continue to vary, and even developed countries display markedly disparate approaches and, although in 2009 it was recorded that 97 percent permit abortion to save the woman's life, this amounts to a very stringent pre-requisite that rarely arises. In reality, the additional regulatory demands and procedural requirements peculiar to nation-states, including gestational limits, spousal consent and third party authorization, dictate that policy is far from standardized across the globe and is instead a field littered with an array of cultural, religious and societal considerations (UN 2011). The introduction of the 1967 Abortion Act in the UK served to create one of the most liberal systems in Europe, in principle permitting abortion up until 24 weeks of gestation, double the limits in France and Germany, and six weeks later than in Sweden and Norway. Unlike other member states such as France, Italy and Spain, however, under the Veil Law of 1975, Law No. 194 of 1978, and Article 417 respectively, where abortion is available upon request within the first trimester, the termination of unwanted pregnancies in the absence of legally defined justification remains an offence. This disparity is perhaps not especially surprising given that, by virtue of Article 152 of the EC Treaty in which it was stipulated that the EU has no absolute powers in the field of health, abortion is indeed a member state competence. This strict retention of abortion as part of the criminal law across the UK, however, appears at odds with the popular perception of a permissive approach in the region. Granted, the termination of pregnancy is far from an open and shut case in many countries across the world, and various domestic regulatory schemes are attached to the process. However, it is the governance of abortion in the UK, except in the region of Northern Ireland, that is frequently depicted as offering relative ease of access when an end to a pregnancy is sought, and the number of women receiving treatment each year does indeed reach a comparatively high total within a global context. Often overlooked in these discussions, however, is the fact that much of the laissez-faire critique relies substantially on citing the higher than average upper time limit for the procedure that is permitted in the UK, rather than acknowledging that free and easy recourse to termination under the 1967 Abortion Act, and a situation of abortion on demand, is never an option at any stage of gestation. Such perception of a seemingly lax nation-state is nevertheless frequently quoted in the popular press, and newspapers appear rife with anecdotes of 'quickie' terminations, or claims that in comparison to its EU neighbours, the UK is the European capital for 'free and easy' abortion (Doughty 2005).

Interestingly, however, this absolute right to access, although apparent in neighbouring EU countries, is not enshrined at the level of supranational law and can be seen to contribute to the limited societal outcry for this position. In *Bruggemann & Scheuten v. Germany* [1977] EHRR 244, the ECtHR held that although legislation restricting abortion does engage Article 8 as its intention is to protect the right to establish relationships with others, including sexual relationships, there is no breach of the article in circumstances when abortion is denied. Abortion does not fall solely within the private sphere of the mother; thus access to the procedure is not an absolute right and rules restricting abortions beyond a certain point can be legally justified. This point was reiterated in the second, and more recent case, of *A, B and C v. Ireland* [2010] ECHR 2032 in which the court distinctly provided that Article 8 cannot be interpreted as conferring a right to abortion. It is of importance to acknowledge, however, that the extent of medical control over the matter is nevertheless acknowledged by the EU and addressed with some level of concern; a trend that is not mirrored by wider society in the UK. The parameters of the conscientious objector clause in the closely related field of contraception, for example, were addressed by the ECtHR in the judgement in *Pichon and Sajous v. France* (Application No. 49853/99). The case concerned two French pharmacists who claimed that their freedom to manifest their religion had been violated when they were convicted by the French authorities for refusal to dispense oral contraceptives to three female customers. The Court stated that the right under Article 9 was not contravened, as a pharmacist's refusal to sell contraceptives did not fall within the scope of right to manifest a religion or a belief, and emphasized professional obligations over personal beliefs. Furthermore, the concept of abortion as a service, a matter that is not reflected in the 1967 Abortion Act, has in fact been recognized at the supranational level. The case of *Society for the Protection of the Unborn Child Ireland Ltd v. Stephen Grogan and others* (Case C-159/ 90) involved the circulation of information by Irish students on abortion services outside of the Republic of Ireland. SPUC challenged the publications by University College Dublin and Trinity College Dublin contravened national law by providing names, addresses and telephone numbers of clinics providing terminations in the UK were then included. Importantly, the Court obliberated the meaning of 'services' under Article 60 of the Treaty of Rome. Attention was drawn to the first paragraph of the provision, which states that definition rests with the question of remuneration; an action constitutes a service if it is paid for and is not governed by the provisions relating to freedom of goods, capital or persons. The Court also highlighted indent (d), which expressly details that activities of the professions fall within this definition of services. The judgement therefore continued that the termination of pregnancy, as lawfully practiced in several member states, is a medical service, which is normally provided either for remuneration or carried out in the course of a professional activity. Support was provided from the previous judgment in *Luis and Carbone v. Ministero del Tesoro* 919840 ECR 377 in which it was adjudicated that medical activities do indeed fall within the scope of Article 60. Despite SPUC's claims that abortion, as a grossly immoral action, could not be regarded in such a manner, the Court reiterated that domestic courts should not substitute its assessment for the legislation in those Member States where terminations are conducted legally. Thus, it was clearly stated that the medical termination of pregnancy, in accordance with the law of the State in which it is carried out, is considered a service.

The acceptance of abortion as a medical service at the supranational level marks an important facet in the search for an EU policy field. Although lacking the purpose displayed in some of the ECtHR rulings, the judgement does expound the sentiment that abortion is a medically necessary treatment for the EU. This raises questions in regard to possible welfare concerns, such as social inclusion, that can be linked to this type of treatment. Indeed, in 2001 the Laeken European Council adopted a set of commonly defined indicators, including access by all to resources, rights, goods and services, and these have come to play a central role in monitoring the performance of Member States (Commission of the European Communities 2002). Although clearly none directly reference medical treatments, health is a primary indicator, and this may have subtle ramifications for the administration of abortion services at the national level (Atkinson et al 2004). The judgement further goes beyond this point of law and touches upon a 'service for remuneration', additionally evoking ideas of a customer and an offer that can be acted upon out of choice; as such it opens the floodgates to challenges on the basis of, for example, appropriate consumer welfare.

Consequently, as abortion is not considered to be a right in supranational law, UK's legislative scheme does not contravene the EU in this manner. Of interest, however, is the fact that the region is in the minority of member states to deny abortion on demand and it appears that this is a fact that largely goes unnoticed amongst the general public. Indeed an acceptance of the current legislation, and failure to challenge the limitations placed on innovation, is apparent at the grassroots level across England and Wales, and Scotland. The termination of pregnancy undeniably remains an emotive and value-laden issue, and the ideational aspect is inescapable; unlike the simple yes/no debate presented prior to reform, however, a plethora of clinical and scientific dialogue now ensues on the appropriate administration of the procedure. As a result, the general public is progressively alienated from such elite debates and increasingly discouraged from challenging the existing status quo, even when their needs are not being met. The introduction of legal and safe methods to terminate a potentially harmful pregnancy in the 1960s was supported by a favourable climate of opinion. In the years since decriminalization, however, the abortion paradigm has inevitably evolved beyond a straightforward question of 'for' or 'against' and has become fractured (Entman 2002); multiple frames now exist on the role of the practitioner and the implementation of clinical developments, and a disparity is emerging between political knowledge and scientific expertise on the one hand, and civic appreciation of the issue on the other. Within this ideational domain, the UK public is thus increasingly alienated from elite policy debates (Fischer and Forester 1993), and consequently its attention for abortion governance is limited.

The clear framing (Rein and Schön 1993) of the abortion debate as a matter of public health necessity induced private attitude, and personal conscience, into public support for reform. Although a multiple-streams approach (Kingdon 1995) has previously been engaged to explain the overhaul of the law, and in particular the problem of maternal mortality had grown in recognition among the medical profession in the decades before, arguably the thalidomide tragedy of the early 1960s really served to punctuate the equilibrium (Baumgartner and Jones 1993) in the policy field. Prior to these events, only incremental changes to the legislation had been apparent, and the historical association of abortion with the criminal law persisted regardless of a number of campaigns. The crisis around the 'morning-sickness' pill, however, was engaged as a symbolic device by the reform lobby as to whether women finding themselves in such unfortunate circumstances should be treated as criminals or patients, and accompanied by a general air of liberalism in 1960s Britain, the formation of mass public support around the simple sentiment of decriminalization quickly ensued. When National Opinion Polls in 1962 asked the question 'Would you be in favour of a change to the law allowing doctors to terminate pregnancy where there is a good reason to believe that the baby would be badly deformed?', an overwhelming 72 percent answered 'Yes' and favoured decriminalization. By 1965, this had risen to a crushing 91 percent (Hindell and Simms 1968). Further, the younger spectrum of the population became engaged with the subject and, after the unnecessary death of a female undergraduate student, over a thousand Oxford Union students sent a petition to the Prime Minister demanding the legalislation of abortion. Later, the Oxford Union Society passed a motion condemning the existing laws by a 3 to 1 majority (Hindell and Simms 1968).

Previous studies have shown that when there are clear beneficiaries of policy, public support is far easier to galvanize than when multiple frames are presented to the public (Nelson and Kinder 1996). As such, the 1967 Abortion Act objectively fulfilled the public's simple demand for access to appropriate reproductive healthcare and silenced a baying crowd. For its stipulated purposes, therefore, national statistics demonstrate that it continues to suffice these aims to this day, and thus the government has been able to declare the policy a success. From an even more rudimentary standpoint overlooking an evidence base of facts and figures, however, society in the intervening years has appeared sufficiently appeased by the fact that abortion has become a reality of everyday healthcare for those women that need it. In this vein, the public, just as sub-national and institutional actors, operate in a rational, self-interested manner and, as a consequence, little motivation has surfaced to reignite a grassroots push for reform (March and Olsen 1984). Indeed, public health warnings with implications for abortion have certainly emerged since the implementation of the legislation; however, they have failed to attract the gravitas of the thalidomide tragedy. In 1995, for example, there was a 'pill scare' in which the UK Committee on Safety Medicines submitted that oral contraceptives containing gestodene or desogestrel were associated with a higher risk of venous thromboembolism. As a result, a significant number of women either switched brands or ceased contraception altogether, resulting in an increase in costs from abortions of over £46 million to the NHS (Furedi 1999). Unlike the punctuation to the equilibrium (Jones and Baumgartner 1999) that occurred in the 1960s, however, such events followed a much more conventional issue attention cycle (Downs 1972) in which 'fads' in challenges to the abortion law leap into prominence, but remain on the public agenda for only a limited time. Indeed, the warning around the oral contraceptive pill received massive media coverage in the days immediately following the announcement and, although the ramifications were considerable, the fact that the studies which had motivated the health warning were later disproved received less acknowledgement, and the issue slowly faded into the background.

Although the evolution of the abortion issue in mass consciousness thus originally reflected elite debates around a matter of public health, this has vastly depreciated in the decades since. As the policy field has gradually become the occupation of those with scientific and expert knowledge, the discussions around the termination of pregnancy have slowly failed to resonate with the public, and the issue of abortion largely appears resolved. Certainly, unlike the compelling argument for making abortion legal, elite policy discourse around the specifics of regulation does not resonate at the same emotive level with the public. Contrary to the overwhelming majority in favour of decriminalization prior to reform, for example, when Social Surveys (Gallup) polled the public in 1967 on amendments to the Abortion Bill concerning the approval of doctors and the grounds for abortion, there was an abnormally high percentage of 'Don't knows' (Hindell and Simms 1968). In the years since, this confusion has been a rising trend in opinion statistics relating to the specifics of abortion legislation. MORI, for example, has examined the attitudes of the UK public on the termination of pregnancy for BPAS by virtue of three studies conducted in 1997, 2001 and 2006.

The multiple conditions included in the question 'Do you approve or disapprove of abortion under the following circumstances?' all reflected an increase of 'Don't know' responses between 1997 and 2001, from 13 percent to 15 percent. In comparison, the simple statement 'Abortion should be made legally available for all who want it' was met with only 9 percent indifference in 1997, which rose by just 1 percent in 2001. The problem of the perpetuation of multiple frames, and the threat of alienating society, is further evidenced in a study conducted in the United States in 2000, in which college students, once a principal demographic in the debate, reported only a moderate degree of commitment to the issue of abortion (Carlton et al 2000). Consequently, interest groups have increasingly encountered difficulties of gathering support for their campaigns, particularly when it is additionally appreciated that these results are induced from the public though the course of interviews and do not demonstrate actual behaviour (Wicker 1969); thus it can reasonably be expected that in terms of proactive support for campaigns, the level of 'Neither agree or disagree' would rise.

2.6. CONCLUSION

The UK's statutory scheme dictating access to a termination of pregnancy is a fractious blend of the criminal law and healthcare domain, in which medical practitioners have assumed a key role in determining the level of access for women. Rebutting the popular view of a liberal regulatory field, therefore, the important absence of explicit right to abortion, at any point of gestation, can be extrapolated from analysis of the key statutes, and its status as an offence, promulgated on the strong idea of wrongdoing, can instead be viewed as an institution dating back to early common law. Bolstering this rationale, such path dependence (Krasner 1984) on the underlying element of criminality has been continually reaffirmed in legislative updates over the years that have served only to tinker with considerations over time limits and similar clauses, and refused to completely remove the procedure from the criminal law. The evolutionary underpinnings of historical institutionalism have thus provided much insight in this regard, and it has been demonstrated that only in times of great pressure, in which the difficult conflation of policy streams can open a vital window for change (Kingdon 1995), inducing punctuation to the equilibrium, can a divergence from history be evidenced. Demonstrating such a critical juncture was indeed the 1967 Abortion Act that served to provide a series of healthcare defences to the termination of pregnancy in response to a number of exogenous pressures. Importantly, however, the statute refused to completely remove its misdemeanor status, instead serving to medicalize the crime of abortion, and the regulatory tone of the procedure has endured throughout. Strongly reflected in the debates concerning the HFEA in 2000 and 2008, for example, parliamentarians are keen to keep radical measures off the agenda.

Legislative amendments in the field are of more than academic interest, however, and this halfway house, straddling both the criminal law and health policy domain, harmfully serves to constrain future innovation and change. Although pushing the procedure into the medical world, the failure to fully banish its illegal label has negatively impacted upon the woman's status as a patient, and defines her solely as a criminal until a third party states otherwise. The institutional barriers to accepting abortion as a legitimate therapeutic procedure in both public and private healthcare in the UK that inevitably ensue from this position therefore create a sub-optimal standard of care for women in situations of either elective or even necessary terminations at the point of delivery. Further exasperating this situation is the incorrect perception of the UK as the EU's capital for abortion. A broad study of this region instead demonstrates the high level of medical hegemony in comparison to neighbouring member states; although not appearing to impact heavily on the significant number of domestic abortions undertaken, this international context nevertheless indicates the arduous and subjective process of seeking a termination in the UK and distinguishes this national postcode lottery to the 'on demand' clauses of other countries. Grassroots activism in the UK over these matters, however, is discouraged through public alienation from overly scientific debates. Assuming the matter to be resolved, and abortion free and easy, the technical deliberations that proliferate over regulation are overlooked by the public, and important societal challenges that ensure the proper workings of the law are restricted and a woman's voice in the UK is increasingly dulled.

In summation, therefore, heavily constraining the status of a woman as a patient in the course of terminating a pregnancy strongly contributes to a negative image of the gender in times of abortion. Thus the idea that history matters in this policy domain, far from conjuring up a nostalgic take on quirky British laws, actually demonstrates an antiquated system for managing a legitimate clinical need for women. Although in practice, access to abortion in the UK is comprehensive, and managed by a number of service providers, this does not dictate that this is only a matter of principle. Indeed, such statistics obscure a multitude of other factors, such as the arduous process women must endure to be permitted the procedure. Drawing together the rules, practices and narratives (Lowndes and Roberts 2013) that shape the regulation of women's issues therefore, a task that will be more copiously covered in chapter 6, the problems that arise in instances in which the pregnancy is the result of rape, for example, are significant and should be of concern to the everyday lives of women.

Chapter Three

Balancing Protection and Prosecution: The Rationality of UK Prostitution Legislation

The global sex industry is a broad policy domain that houses a myriad of activities, many with contrasting statutory positions. To illustrate this point in the literature, a 2005 study conducted in Australia, with the intention of illustrating the variety of contexts in which prostitution can occur, identified a non-exhaustive list of 25 different types of sex work, each grouped under the headings of either 'direct' work, such as escort services, or 'indirect' labour, including telephone sex and massage parlours (Harcourt and Donovan 2005). Furthermore, this spectrum is constantly expanding, with the range of conduct being heavily assisted by the proliferation of modern technology (Sanders 2010), and now, by virtue of the Internet, constituting an even more diversified and exaggerated enterprise than ever before (Sarikakis 2015, 212). A communal heading for such trade consequently tells us little about the realities of contemporary governance over the topic, and the regulation of the issue is unquestionably complex across the legal jurisdictions in the UK. Although Northern Ireland has recently increased its criminal measures in regard to third parties engaged in prostitution and distinguished itself from the other regions on the matter, particularly stark across England, Wales and Scotland is the continued criminal ban placed on the solicitation of sex on the street. With punishment for those offering such services ranging from a non-statutory caution to a financial penalty, the continued perception of the behaviour as a public nuisance is prevalent. Putting this in everyday terms therefore, in 2012, in the months prior to the Olympic Games in London, police underwent a 'cleaning up' of the local boroughs, with the number of arrests for public prostitution in Tower Hamlets in the first few months alone far exceeding the previous yearly total (Furness 2012). In an increasingly sexually liberated society, however, in which lap-dancing bars and strip joints are no longer confined to the backstreets (Sanders 2006, 92), and simple searches of the Internet can open up an array of 'arrangement' web-sites in which 'sugar daddies' can connect with 'sugar babies' (Padawer 2009), the specific rigidity with which this outdoor activity continues to be entirely prohibited is certainly conspicuous and entices further investigation.

In contrast to the misinformed liberal perception of abortion legislation uncovered previously, therefore, it is this curious contradiction over 'sex for sale' within the policy field itself, and the lines drawn between legal and illegal behaviour, that is instead at the heart of this chapter. When viewed in the context that prostitution is now calculated to generate an estimated £5.3 billion for the economy every year (ONS 2014), the rationale underpinning the continued criminal status of street prostitution is a point of both empirical and academic interest that demands closer espousal. A focused institutional analysis of the behaviour of parliamentarians in this domain, therefore, ex-ploring the rules that determine rationality in the decision-making process (Duquech 2011), suggests a 'logic of calculation' undertaken by such agents operating in the context of both the procedural rules of the legislature (Nor-ton 2001) and the electoral arena (Denzau et al 1985). At the base level, acceptance of this matter rests heavily on standards of social order and de-cency, a frame elites readily perpetuate; from merely a cursory glance of history in the UK from the time of the Victorians, citizens and political elites alike have long distinguished between an individual's private life and the community's public action (Harris 1994), with the latter providing the ac-ceptable face of conduct. To not air one's dirty linen in public, a suggestion oddly first made by Napoleon (Lerman 1994), actually became a guiding principle in the nineteenth century and although this was a trend not confined to domestic shores, even reaching as far as the United States (Levinger and Raush 1977, 54), it became closely tied to a very British approach to the degree of constraint in matters of a sexual nature. Unsurprisingly, this same principle distinguishing acceptable and closeted behaviour was extended to prostitution legislation during this period and has certainly been explored previously in the surrounding scholarship (e.g., Kantola and Squires 2004, Sanders 2004). Working to enhance their own careers (Fenno 1978), there-fore, parliamentarians have long been acutely aware of the costly nature of morality politics, thereby in turn dictating the low priority afforded to prosti-tution legislation. Recent statutory amendments in Northern Ireland adopting a radical neo-abolitionist approach to the policy domain evidenced in addi-tional EU states (Jackobsson and Kotsadam 2013), however, suggest a key role for political ambition, and as the realities of the danger posed to street workers is increasingly exposed, the veracity of the public harm principle is correspondingly eroded, and an emerging impetus for reform from the grass-roots up is suggested.

Beginning by charting the history of prostitution in the context of three policy categories (Outshoorn 2008), the chapter addresses the development of the UK's early statutory scheme and the distinction in protective language housed in the Sexual Offences Acts and treatment of prostitution as a street crime. Current regulation through the Policing and Crime Act 2009 persists with this conspicuous indoor/outdoor distinction, and this can be directly contrasted with diverging legislative measures introduced into Northern Ireland in 2015. Closely following the Swedish model, and concentrating punishment on those purchasing sex, an outline of these now diverging schemes will feature in the second sub-section. By engaging rational choice institutionalism to examine the decision of parliamentarians, both in the context of the legislature and the electoral arena more generally, the refusal to adopt this classic abolitionist approach in England and Wales, and specifically afford a labour rights regulatory framework to street prostitution, is examined. Following a 'logic of calculation' (March and Olsen 1984), it is clear that sufficient incentive for individually driven legislative change has failed to emerge in previous years, and such inertia has been preserved by a clear social order and decency frame, a perception that largely overrides concern for individual damage, and additionally constrains increased liability for clients of prostitution. In the wake of high-profile cases such as the 'Bradford Murders', however, the mounting potential for a paradigm shift at the grassroots level, and corresponding political ambition to incite change, demands consideration. This possibility of future adaptation to the law, however, necessarily entails a full appreciation of alternative policy schemes beyond Northern Ireland, and the last section considers the lessons that can be drawn from foreign approaches to the matter, particularly in regard to the benefits of a stricter neo-abolitionist approach.

3.1. THE LAW ON PROSTITUTION: FROM 'STREET OFFENCES' TO 'SEXUAL OFFENCES'

Prostitution is a booming business throughout the world, and an endeavour subject to an abundance of tales across the centuries. Expansive research among legal scholars, for example, has already paid much attention to the intricacies of the law in this field, and directed large efforts towards classifying precisely what amounts to prostitution, not only domestically but across the globe (Weitzer 2010). Interestingly, a consensus over the definition of a prostitute as one which offers themselves to another as a sexual partner is easily garnered and relatively unproblematic, and alone contributes little to the negative labelling of women. Importantly, however, the law principally governs the act of prostitution, and the next crucial step of surmising what in fact constitutes this action is actually plagued with far greater ambiguities. Indeed this hesitancy to provide a strict statutory formulation has been recorded throughout history. The seemingly logical and basic definition would be an act of sexual relations between the aforementioned prostitute and a paying customer, and is a characterization posited by many (Flowers 1998). Perhaps an obvious point, but according to Roby (1969), however, persons are not criminals unless the law defines their behaviour as such, and this is where a divergence in classification is apparent. As a baseline principle, therefore, illegal prostitution in the UK as solicitation on the street can be distinguished from more social formulations that encapsulate permitted behaviour, such as Goodall's definition of earning a living wholly or in part from the emotionally indifferent provision of sexual services (1995). In two contrasting examples, therefore, a Bristol-based initiative in the early month of 2014 saw multiple arrests for kerb crawling as an illegal aspect of outdoor prostitution (BBC News 2014a). In a startling case from 2012, however, a 29-year-old self-employed 'escort', who reportedly earned in excess of £300,000 over two years by way of selling sex, attracted criminal liability and a prison sentence solely for tax evasion of the money earned, rather than principally for such conduct performed, as it was, behind closed doors (*The Telegraph* reporters 2012).

Globally, prostitution regimes have comprised varying degrees of regulation, prohibition and abolition (Outshorn, 2004, 8). Placing this in domestic statutory terms, attempts to address the activity have run in two veins with contrasting underlying intentions. The first legislative stream to address the burgeoning trade in the UK was introduced in the Sexual Offences Act 1956; the measure detailed 10 illegal activities concerning prostitutes, most of which involved the behaviour of third parties. Thus ranging from procuring a girl under the age of 21, to a man living off the earning of prostitutes, the statute was heavily entrenched in the desire to protect sections of society perceived as vulnerable. Stipulating the offence of brothel keeping, for example, the law increased the reach of prosecution beyond just street workers, a theme that was taken further still in subsequent acts. Indeed, in 1985, the offences of kerb crawling and persistently loitering for the purposes of prostitution were both outlined in section 1 and 2. A movement towards addressing the gender bias in this series of acts is also of note and, reflecting the demands of an expanding domain, and in part the complications imposed by a globalized world, the issue of forced prostitution was significant feature of the third iteration of this collection of statutes. Indeed, sections 57 and 58 respectively detailed the liability for trafficking into the UK, and within the UK, for sexual exploitation with the accompanying sanction of either imprisonment or a fine.

The second stream comprises the Street Offences Act 1959, which submitted a wildly different agenda significantly driven by prosecution, and still remains in force to this day. Explicitly addressing the problem of the 'common' street prostitute, it outlined criminal liability for the selling of sex in such a manner and created no misapprehension as to the notion of wrongdoing in this regard. Although amended by section 16 of the Policing and Crime Act 2009 to remove the word 'common', now replaced by the term person, the influence of its clauses still remains. Unsurprisingly, therefore, the language used in the two streams adopts widely different tones, with the protective slant of the former to no extent mirrored in the latter. Having at its heart the problem of the prostitute, the Street Offences Act attempted to usher many women off the street and into private abodes, and it is here that the social order and public decency frame, which will be attended to in more detail later, finds much statutory backing. The use of the term 'common prostitute', for example, clearly upheld the antiquated notion of women of disrepute evidenced throughout the Victorian period, and, although now removed from the black letter of the law, arguably continues to influence regulation to this day. The extent to which class-based values of acceptable behavior have historically underpinned the legislative field, therefore, is palpable, with the female worker continually identified as a sub-class in need of segregation from other upstanding citizens and productive members of the community. Recent additions to the statutory landscape in the form of the Policing and Crime Act 2009, and the Modern Slavery Act 2015, however, both of which will be outlined below, curiously continue to reflect these standards.

Uncovering these two interrelated principles of protection and prosecution allows for much plausible explanation for legislative and societal reaction across the ages, a line of inquiry that will be developed later in this chapter. Of brief note at this juncture, however, is that statutory development from the 1950s to the contemporary situation has continually addressed the outdoor presence of women of disrepute within a framework that largely accepted the use of such service by others, predominately men. Although, granted, the Sexual Offences Acts were, and continue to be, entirely necessary for safeguarding vulnerable sections of society, and additionally incorporate violent assaults such as rape, all of which will be explored in the next chapter, this does not mitigate the inadequacies of the Street Offences Act. Indeed no form of protection is envisaged as necessary in the instances of street prostitution, and the woman first and foremost is labelled a criminal. Returning to a point made in the introduction of this book, therefore, it is challenged that adopting such a zero-tolerance approach to the legislation allows for many to fall between the gaps, and the rationale that those that solicit sex on the street are automatically free to make that choice, and consequently should accept criminal liability, is a harmful assumption to make. Unlike the fractious policy domain resulting from the overlapping legislation in abortion, therefore, this action outlines the disparate nature of two distinct forms of 'sex for sale' within the same policy domain.

3.2. THE POLICING AND CRIME ACT 2009

As evidenced throughout history, nothing in the current legislation in England, Wales and Scotland directly stipulates that the exchange of sexual services for money, as a baseline principle, is an illegal act; rather it only becomes so if performed in certain stipulated circumstances. Running alongside the criminality of selling sex on the street, therefore, the Policing and Crime Act 2009 details that it is in fact those publicly living off the earnings of prostitution in England and Wales, or indeed those exercising control over prostitutes, which will attract prosecution. The offering of sex for fiduciary gain by solicitation, therefore, or through owning a brothel, procuring, or assuming the role of a pimp, would fall within this category. In a similar vein, monetary offerings from what is colloquially termed 'kerb-crawling', in which a person, typically a man, solicits sexual pursuits by driving around known red-light areas (Brooks-Gordon and Gelsthorpe 2003), is also against the law; if arranged solely by the person offering the activity, however, and this is conducted in private as opposed to the street, such action is deemed permissible. An overarching jurisprudential imperative can therefore be extrapolated from the current regulatory field distinguishing public and private acts, creating the situation in which the independent prostitute working lawfully from their home, and potentially enjoying good relations with the police (West and Austin 2005), is lawful in their conduct, as contrasted to those occupying the streets at night. This contradictory standpoint filters down into several other anomalies such as the supposedly straightforward example of advertising. By virtue of sections 46 and 47 of the Criminal Justice Act 2001, the use of colloquially termed 'tart cards' to promote the services of prostitutes are entirely barred in public places such as telephone boxes, shelters or hoods (Home Office 2001). As a result, the clamping down on these items has periodically occurred and in 2003, for instance, it was reported that 12 million were removed from the London area alone to the considerable cost of approximately £250,000 (Conway 2004).

Although a seemingly insignificant detail, the level of enforcement of this clause is of interest in comparison to the less overt prostitution activities. The pertinence of such a marketing method is of course eroded in a modern age in which even phone booths are now a rarity, and the practice has been increasingly usurped as the primary portal for sharing information about adult services by social networking sites; interestingly, however, the sanctions and backlash attached to this highly developed form of publicity is, by contrast, minimal, despite of its widespread use. A study of prostitution in New York, for example, unveiled that of the 290 sex workers studied, 83 percent had a Facebook page (Venkatesh 2011), and the United States' 'Craigslist' has netted a reported $36 million income related to the advertising of adult and erotic services (Weiss and Samenow 2010, 243); the UK is no different, and *The Times* newspaper reported dozens of such pages in 2014. According to representatives of Facebook, however, action can only be taken in response to offensive items that are directly reported to the administrators by users (Hamilton et al 2013), and police interjection into this online trend is limited to say the least, the activity not specifically covered in any statute. Again feeding back into this public/private divide therefore, it appears that the principal concern of much of the legislation is towards that which is outwardly noticeable.

In light of this revelation, it is of countenance that the 2009 statute was actually purported to tackle the stigmatization around street work evidenced previously, and create a more egalitarian approach to liability for the customers of prostitution. Indeed, much of New Labour's response to the trade appeared to be underpinned by the notion of social inclusion, forwarded from the 1980s onwards, and a significant degree of the rhetoric engaged in the consultation process of the time focused heavily on multi-agency action (Scoular and O'Neill 2007). In particular, section 17 introduced mandatory attendance at meetings for those engaging in such conduct to discuss, among other matters, how to cease such activity. Thus a key theme in the gathering of data and opinions that began in 2004 was the need for a balanced approach between protection and prevention, explicitly stipulating that one of the best forms of safeguarding for those involved in prostitution was justice (Home Office 2004). Certainly a commendable submission, the extent to which this current legislative instrument has achieved such aims is nevertheless questionable, and will feature in the final sub-section of this chapter. Suffice to say at this moment, however, that the open dialogue that flourished in such a process, David Blunkett himself welcoming submissions of all natures, interestingly highlighted the government's awareness of how the issue should sit within the context of wider policymaking (Home Office 2004, 6), regardless of its subsequent failures to remove the entrenched image of the hardened street hooker.

On a closing point in terms of the current statutory scheme, and alluded to previously, although formerly unified in its approach to prostitution regulation, the UK has recently experienced a division in its stipulation of criminal sanction, and Northern Ireland now provides a distinct legislative agenda for prostitution. As discussed in the preceding chapter on abortion, control over criminal powers in the region has been a complex matter over the decades, and responsibility has devolved to Stormont and passed back to Westminster on a number of occasions as dependent on political conflict, and a distinct statute pertaining to prostitution in the country is not a new occurrence. Indeed, the Sexual Offences (Northern Ireland) Order 2008 previously stipulated the country's framework for sexual offences, but rather than challenging the corresponding legislation in the rest of the UK, it largely mirrored the Sexual Offences Act 2003 and Sexual Offences Act (Scotland) 2009. This was to such an extent that the Policing and Crime Act, as outlined above, amended its provisions to bring the three legal jurisdictions in line on the matter of prostitution with one common statute. From 2013 onwards, however, Stormont has steadily increased its debates around the matter, and a new initiative has been deliberated with the result of a sharp change to the law that now clearly distinguishes the Irish approach from England, Wales and Scotland. Although under the terms of devolution, this latter region is free to pursue its own policies on the matter, and several amendments have been introduced in the vein of Northern Ireland's approach discussed next, these have thus far failed, and the law, for the most part, mirrors the approach of England and Wales.

Specifically, the Human Trafficking and Exploitation (Criminal Justice and Support for Victims) Act (Northern Ireland) 2015 stipulates that it is illegal to pay for sex in the region. The product of a PMB introduced into Stormont in 2013 by Lord Murrow, the controversial stance initially met with mixed reviews, with the Justice Minister David Ford strongly asserting his opposition (McDonald 2014). Despite this, the vast majority of provisions have received Royal Assent, with two sentiments, in particular, of great magnitude. As a result, the new law repeals Article 59 of the 2008 Order, detailing the offence of loitering or soliciting for the purposes of offering sexual services, and Article 64a, outlining the criminality of promising payment for the sexual services of a prostitute, and provides the offence of obtaining sexual services from a person in exchange for financial gain. In simple terms, therefore, the new scheme dictates that it is an offence to buy, but not sell, sex, and this closely follows the long-standing Swedish model. Introduced as a bill in 1998, and coming into full force in 1999, the 'Kvinnofrid' law has since become the cornerstone of Scandinavian efforts to create a democratic society in which women and girls can live free from fear of male violence (Ekberg 2004). Now similarly adopted in Northern Ireland, the merits of this scheme will be addressed in due course.

It is therefore suggested that despite outward attempts at a more empathetic approach to prostitutes, this modern scheme has again failed to completely remove the preoccupation with the problem of the street prostitute. Although claiming to address a range of offences, and the problem of an inequitable level of sanction for women, and notably tackling sex trafficking, it is suggested that the attempt to move towards social inclusion is actually constrained by the retention of this conspicuous indoor/outdoor distinction. The sharp divide between the pursuits appears to be endemic in various

stages of the policy domain, with smaller conflicting messages further ab-
sorbing this arbitrary standard, and the reasons for such legislative decisions,
and societal reaction, now demands attention. Although the reality of Northern Ireland's new scheme in ensuring a safer sex industry will be debated
later in the chapter, this next section will nevertheless deliberate this alternative 'Swedish model', alongside other options such as Germany's approach to
the matter, in terms of the incentives for change in England, Wales and
Scotland. Stricter legislative controls introduced in 2009 thus certainly question the motives of government, but it is actually analysis of the wider debate
concerning full decriminalization, as explored below, that highlights the
dominant constraints on parliament.

3.3. A PUBLIC NUISANCE OR A QUESTION OF LABOUR RIGHTS?

A state of legislative inertia characterizes the field of prostitution regulation,
with few meaningful changes to the statutory landscape evidenced since the
1950s, and the criminal status of street conduct remaining untouched. In a
contemporary world hosting a problematic economic situation, however, but
in which the sex industry nevertheless continues to flourish, the rationality of
England, Wales and Scotland's decision to persist with this position demands
attention. There are precedents in domestic law of radically overhauling the
statutory position, from the removal of capital punishment to the decriminalization of homosexuality, and by more specifically revealing the lack of a
strict ethical binary over moral and immoral behaviour in the field of 'sex for
sale', it appears that similar transformation to this policy field is at least in
theory possible. Indeed, the incongruence across the various indoor and outdoor acts detailed above results in awkward irregularities and definitional
conundrums in regard to what constitutes lawful and unlawful activity, but
does suggests that the so-called mainstreaming of the sex industry (Brents
and Sanders 2010) has occurred in at least an asymmetrical fashion in the
UK. Thus, when considered in the context of this creeping liberalization, the
regulatory field hints at a deliberate but uneasy trade-off on the part of key
institutional actors between a collective moral framework and an innovative
scheme of labour rights. Attempts to capture an explanation for a public/
private divide have long been attempted and largely centre around the continued reliance upon Victorian measures, originally intended to purify the public world (Bland 1992) and combat a mounting 'social evil' (McHugh 2013),
in the construction of the idea of community (Hubbard 1998). The notion that
the legislation remains infused with this antiquated framework of social order
and decency, and a desire to harness a public nuisance, is therefore engaged
in this section and its ability to constrain the full decriminalization of prostitution, or even consider alternative 'halfway' house schemes, is deliberated.

A full espousal of the incentive structure for policy actors in this domain must go beyond a study of the individual, and it is rational choice institutionalism, taking institutions as scripts that constrain behaviour (Shepsle 2006), which provides an appropriate and beneficial analytical tool in this regard. In contrast to the preceding issue of abortion, therefore, it is contended that the merits of historical institutionalism alone would be unable to fully capture the intricate balance between social order and labour rights in this domain, and of greater significance are the calculated preferences that arise from the interaction of individuals and institutions (Katznelson and Weingast 2005). For proponents of this alternative strain of NI, '*rules are the strategic context in which optimizing behavior takes place*' (Shepsle 1989, 135) and can constitute many forms, with various entities falling within this school of thought. Acknowledging generally, therefore, that it is the formally constructed rules of the game that must be explored, two approaches to rational choice institutionalism, focused on institutional rules (Ostrom 1986) and the operation of individuals within organizations (Niskanen 1971) respectively, will be engaged in this section. Fearing the costly nature of legislating on morality, and strongly swayed by the climate of opinion of the voting public, the institutional shaping of a parliamentarian's desire to act is revealed.

Providing the first wave of corroboration for the continued criminal status of prostitution are the long-standing rules of the legislature. Much work has previously been undertaken into the institutionalization of core legislative bodies such as the House of Representatives and Commons, and these set out a series of important insights into the formal constraints that substantially dictate the rules of the game in lawmaking across all policy domains (Gilligan and Krehbiel 1990). Central to the ethos of this work is the sentiment that '*rational, goal-orientated entities . . . are created to perform certain functions and tasks*' (Cooper 1977, 140). Submitting that institutions absorb specific qualities, and indeed lose others, as they progress and mature, Hibbing discusses that institutionalization embodies the process by which a body adopts a definitive way of performing its functions. Studying the British House of Commons in the 1980s, his research concludes that boundaries have been firmly entrenched in the organization and notes an increasing reliance on universalistic rules. Often referred to as standard operating procedures in neighbouring literature, the author continues that this behaviour is distinct from the surrounding environment and, providing a nod to the work of Jewel and Patterson (1977), is independent of membership and issues of the moment (Hibbing 1988). One such rule is that the capacity to produce policy change generally is heavily dependent upon an agreement to alter the status quo by institutional players. Importantly, however, as the number of veto points and their ideological distances increase, so too does policy stability (Tsebelis 2002). This is evidenced continually across matters of an ethical nature, and specifically in terms of abortion legislation uncovered previously, in which debates are vast and change is minimal. As a result of this unlikely consensus caused by such polarizing matters, ideology will further instigate parliamentary players to act according to the lowest common denominator resulting in change unless guided otherwise (Von Wahl 2008). Indeed, the restrictions on cohesive voting behaviour caused by normative values that cut across traditional left/right divisions, and the unpredictability of conscience in 'free votes', has previously been highlighted in British voting behaviour on a number of social matters such as homosexuality and capital punishment (Hibbing and Marsh 1987), in the European Economic Community issues in the 1974–1979 parliament (Rasmussen and McCormick 1985), and, from an Australian perspective, on euthanasia, stem cell research and, indeed, the abortifacient drug RU486 (Warhurst 2008). At this premature stage, therefore, it can be suggested that any legislative amendments to this field that alter the underlying tone and ideology of prostitution are thus avoided by successive governments due to their costly nature, a trend that has been extolled across mooted amendments to the regulatory field over the years.

Governmental activity around prostitution legislation may have indeed increased throughout the last decade, with consultation papers published in 2000 and 2004, but both documents staunchly refused to depart from the overarching demand for enforcement. As referenced above, the latter, entitled 'Paying the Price: a Consultation Paper on Prostitution', was heralded by the then Home Secretary, David Blunkett, as a starting point for the development of a realistic and coherent strategy to address the activity, and its consequences both for the individual and for surrounding communities. A significant feature of the paper, and certainly the surrounding rhetoric, was the need to tackle those forced to engage in prostitution activities, who were seen as worryingly falling foul of exploitation and the associated pitfalls of the sex industry. Citing that the 2003 Sexual Offences Act had initiated the reform process in terms of trafficking, it was claimed that more still needed to be done in this realm, and specifically in regard to the definition of vulnerability. As such the concept of preventative measures to protect those at risk of being drawn into a vicious cycle was a key driver for the research (Home Office 2004). Although importantly addressing protection, therefore, this did not amount to an extension of existing law, but rather the compounding of a pre-existing approach, and alternatives to the current outlawed status of prostitution were not realistically considered. In this vein, the recent attempts to include the criminalization of purchasing sex, as an alternative to full decriminalization of street prostitution, in the 2015 Modern Slavery Bill through an amendment tabled by Fiona Mactaggart, MP, was swiftly dropped after facing tough opposition in the Commons. Marking a radical departure from the law, and adopting a Swedish model of regulation, as is the case in Northern Ireland, it again appeared a step too far even for substantial debate. Clearly evident across a range of interventions, therefore, the polarizing nature of the topic permits some minor developments, but significantly constrains notable change.

Despite its failure, however, the principle enshrined in Mactaggart's amendment is important to acknowledge, particularly in the context of its increasing global acceptance. Various models of prostitution regulation can be identified across the world, from the Swedish model discussed above—to which this failed amendment is most akin—through to the German framework of complete decriminalization. In this latter, radical example, its absence from parliamentary debates in England and Wales is conspicuous, particularly in the flourishing economic climate referred to previously. In the region, a sophisticated web of labour laws now shroud the activity, deeming prostitution to be a legitimate occupation that requires appropriate legal protection. Interestingly, it has been argued in some quarters that the success of this legislative change can largely be attributed to the definition of prostitution, seen as construing different activities in Sweden and in Germany. In the former, it is perceived as unacceptable, with significant parallels drawn to slavery, and identified as a variant of rape and abuse, with tangible health-care concerns such as the spread of disease. By way of contrast, Germany identifies prostitution as multi-faceted and not existing as a problem of itself; rather, a multitude of women can assume the role of prostitute, and variations in status invariably ensue (Dodillet 2004); allowing this statutory change of full decriminalization to come to fruition, this perception of prostitution is a theme that will be explored not only in regard to the UK's view of the activity in more detail below, but also has consequences for the stereotypical imagery of women that has run throughout the analysis of women's issues in this book. Indeed it is a marked deficiency in legislation that addresses the issue rather than the individual that dominant stereotyping is allowed to flourish which, in turn, allows women to fall between the gaps. In terms of the continued criminal status of prostitution, this often manifests in a plethora of myths such as a women cannot be raped (CPS 2012), or a blind eye turned when a violent crime against a street worker is committed. By turning this statutory focus on its head in the manner conducted in Germany, therefore, it becomes the priory of regulation to address the woman in a specific realm, rather than defining her solely by her activity. Prior to this aggregate analysis, however, which will feature in more detail in the concluding chapter, the opposing definition around prostitution in England, Wales and Scotland requires espousal.

Sitting aside from Sweden's concern for harm to prostitutes, and Germany's innovative labour perception, the UK's approach to prostitution, save Northern Ireland who, although sharing much history on the matter, will be dealt with in turn later, rests heavily on a social order and decency framework. Societal concern for the street prostitute has long existed across these two jurisdictions and can find its routes in a series of misinformed assumptions that appear ubiquitous in the historical perception of the act. First, and going against the grain of other matters covered in the course of this book, its sequential development is not principally characterized by an overarching statutory ban on the activity as is so often presumed, but largely focuses on the micro-level problem of the female prostitute. Second, the enduring definition of prostitution as a profession, indicating a deliberate and free choice on the part of the woman, is unveiled as deeply flawed. Finding little corroboration in historical text, it is evidenced that the public far from accepted the activity as legitimate and instead objected to the sight of the working-class prostitute. Referring to the early account of the law stipulated above, therefore, it appears that despite 'street offences' being supplemented by concern around prostitution more generally in 'sexual offences', these two principles are enduring both at a legislative level and in societal attitude.

First, as opposed to the strong element of misdemeanour infused in the history of abortive procedures and rape, for example, descriptions of street solicitation are not heavily legalistic in their tone. Anecdotes instead largely recount the inappropriateness of prostitution in the community more generally, and it is the marginalized status of sex workers from the rest of society that is commonly the focus of such narrative. Reference to the activity is therefore still rife in historical documents, but is deeply infused with critiques of the woman's immorality and poor standing as opposed to criminal conduct; in this sense, it is prostitutes that have long been identified as the problem, rather than the act of prostitution itself being problematic. One classic example of this situation emanates from the New Testament and the story of Mary Magdalene, the woman of central importance in the crucifixion of Christ. Biblical accounts focus heavily on this character's status and her image as a woman cured of evil spirits (Luke 8:2), as opposed to recounting her life story (D'Angelo 1999), and it is Magdalene's subsequent sanctification, supposedly illustrating that confession, contrition and penance can wipe away even what is regarded as one of the worst of sins in Christian teaching (Mazo Karras 1990, 3), that is of vast religious significance. Furthermore, Ancient Rome appeared to proffer no specific legislation on prostitution (McGinn 1998), but instead grouped such women in statute as infamis, or 'lacking in reputation', and prescribed a range of legal disabilities to which they were to be subjected (Edwards 1997, 66). This included the elimination of certain political rights, as well as exclusion from religious celebrations (McGinn 1998, 23) and had the effect of positioning prostitutes alongside other socially marginal groups, such as gladiators and actors, as noncitizens (Bohle 2013). This identification of immorality was thus a key defining feature between Romans (Edwards 1993) and served to set individuals apart. Interestingly, the prolific use of these prostitutes as courtesans by the elite (Faraone and McClure 2008, Sanger 2013) and arguably the early problem of an emerging sex industry were, in comparison, largely overlooked.

This isolating approach to the woman was similarly evident in Victorian England. Aimed at protecting servicemen vulnerable to the spread of infection, and taking inspiration from the treatment of women abroad, the introduction of a sequence of Contagious Diseases Acts sought to control the domestic use of prostitutes. An activity heavily engaged with by the British Army throughout the 1800s in which a high incidence of venereal disease was evidenced (Ramanna 2000), the use of commercial sex was most clearly evident in the colony of India. In order to prevent the spread of infection among the forces, medical officers would routinely test these women for venereal disease, sending away those who were found to be carrying an illness. This practice soon spread to protecting soldiers and jailers in towns in England (Walkowitz and Walkowitz 1973), and the first act in 1864 detailed that any woman suspected of being a common prostitute was obliged to submit to an internal genital examination. Refusal to comply with these terms was made difficult for women, and could potentially result in a prison sentence of three months or, alternatively, hard labour. Two years later, this statutory instrument was extended to the civilian population (Walkowitz and Walkowitz 1973), and in 1869 the penalty was doubled to six months. Although granted, legislation against public nuisance had already made reference to brothels in 1751, and the Vagrancy Act of 1824 introduced the term 'common prostitute' into the legislation and criminalized prostitution for the first time; this specific series of instruments was crucial in compounding the isolated status of women selling sex on the street, in the context of an overarching acceptance of the activity. Certainly, by providing statutory protection for men against the risk of disease, the activity of prostitution, by deduction, was widely considered permissible, and this period of legislative intervention arguably marked an attempt to domesticate the problem (Howell 2000) and remove the nuisance from public glare.

Condemnation of the worrying statutory interjection was at first limited (Smith 1990), due in large part to parliament deliberately passing the statutes quietly without any debate in the HoC (Smith 1971, 119). With gradual awareness, however, came creeping outrage from a range of perspectives, and legislative challenges began in earnest; some, such as William Fowler, the liberal MP for Cambridge, considered that the regulation in effect legalized prostitution, others, led largely by Josephine Butler and the Ladies' National Association for Repeal of the Acts, centred their argument around the violation of English women's basic liberties (Hamilton 1978). Having gathered much notable support, including from the renowned philosopher John Stuart Mill (Hamilton 1978, 17), repeal of the instruments was finally achieved in 1886, and the Criminal Law Amendment Act 1885 assumed the role of principal statute over prostitution, prescribing terms such as the raising the age of consent from 12 to 16, and more explicitly addressing the prevalence of brothels. It is here, therefore, that the counterfactual causal narrative that has loomed over this chronological account of the legislative field can be partially dispensed with. Indeed, it has appeared at junctures that the divide between indoor and outdoor activity could be more readily assimilated to the convention type status of abortion as a crime evidenced previously, existing as it has across vast time spans. It is considered, however, that such a path-dependent approach (Krasner 1988) is not an accurate portrayal of this situation, and in fact parliament has indicated its desire to combat the expanding problem in a variety of manners. Thus, although the divide between activities may be clear throughout, this can be more accurately seen as decisive legislative action rather than a determinate decision at the point of policy formation.

The second, and interrelated, flawed conjecture that persists around the perception of street prostitutes by society more generally is the title afforded to prostitution as the 'world's oldest profession'. Many researchers have laid claim to the existence of such activity in nearly all ancient and contemporary cultures (e.g., Drexler 1996, Whelehan 2001), but a challenge to this popular declaration can be mounted not only in respect of the empirical authenticity of the assertion, but also in terms of the veracity of the definition. The reality of the statement has indeed become a bone of contention in the literature, and scholarship has instead come to shed light on a slightly different narrative of prostitution across the ages, challenging such a cliché. A seminal work in the *American Historical Review*, for example, contends that the sale of sexual services was far from a salient feature across all of antiquity (Glifoye 1999), a statement that has since been corroborated in various sources (e.g., Vishina 2005). More importantly, however, the term profession is inappropriately engaged here, and the review of the Victorian statutory position above pays testament to this. The strict penal measures were seen as a way of purging 'material nuisance' and avoided the problem of prostitution (Walkowitz and Walkowitz 1973), rather than acknowledging any form of industry. Often reputed to be the "unskilled daughters of the unskilled classes" (Flexner, cited in Walkowitz 1980, 15), prostitutes were not afforded professional standing in society as the quote suggests, but were an occurrence that seemingly demanded eradication. Furthermore, prostitution was largely viewed as a necessity for certain groupings, rather than a privileged choice, a fact that has continually found little empathy in statute. Instead, as highlighted throughout literature in which boys were often depicted as pickpockets, and girls as prostitutes (Wolff 1996), a gender-specific need to turn to such action has long characterized the field. In this vein, the consequences of venereal disease for the woman was also largely overlooked, and those contending to try to improve the sector often rested their case on the need for moral salvation for such women, rather than the protection of their healthcare needs. A key example of this comes from Scotland in which a non-statutory female penitentiary movement, entitled the Glasgow Magdalene Institution, set about trying to encourage moral reform of such women (Mahood 1990), rather than addressing the underlying reasons for turning to prostitution.

Such long-standing assumptions around prostitution as the free choice of the morally corrupt, therefore, have been continually reflected at all stages of legislative development. 'Sex for sale' itself has never been heavily regulated, but the problem of female prostitutes in terms of public order and decency, and more pragmatically in terms of the spread of disease, have continually been at the heart of governance. It is here that the persistent tag of 'profession' that has accompanied prostitution is eroded, and far from a free choice by the majority of workers, the offering of sex for financial gain was a necessity of the working-class women and thus one that Victorian Britain did not want to draw attention to. Arguably these interrelated pursuits have consistently underpinned legislative societal reaction to the policy domain, as exemplified by the 'Street Offences' tag that remains in force to this day. Vastly mirroring the strict retention of the element of misdemeanour extolled in abortion legislation, and returning to an aforementioned point, it could be suggested that a path-dependent (Krasner 1988) approach has similarly come to characterize this arena. Unlike the termination of pregnancy, however, this domain has not experienced the same critical punctuation of decriminalization, and the current statutory scheme amends little from the past. Bringing into focus again to the lens of rational choice institutionalism, therefore, to unpick the incentive structure of the legislature in isolation is certainly inadequate at this point. Rather studies have demonstrated that the rules exacted upon parliamentarians do not emanate solely from the institution in which they perform their formal duties, but further they have a responsibility to wider society (March and Olsen 1984).

Indeed, at a more party-political level a number of objectives are held by parliamentarians, such as reselection, re-election, party office and legislative office, which are affected by these institutional rules (Strøm 1997). Moving beyond the career desires of politicians within the context of the legislature, however, their representative position for the public, and demand to curry favour with such a voting body, is of significance here (Bräuninger et al 2012). Incorporating prostitution into legislation addressing sexual offences supposedly marked a turning point in attitudes towards the activity; putting to bed the idea of nuisance so heavily embedded in Victorian attitudes towards street solicitation, and the fear for order and decency exemplified by instruments such as the Contagious Diseases Act, the instruments claimed to introduce a level of protection in regard to tougher measures on clients. In reality, however, the continuation of the 'Street Offence' tag alongside these amendments resulted in very little change for the individual and can arguably be attributed to this endemic public/private and a rational trade-off on the part of parliamentarians. This may appear strange when, on the surface at least, mass public opinion appears to readily group all 'sex for sale' acts into one class of behaviour. A survey conducted on behalf of the Government

Equalities Office by Ipsos MORI in 2008, for example, charted that 59 percent of a representative sample of British adults agreed with the perception that prostitution is a perfectly reasonable choice that women should be free to make (Government Equities Office 2008). That said, a 'not in my backyard' (NIMBY) approach seems to be taken and reflected in areas further than purely the black letter of the law, and the stigma attached to outdoor prostitutes is evident across numerous sections of society, from vice squads 'cleaning up' red-light districts in the aforementioned example of areas of London for fear of degrading the Olympics (*The Telegraph* 2012a), to popular media portrayals of the modern-day Cinderella tale of the needy but thankfully rescued 'Pretty Woman' (Kelley 1994), right down to community fears at local council meetings linking known red-light districts to increased drug use (*Manchester Evening News* 2010). Indeed, according to O'Neill, 'the word "prostitute" is the "end stop" in discourses on good and honest women' (2001, 186), and street solicitation is far more likely to garner citizen complaints than the more, as Weitzer terms it, 'clandestine, indoor varieties' (1999, 84). Pandering to a voting public, therefore, that appears to rid their local area of any public activity, it appears that a focus on the protection aspect of legislation in regard to exploitation and trafficking is a far less costly activity for the career politician.

Although entirely plausible in its statement on causality, this suggestion does beg the question of how change was conversely possible in Northern Ireland. A further benefit of the theoretical lenses of rational choice institutionalism, however, are their comparative utility, and, having outlined a link between this public order and decency framework and the institutional constraints faced by parliamentarians, attention is naturally then drawn to the innovations of late in the third legal jurisdiction. Formally under direct rule from Westminster, the region shares much of the same history of prostitution uncovered above, heavily dominated by a desire to remove the 'infectious creature, a carrier of disease and immorality' (Luddy 2007, 7) from public glare. If this chronology can be supposed to have a discernible impact upon the actions of the legislature, therefore, the reasons for the country's breakaway challenges the assertion that policy change is too costly a pursuit for parliamentarians. The causal hypothesis that has been so carefully garnered throughout this section, however, should not be disposed of in haste; rather the distinct religious tradition, as was so instrumental in abortion policy previously, again comes to the fore in this instance, albeit it with a slightly more radical stance. Certainly, religious tradition, far eroded in the rest of the UK, occupies an integral role in the formation not only of political incentives but also in galvanizing grassroots support.

Arguably born from an emerging moral panic that readily equates all prostitution with trafficking, religious support has been galvanized by the framing of the issue and, returning to Sweden's concern for the proliferation of harm from the trade, promoting the evils of street work has been crucial in these legislative changes. Ruhama, for example, a Dublin-based NGO that works with women affected by prostitution, has focused its campaigns around the high levels of trafficking for reasons of sexual exploitation in Ireland; a submission to the European Communion specifically highlighted this number to be 69 percent (Ruhama 2015). Similarly, the dominance of organizations such as the fundamentalist Christian charity CARE, and the European network affiliated Act to Prevent Trafficking (APT), in projecting a 'rescuer industry' in which all aspects of the sex industry reflect vulnerability, has been noteworthy (Ellison 2012). This saviour complex is at first surprising given the fact that societal attitudes in Northern Ireland have always been comparatively less tolerant of prostitution than its other UK neighbours (Sneddon and Kremer 1992). Indeed, the intent to clear the streets of such ill behaviour arguably extended beyond the impact of the Contagious Diseases Acts, and workhouses, termed Magdalene laundries, were established in large numbers to effectively imprison those perceived to be a threat to the moral fibre of society (Smith 2007). Running alongside this proactive approach, however, has been a long-standing empathy for the prostitute as an abandoned woman in need of rescuing (Luddy 2007, 7), and bridging the gap between these positions has largely been the religious congregations and missionary societies. While formerly religious organizations were the convenors of these workhouses, therefore, with the Irish Church's Ulster Magdalene Asylum of particular note, such organizations have since been disbanded, and religious approach to the matter has shifted focus to the notion that prostitution has the potential to be completely eradicated from the region. A poll conducted by CARE, therefore, evidenced 78 percent support for the criminalization of purchasing sex, with 83 percent of Catholics surveyed agreeing with this (CARE 2014). As a result, the influence of public order and decency paradigm is not lost across all regions of the UK, but is conversely approached in a manner that is perceived as having the potential to rid the region of the problem in Northern Ireland rather than purely confine it to the backstreets. As a result, however, and has been the case with other matters of social policy, most clearly evident in the instance of the smoking ban (Cairney 2009), the possibility for lesson drawing and policy diffusion (Dolowitz and Marsh 1996) is raised. To be sure, the potential of cross-boundary movement across such close geographical nexus, and a similar road to statutory overhaul in England and Wales, cannot be ignored in the case of prostitution, but will of course rest substantially on the perceived success of the model in the coming years.

It can be widely accepted, therefore, that the regulation of street prostitution rests heavily on a framework of social order and decency in England, Wales and Scotland. Indeed, the progression of prostitution through the criminal law, and the development of statutes governing such activity, have ostensibly moved from a position of viewing the industry purely in terms of 'street offences', as recorded in earlier legislation, to a complex and nuanced field of 'sexual offences'. Interestingly, however, it is the former categorization that still attracts the burden of sanctions, and solicitation of sex in public, in addition to its purchase, is the focus of the law to this day. The persistence of this Victorian standard in an ever-expanding financial climate, and sex workers' rights highlighted through a labour framework in neighbouring EU countries, is rightly challenged. In acknowledgement of the dual facets of the re-election desires of MPs, however, acceptable levels of public order and decency place a premium price on the decriminalization of public prostitution; these deeply entrenched parameters of behaviour (Peters 2011, 48) strongly constrain any form of innovation by members of the legislature and result in an antiquated policy domain, that will need substantial impetus from the grassroots up for reform. Indeed, partially engaging Calvert's view that actors in such a scenario can be inclined to push for change if the circumstances are ripe (1995), therefore, it is thus civil society that is crucial in limiting the actions of individual parliamentarians in this regard. Now further focusing attention on the public's role in shaping this incentive structure, the risk of violence from street prostitution is already of great anxiety to those directly engaged in the activities (Sanders 2004), and it has become generally accepted those who solicit customers online, for example, are more likely to engage in lower risks than their street-based counterparts (Cunningham and Kendall 2011), yet currently such factors do not appear to be copiously reflected in the legislation. Questioning if greater awareness of these associated risks can incite a change in the definition of prostitution, therefore, the next sub-section explores the construction of Mill's infamous harm principle (1859) in greater detail.

3.4. POLITICAL SELF-INTEREST AND FUTURE REGULATION: THE CASE OF THE BRADFORD MURDERS

The fickle nature of political self-interest poses the possibility of future amendments to prostitution legislation. Certainly, the insights garnered from rational choice institutionalism are invaluable for suggesting that a social order and decency framework induces the legislative inertia that typifies this policy domain, but it additionally hints at how this might be punctuated (Jones and Baumgartner 2005) in the future. In particular, by highlighting the career desires of individuals within these bodies (Fenno 1978), it illustrates that the current, costly nature of morality politics could be eroded, and an inducement for innovative political action posited, if a change to this climate of public opinion occurs. As previously studied, overhaul of a value-infused field, as was evidenced through the 1967 Abortion Act, is possible if a number of factors coalesce to create a policy window (Kingdon 1995). Although contemporary societal mood in regard to street solicitation appears to hold little promise in contrast to the liberalized attitude and grassroots push for reform in 1960s, there is nevertheless potential for this current public sex for sale framework to shift and redefine the matter, as was evidenced in Sweden and Germany. For this to occur, however, it is contended in this subsection that a key catalyst is required, that moves the principle of harm away from a formulation based on public order and decency and towards the broad range of risks posed to the individual prostitute. In light of the example of the 'Bradford Murders' therefore, and in recognition that protection, albeit in regard to trafficking, has nevertheless been a key theme throughout discussions and amendments to the law, the potential erosion of this framework is explored. By humanizing the prostitute, and considering prostitution the problem as opposed to the individual woman, incentives may arise to introduce a novel and groundbreaking piece of legislation, and the UK can legitimately look abroad for alternative regulatory measures.

In order to appreciate the impact the awareness of associated risks in prostitution may have upon the public order and decency frame, it must first be evaluated if this is in fact predicated upon a wider, collective morality that underpins the very action. Students of law will often be taught that for an act to be criminalized, the requirements are threefold; the conduct must be wrongful, it must be necessary to employ the criminal law to condemn or prevent such conduct, and it must be permissible to criminalize the activity (Clarkson, Keating and Cunningham 2010). It is in regard to the first demand of wrongdoing, and the dependence upon the concept of morality this incites, that is of particular interest when exploring the reasons for why certain aspects of sex for sale are viewed as lawful and others as not. Hart, the first theorist to coin the phrase 'legal moralism', addressed the importance of society's collective agreement of what constitutes moral or immoral action in the classification of criminal activity (Hart 1963). An accessible and workable definition is provided by the assimilation of contemporary works in the stipulation that the immorality of an act of type A is a sufficient reason for the criminalization of A, even if A does not cause someone to be harmed (Peterson 2011). Such a principle appears to be applied in a patchy manner in the field of 'sex for sale', however; indeed as aforementioned, no overarching principle in this vein exists, so ostensibly identical acts, that are distinguished purely in terms of the setting in which they are conducted, are adjudicated differently in statute.

Attention must therefore be turned to Mill's submission that it is instead the demonstration of harm that should be the basis of defining a crime, and therefore the basis of law (1859). Harcourt (1999) summarizes this position eloquently with the example of a new approach to alcohol policy that was introduced into a number of neighbourhoods in Chicago in 1998. Within the scheme, the residents voted to shut down all liquor stores, bar and lounges, 15 percent of which subsequently declared themselves to be alcohol-free, while other related businesses consequently shut. Importantly, however, drinking in the privacy of one's home was not restricted in the regulation, and not adjudicated upon in any sense. The focus of harm in this example was thus upon those risks that drinking establishments can cause, such as binge drinking, brawling and drunk driving, rather than submitting a moral judgement over the consumption of alcohol itself. The author continues to helpfully draw a comparison with prostitution, citing the example of former Mayor of New York City Giuliani's policy of zero tolerance to so-called 'quality of life' offenses. As a result of this approach, a crackdown of street prostitution began in 1994, resulting in over 9,500 arrests. It was widely acknowledged that this did little to prevent the trade, however, as much of the activity was instead moved onto Internet sites, with little challenge from the authorities (Cunnen 1998). Extracted from these two examples, therefore, is the principle that it is the harm the activity causes, and not its immorality, that is the focus of regulation. This can readily be assumed to be the case in England, Wales and Scotland; it is the notion of risk that guides regulation on street prostitution in regard to the attrition on public order, and not a moral judgement. Continuing with this logic, therefore, the parameters of this definition of harm are of great importance here, and the ability of it to be extended to cover a wider remit of factors demands deliberation.

To accept standards of socially acceptable conduct as the sole harm embodied in prostitution indeed appears to be a rather narrow view of the notion of 'threat of danger' and relies heavily on a one-dimensional view of the situation at hand. Although some argue that the sale of sex is a victimless crime and therefore should be lawful, opponents have conversely cited that it does have victims in the form of those who do it, particularly if driven by economic necessity, or coerced by a third party (O'Neill 2013). Much attention has been paid to this latter grouping, particularly among feminist critics, and has been extended to additionally acknowledge that self-loathing, interference with personal relationships, and barriers to the uptake of social, educational and economic opportunities can all arise from this industry. In retaliation, however, opponents claim that the introduction of legislation based on such reasoning alone draws worryingly close to symbolizing a paternalistic approach by the government (Marneffe 2009). Other feminist thinking argues that violence within prostitution is not merely incidental to the conditions in which such activity is conducted, but endemic within a structure that promotes women's sexuality as a commodity to be purchased (Munro and Della Giusta 2008). It is submitted here, however, that all of these arguments overlook a more tangible class of risks in the form of further crimes committed against prostitutes, such as rape and murder, due to the vulnerable context in which they operate. Indeed, even among the fractious viewpoints of femi-

nists on the matter (Shrage 1989), limited attention is still paid to the reduction of adjacent crimes, and, similarly, the experience of prostitutes in studies
of violence and rape comprise a shallow field of scholarly work (Miller and
Schwartz 1995). Granted, some links can be seen in the surrounding literature between working conditions and ideas of occupational health, but this is
often restricted to controlling client violence (Barnard 1993), as opposed to
affording full recognition to the surrounding climate in which prostitutes are
situated, leaving them vulnerable to third-party attacks.

Moving beyond the theoretical, therefore, a study of this field unveils a
broad range of potential risks for those engaged in the sector. The dangers
associated with the industry are undeniably vast in their number and nature,
including numerous threats to the sexual health of the female worker, emotional risks, both in the course of such work and in the future, and the
continued threat of physical violence from customers and third parties. As
alluded to above, however, much of the literature has focused upon the first
grouping and the considerable hazard of sexually transmitted diseases
(STDs) for those engaged in such conduct, with recognition long being
awarded to the fact that workers in the sector have been among the populations most heavily affected by HIV since the start of the epidemic more than
30 years ago (WHO 2013, XIV). In a study conducted in the highly regulated
region of China back in 2001, for example, it was hypothesized that the
potential for the fast spread of HIV among a group in which the prevalence
of STDs was already elevated was vast (Van den Hoek et al 2001). Furthermore, a study comprising 320 women working as prostitutes in the inner
London area over a period of nine years uncovered that the frequency of a
range of STDs was indeed significant among the sample. Genital herpes and
chlamydia, for example, were apparent in 16.8 percent and 8.2 percent of
cases respectively, and 1.3 percent (amounting to four of the sample size)
tested positive for HIV, eight times higher than women having babies in the
same area between 1988 and 1993 (Ward et al 1999, 342). Although much of
this research must be viewed in the context of its time, and the now increased
awareness of AIDs and condom use, the stigma around sex work remains a
salient barrier for effective health intervention in HIV/AIDS (Scambler and
Paoli 2008). Many key organizations have submitted their explicit support
for the decriminalization of prostitution; in a 2014 report housing guidelines
to help prevent the spread of HIV, for example, the World Health Organization (WHO) has urged countries to work towards the removal of legal sanctions against sex workers (WHO 2014).

In comparison, therefore, it is somewhat troubling that scant exploration
of the verbal, sexual and physical violence faced by street prostitutes on a
daily basis has emerged in the same body of literature (Church et al 2001)
and is equally absent in studies of violence and rape (Miller and Schwartz
1995). Returning to the aforementioned study by Ward et al, however, this

oversight is gradually being acknowledged in the data, and the same study additionally highlighted the mortality from violence rate for such grouping with two of the studied cohort of 320 being murdered in the time frame of observation (1999). Furthermore, a survey of 240 prostitutes working across three major British cities conducted in 2001 indicated that prostitutes working outdoors in Glasgow were six times more likely to have experienced violence by clients than those working indoors in Edinburgh (Church et al 2001). Uncovering that disease-associated factors are not the only occupational hazards encountered by street prostitutes, therefore, and that the threat posed to these workers cannot solely be confined to exchanges with customers, the potential for statutory change on this evidential basis must be considered.

Evidence to highlight the lack of protection and potential for danger associated with failing to decriminalize street prostitution is indeed mounting and increasingly spurred on by the uptake of alternative schemes across the globe. The potential for domestic legislative change at present is of course hypothetical, but consideration of the options available for political innovation is an interesting point. Global debates on removing a ban on prostitution frequently cite the problematic position this may lead to for women in terms of, among other factors, a proliferation of sex trafficking (e.g., Raymond 2004), and this should certainly be a concern for policymakers. Granted it is a significant and persuasive regulatory problem, but a myriad of alternative literature and real-world examples, as referred to above, also exist to suggest that sustaining a position of illegality inadvertently strengthens the treatment of prostitutes as a sexual commodity, removed from a personal identity and familial relationships. Street workers throughout literature, for example, as so astutely pointed out in the work of Hirschman and Stern, are often reductive, comprising a collection of sexual parts, rather than a complete human being (1994). Certainly, preserving the criminal status of this form of solicitation has a discernible impact upon the common perception of these women, and, with more radical tone, Andrea Dworkin stipulates that it is impossible for a prostitute to remain 'whole', that she has been turned into a 'sellable commodity' and that the industry reflects a contempt and hatred for women so deep that she is 'reduced to a few sexual orifices' (1993, 6). Certain studies have further correlated a risk-taking disposition with the use of prostitution services (Cameron and Collins 2003), and scholarship in the academic domain of psychology has charted a correlation between alcohol consumption and prostitute use (Sawyer et al 2001). Thus studies such as Brent and Hausbeck's research into legalized brothel prostitution in Nevada strongly concludes that the legalization of prostitution can actually amount to a beneficial level of public scrutiny, official regulation and bureaucratization that can, in turn, reduce this risk of violence (2005). Conversely, other writers have argued that the tougher line on clients of prostitutes enshrines a deeper level of deviant behaviour and a new Trojan horse (Brooks-Gordon and Gelsthorpe 2003). Such studies are not of solely academic interest, however, and innovation has been evidenced in other countries, the most notable example of which clearly is the aforementioned Swedish model. Emerging from a radical feminist perspective, the push for criminalizing the purchase of sex in this instance actually illustrates the successful rationale linking drugs and prostitution in permeating the agenda (Gould 2001). Although it could be suggested that this symbolic discourse could therefore gain equal traction in the UK, the contention over its success remains prominent in the minds of domestic policymakers; examining application at a local level, for example, one research paper highlights the decrease in clients and the appearance of prostitutes on the street, but conversely notes the rise in Swedish Internet pages offering sexual services (Danna 2012).

Unequivocally, these factors will have not gone unnoticed by Westminster, yet up to now, limited pressure for change has been exerted. Indeed, in the absence of a clear and positive data haul, the deeply entrenched 'rules of the game' (March and Olsen 1984) are likely to again constrain innovation and in this sense, have thus far served to neglect sustained discussion on the vulnerability of UK prostitutes in several aspects of potential harm. Precedent for legislative action predicated on ideals of protection have previously been evidenced in this domain, however, through the introduction of the Sexual Offences Act, and the Policing and Crime Act's approach to trafficking. Certainly, if vulnerability is a key driver in the formulation of prostitution legislation, an argument can be submitted that this should take into account not only the need to safeguard those forced into the industry, which presently the statutory law of the UK rightly attempts, but should also have regard for the possibility that the current illegal status of streetwalking is not necessarily best protecting women. Returning again to a 'logic of calculation' as largely derived from the electoral arena in which parliamentarians operate, therefore, and the recognition that it is the dominant public order and decency frame that provides little impetus for reform, it is submitted that it is at this grassroots level that change can originate if significant awareness to an issue is raised. In this sense, citizens can be viewed as a thermostat for elite attention (Wlezien 1996), highlighting the salience of an issue and pushing for government action, and a series of high-profile criminal attacks on women pose this very possibility. In practice, it is becoming increasingly exposed to the eyes of the public that the stigma attached to streetwalkers, leaving them vulnerable to harm and attack through other crimes, is a mounting problem in the UK.

The recent shocking case of the colloquially termed 'Bradford Murders' exemplifies this broad spectrum of harm posed to those soliciting on the street, involving as it did the serial killings of three prostitutes at the hands of Stephen Shaun Griffiths. Pleading guilty to all three charges, and responding in court that he was to be referred to as the 'Crossbow Cannibal', Griffiths was sentenced to life in 2010 (Carter 2010). His attacks involved the murder of three prostitutes in the Bradford area, who had accompanied him voluntarily to his nearby flat before the atrocities took place, and the circumstances that surrounded all three deaths drew out two crucial features of the vulnerability of sex workers. First, much attention has unsurprisingly been heaped upon the situation by the media, and a range of theories and rationale for the brutal serial attacks pondered. Curiously, however, they all appear united in their observation that the red-light district in which this took place afforded a certain amount of protection for Griffiths, providing an ideal world for him to go undetected, and in which he was able to fit in comfortably (Dixon 2011). Thus related to this observation, the second feature of note was the corresponding failure of relevant agencies. According to the UK Network of Sex Projects' Good Practice Guidance, the importance of 'ugly mugs and dodgy punter' schemes are significant to improve the safety of sex workers (2011). Agencies engaged in the sector are therefore encouraged to have a strong circulating mechanism in place that disseminates important information, including those potential clients that are perceived as risky, in the form of, for example, notice boards erected in drop-in clinics. In the case of Griffiths, the offender had previously been imprisoned for holding a knife to the throat of a girl, and it has been mooted in the press that he discussed his desire to kill with his probation officer, and revealed his idolization of the Yorkshire Ripper to other professionals working with him (Johnston 2010). In addition, such 'dodgy punter' policy was in force in Bradford at the time of the horrific crimes, yet it is noticeable the two were not linked, and images of Griffiths were not made aware to prostitutes in the area. Although the joining of the two features may be a stringent link, particularly if he had not previously been seen in such red-light districts, the lack of unity across the agencies is still worthy of note. A strikingly similar circumstance manifested in the case of the Ipswich killings, which again involved the violent attack of prostitutes, and in which it was reported that the attacker killed because it was 'easy' (Harrison and Wilson 2008) and runs concurrently to further research that has highlighted their vulnerability in this regard, and the lack of action taken by the government (Canter, Ioannou and Youngs 2009).

Again focusing the potential for change upon an innovating individual, David Cameron's response to the 'Bradford Murders' highlighted the potential for statutory change. In a perhaps somewhat flip remark with a media outlet, the PM stipulated that the decriminalization of prostitution should again be looked at (BBC News 2010). Mirroring strong declaration made by Lord David Steel in the road to the decriminalization of abortion, this action was isolated from other political concerns at the point at which it was made; however, when placed back within the structure of government, and the wider legislature, those around Cameron were quick to rebut the claims, and reframe his comments towards the problems of kerb crawling and drug abuse, both debates of far less magnitude for the party to deal with. Elite attention did not end there, however, and the government in 2010 undertook a review of effective practice. Explicitly referencing the danger and risk of violence faced by street workers, the paper estimated that at least 137 prostitutes had been murdered since 1990, dictating that female workers are 12 times more likely to be murdered than a woman of a comparable age (Home Office 2011, 3). In a nod to the public order and decency paradigm framework that has been referred to throughout this analysis, the document also engaged with the notion of the community as the impetus for action, while additionally recognizing that the most effective responses should incorporate a broad range of vested interests, including those directly partaking in prostitution (Home Office 2013, 8). It is at this point, however, that acknowledgement should be afforded to the transient nature of public attention, and the due recognition that this is given by the government. Certainly, the case provided a shock to society and an explosion of attention to the issue at hand but, as so astutely captured in Downs' 'issue attention cycle', sustained focus from the public is unlikely to ensue when the personal costs of implementing policy change are eventually realized. In his article, Downs refers in this sense to the idea not just of monetary concerns, but the concept of a constraint on a civil liberty, a factor that is of pertinence here (1972). Although public sympathy for the murders was clear, the tackling of prostitution, and perhaps the outlawing of purchasing sex in the manner evidenced in Northern Ireland, comes with associated restrictions on what citizens perceive to be social order. It is instead contended at this juncture, therefore, that it is at first an erosion of this dominant paradigm that needs to be achieved in a more sustained manner before real change will be demanded. Parallels can be drawn here with a study completed by Baumgartner, de Boef and Boystun of the death penalty in the United States, in which a decline in the figures of death sentences in the United States since 1996 can be attributed to the reframing of the debate. Although mistakes within America's criminal justice system have always occurred, the introduction of this concept into public discussion, largely due to stories of DNA evidence used to exonerate death row inmates publicized by the mass media, has seen a paradigm shift in public perception and has had a knock-on effect upon practice. The authors submit that framing the debate along a particular dimension, and similarly the exclusion of alternative hypotheses, has had a significant impact upon the issue at hand (Baumgartner et al 2008). Of note in this instance, therefore, is the development of the issue in light of a growing realization from members of the public, a situation that could feasibly occur around prostitution regulation in England, Wales and Scotland that could distinguish people's NIMBY approach from their cognitive realisation of a problem that demands action.

The protection of prostitutes from crimes against the person is indelibly coloured by their principal status as a criminal, and the present refusal to overhaul this aspect of the law in the UK perpetuates an alternative category of incidental harm to women. The pressing demand to provide appropriate protective legislation for those forced into prostitution has been duly recognized in the last decade and, arguably, has been substantially met by the reforms housed in the Sexual Offences Act and Policing and Crime Act detailed previously in the chapter. Addressing vulnerability in this manner, however, reflects a narrow construction of harm and overlooks the significant threat of violent crimes, such as rape and murder, committed against prostitutes. Recent reporting on significant cases such as the 'Bradford Murders' signal a challenge to this ignorance and provides potential impetus for political innovation if enough erosion to the social order paradigm is induced by such events.

3.5. DERIVING INSPIRATION FROM OVERSEAS: NEO-ABOLITIONISM IN EUROPE

The drawing of lessons from arrangements in one political setting for use in another is a trend heavily acknowledged in the literature (Dolowitz and Marsh 1996). In addition, research around prostitution specifically has noted the increasingly pervasive neo-abolitionist measures that are sweeping across the EU (Scoular and Carline 2014), and the recent uptake of criminalizing the purchase of sex in Northern Ireland is indicative of this very situation. With that in mind, this is just one typology of legislation on the matter, however, and a country's market for commercial sex (Jackobsson and Kotsadam 2013, 88) can additionally be characterized as one of regulation, decriminalizing the activity as evidenced previously in the case of Germany, and providing a scheme of labour rights for the profession. Having therefore identified a spectrum of approaches to prostitution regulation as ranging from the traditional criminal approach, to prohibition of its purchase, to complete decriminalization, the extent to which the operation of these approaches has elicited varying results is an important point of consideration. Although the incentive for adaptation to England, Wales and Scotland's scheme is heavily constrained by normative reasoning concerning social order and decency, and has thus far been only partially eroded by individual concern for the prostitute, it must now be questioned if perceived benefits housed in varying schemes across the EU provide a more robust motive for reform. Thus the array of merits and corresponding deficiencies that are apparent across the EU's varying schemes and the impact of legislation in terms of reducing levels of sex trafficking should be considered. Indeed, an evidenced-based approach to policymaking is an ideal strongly promoted in the concluding chapter and has been at the forefront of much research into prostitution legislation (e.g., Weitzer 2011), and a comparative appreciation of criminal justice systems that allows us to look outside the boundaries of our own country to take into account foreign ideas and experiences is a worthy pursuit (Terrill 2012).

Turning attention to the increased measures aimed to eradicate prostitution in its entirety, a key driver for the 'Swedish model' referenced previously in which the purchase of sex is criminalized, many of these decisions are based on insights gathered from economics. Acknowledging trafficking as a money-seeking activity, it has been asserted that the profitability of such a pursuit in a given country is dependent upon that state's market for commercial sex (Jackobsson and Kotsadam 2013). According to a 2014 UN report, therefore, Western and Central Europe is both an origin and a destination for trafficked persons, with the richer countries in Western and Southern Europe often the destination for those extracted from Asia, Africa, the Americas and Central Europe (UN 2014, 59). Concentrating on those that have adopted a neo-abolitionist approach to the law, therefore, namely Iceland, Norway and Sweden, the recorded levels of activity are seemingly low in comparison to countries in which prostitution is legal and regulated. Beginning first with the 'world's most feminist country' (Bindel 2010), the Icelandic parliament has adopted such a programme since 2009 but with mixed results. According to the popular English language magazine 'The Reykjavik Grapevine', the demand for sexual services of this nature are indeed high (Fontaine 2011). Although there is certainly a dearth of reliable sex trafficking data, the United States' Trafficking in Persons (TIC) 2014 report, however, has indicated only 17 potential cases of trafficking reported by the government, compared to 6 in 2012. Norwegian authorities similarly initiated only 30 investigations into alleged sex trafficking in 2013 compared to 26 in 2012 (TIC 2014, 299), and Sweden additionally mirrored such low levels with 40 inquiries in 2013, compared to 21 in 2012 (364). On the other hand, in those countries in which prostitution is legal and fully regulated, comprising Austria, Germany, Greece, Hungary, Latvia, Netherlands, Switzerland and Turkey, the statistics are slightly different. In Austria in 2012, for example, 134 cases were investigated, increasing to 192 in 2013; Germany demonstrated even higher levels in 2012 at 491. Prosecutions in the Netherlands in 2013 for trafficking generally—the county not disaggregating labour and sex forms—reached 236 (TIC 2014). Returning to the aforementioned point centered around the failure to reduce harm in Iceland, however, many equally fear the problems associated with pushing the activity underground. In Sweden, in particular, a reduction in access to social services for victims of the sex industry is of note (Thompson 2013) with service providers often withholding help within the overarching aim of encouraging such people to cease their sex work (Levy 2014, 152).

3.6. CONCLUSION

A domestic division in the way sexual acts are regulated in England and Wales, and furthermore in Scotland, far from reflects a strict binary judgement over 'sex for sale'. The clear divide that can instead be extrapolated from the legislative situation is in fact between public acts and private matters, creating a policy field that adopts a mix of abolition and prohibition measures. Previous studies have long attempted to provide for justification for this position, and it is in Victorian standards of social order and decency that much rationale can be found. Upon analysis of a number of institutional and decision rules operating with the legislature, it can be more specifically observed that parliamentarians, already pre-conditioned to place morality politics low on their personal priorities, are collectively heavily constrained in their abilities to innovate the policy domain due to the proliferation of veto points. Drawing lessons from neighbouring spheres such as abortion, however, in which partial decriminalization, and radical overhaul of the law, has been evidenced, it is contended that change is clearly possible in alternative value-based schemes, and thus this situation of inertia requires further justification. Returning to the indoor/outdoor divide, therefore, the public order and decency frame prevalent in wider society for centuries, and the deeply entrenched desire for 'not in my backyard', still retains its significance, and contributes to this ordering of incentives for parliamentarians. In light of alternative schemes, therefore, the complete decriminalization of prostitution, and a scheme of regulation of sex for sale as demonstrated in Germany, is a step too far in the region. By way of contrast, however, the new abolitionist measures introduced by Northern Ireland, and the penalties imposed upon those purchasing sex, house greater potential for introduction in England and Wales.

Although the full recognition of labour rights indeed appears out of reach for successive governments, the harm posed to prostitutes, as exemplified by the case of the 'Bradford Murders', creates further impetus to unify the UK in these new measures. Granted, the calculation of costs in decriminalizing prostitution remains insurmountable at present, but the increasing amount of media coverage of violent crimes against prostitutes creates awareness among the public of a broader spectrum of harm to street prostitutes. In order for this to occur, however, a paradigm shift at the grassroots level, moving away from ideas of social decency and towards concern for the individual, is demanded. Although such high-profile cases inevitably erode this situation, a successful change in perception of the problem is heavily constrained by the deficiencies highlighted in the so-called Swedish model in tackling the issue of harm reduction, a point that is acknowledged by both the public and elites alike.

To some extent mirroring the harmful stereotyping evidenced in the last chapter in which a prevalent view of the abortion pill as a quick fix overlooks many legitimate aspects of women's health that are not appropriately met, the preponderance of legislation to classify prostitutes as either vulnerable to exploitation, or hardened criminals soliciting sex in public, dangerously overlooks an increasing number of violent crimes committed by both clients and third parties against these women. Arguably, the deviant label on those voluntarily working the streets has become well and truly stuck, and institutional inertia around the issue significantly contributes to a one-dimensional view of these women. Without devoting large attention in this book to the psychological reasons for committing violent crimes, even a cursory look at the surrounding literature highlights a strong causal link between a lack of respect for prostitutes and violent acts committed against them. In addition to warding off the possibility of harm inflicted through exploitation, therefore, policymakers should have additional regard to how failing to provide state legitimacy to the work of prostitutes by fully deeming it a legal industry, restricts the rights of women, and not only in terms of labour laws. The cases explored above are extreme examples of common experiences among prostitutes, who face a continuum of risks (Sanders 2004). Providing fodder for the comparative analysis in chapter 6, therefore, the inflexible nature of this criminal label, and the isolated manner in which it is constructed, has harmful consequences for the gender.

Chapter Four

Demanding a 'Proper Victim': The Culture of Rape Policy in the UK

The brutal incident of rape has devastating physical and emotional consequences for victims, both at the time of attack and in the years subsequent. Horrifyingly, these events are not an uncommon occurrence and take place in significant numbers across the world, with the UN estimating that one in five women will become the victim of rape, or attempted rape, in their lifetime (2015). Furthermore, claims of such attacks in England and Wales, based on aggregated data collated from crime surveys between 2009 and 2012, paint a similarly harrowing picture with 473,000 adults reporting such an offence (Ministry of Justice et al 2013a). Although it is appreciated that men account for 72,000 of this total figure, and is undeniably an offence of equal gravitas, the significant number of women—hereinafter comprising the victims referred to throughout this chapter—forms the focus of study. Certainly, the overarching objective of this book is to fully espouse the regulation of women across various policy domains, and it is with the sentiment that there is no gender equivalence in sexual violence (Burke 2009) that this account finds much of its rationale. When addressing the legal process after attack, therefore, the actions of reporting the crime, attending trial and later living with the verdict delivered can be an additionally distressing experience for the claimant, with its own unique set of demands and attribution of responsibility. When the reporting of a case is exposed to the wider public, for example, popular rhetoric is often quick to incorporate acknowledgement of peripheral and unrelated factors such as what the woman was wearing, how much alcohol she had consumed and the extent to which she already knew her alleged attacker. This judgement around the credibility of the victim, as opposed to the veracity of the claim, is a common occurrence and is reflected not only in the popular press, but is an alarming trend that is further evidenced at various stages of the criminal justice system, including street-level interactions with the police. Regardless of statutory wording purporting to outlaw such activity, therefore, the perceived integrity of the complainant, however distasteful and crudely adjudicated upon, continues to occupy vast space in both formal discussions and societal debates.

This presence of a set of standards to which a woman must conform at varying stages of the policy process is therefore of great interest in the course of the chapter and is at the heart of a study of structural forces. Despite its current modish deliberation across high-profile media cases, a 'proper victim' image is certainly not a new revelation, and an array of inaccurate perceptions around rape, including the scorned woman out for revenge, has long been the fodder of urban legend. In an interesting study of prime-time television programming in the 1970s, for example, the depiction of sexual assault in detective shows frequently concerned a violent perpetration by a stranger (Cuklanz 1998), a pattern that far from reflects the reality of the crime. Furthermore, studies of the experience of victims have repeatedly submitted the negative and distressing situation faced by women in claims of rape, with their journey through the criminal justice process subject to an array of judgements about their own behaviour and conduct (Payne 2009). Importantly, however, the sustained influence of these factors in formal processes and public debate goes against the grain of contemporary legislation that purports to mitigate the once onerous burden of proof that was demanded of victims, and this disconnect between law and practice demands espousal. From the outset, it is suggested that reasons for such an observation will not be successfully captured by rational choice institutionalism (March and Olsen 1984) alone, and rather it is here that the normative strain of NI, ascribing central importance to rules, understandings and routines (March and Olsen 1989), and specific works extolling the importance of myths in defining acceptable behaviour (Meyer and Rowan 1977) provide more exacting theoretical value and causal suggestion as to why the apparent sincerity of the complainant continues to feature in a disproportionate manner in cases of rape. Appreciating the varying influence of a range of organizational structures, it is most significantly contended that the marriage of poorly defined legislative intentions, and a pre-existing cop culture (Myhill and Bradford 2013), focuses the attention of the SLB on a likely victim rather than a probable criminal. This apportioning of responsibility is an important observation for the proper workings of the criminal law, not just at the point at which an individual comes into contact with the police, but the barriers this puts in place for future victims when coming forward.

The chapter first presents the origins of the law on rape, outlining the demands placed on those submitting allegations of sexual assault at common and early statutory law, and particularly focusing upon the burden of proof imposed upon the woman in the course of trial. Within this section, the now

outdated subjective test of honest belief in consent on the part of the defendant is explored. Closely followed is an espousal of the current legislative
scheme, with particular attention afforded to the Sexual Offences Act 2003,
and corresponding instruments in Scotland and Northern Ireland. Having set
the regulatory scene, therefore, the succeeding section will discuss the contemporary attribution of responsibility to the victim of rape and, utilizing the
conceptual framework of normative institutionalism, the respective influence
of the legislature, judiciary and police force in creating and perpetuating a
dominant assumption of a 'proper victim' will be explored. The penultimate
section will specifically engage this latter organizational structure, however,
and address the impact of deeply embedded norms on the fear of coming
forward for victims of marital rape. In acknowledging an emerging trend of
'contestable crimes', therefore, it is additionally questioned if the comparative disparities in criminal law across the EU, and specifically the plurality
with which definitions of mens rea manifest across member states, further
exasperate this situation. A conclusion last asserts that the harm to accurate
and appropriate forms of justice caused by the stereotyping of credible victims, driven by a 'logic of appropriateness' (March and Olsen 2008) reflected
through all levels of the police force, is of even greater gravitas in constraining the proper implementation of rape policy across the UK than the wording
of the law.

4.1. RAPE AT COMMON LAW: THE WOMAN ON TRIAL

Even the earliest recorded cultures make explicit reference to sexual offences
and their punishment, and it is here that the roots of the UK's regulatory field
can be traced. Prior to formalized statutory control, however, the idea of
wrongdoing, and the notion of harm, was constructed in a manner wholly
different to that of the contemporary Western world. In Ancient Babylon, for
example, the rape of female slaves was fundamentally considered to be an
instance of property damage, and corresponding sanctions demanded that the
assailant pay a fine to the husband or father of the victim (Cook 2007, 127).
Legal discourse in the Athenian courts displayed a more civilized focus upon
acceptable patterns of sexual behaviour, although the action was still viewed
as a concern for society more generally, as opposed to the victim being of
central importance, and it was levels of normative civic standards that dictated problematic sexual action (Omitowoju 2002, 2). Narrative accounts of
sexual violence against women from antiquity onwards therefore unveil a
worrying oversight of the severity of the act both in terms of the assault made
upon the woman, and the level of her consent, as the primary indicators of an
offence. In modern legal practice, it could easily be assumed that this is no
longer the case, and the once piecemeal regulatory platform would have

experienced egalitarian transformation into a sophisticated statutory scheme. In light of the reluctance of the legislature to discard entrenched ideology on matters of abortion as just one example evidenced in chapter 2, however, the ability of the past to frame current legal parameters cannot be dismissed out of hand. Thus in appreciation of such historical disregard for the impact of rape on the woman, this section charts the development of these various regulatory instruments from their origins in key historical texts to statutory interventions in the UK from the eighteenth century onwards. Across these periods, it is questioned if embers from this previous failure to place the victim at the centre of considerations of harm and justice have continued to burn in the current, Western policy domain.

Archaic conceptualizations of rape, and attention to the consequences of the attack for parties other than the direct female victim, are exemplified in instances outlined in two seminal writings. The first of these is provided by the Old Testament in the example of Dinah, Jacob's daughter, who is raped by the young prince Schecham. Upon hearing that she has been defiled, Dinah's brothers, Simeon and Levi, begin the journey to retrieve her and, in addition to looting various items from the city in which she was being kept, bring her home. When they return, however, Jacob criticizes the brothers for inciting trouble for him and his family, to which they retort 'should he have treated our sister like a prostitute?' (Genesis 34:31). Indicative of biblical translations of rape more generally, therefore, the response indicates that that the action is largely determined to be one of 'theft of sexual property' (Thistlethwaite 1993, 62), thus akin to the robbing of goods or chattel, rather than a violent attack against a person. Certainly, the principal violation in examples across this time period was repeatedly determined to be against the man's rights, as either a husband or father, to a woman's sexuality as if it were one of many forms of property (Gravett 2004, 280). Furthermore, and of even greater harm to the perception of victims of rape in history, Dinah is often attributed blame for her attack and is frequently labelled a whore as a result (Schroeder 1997, 775). The second example, published in 8 AD, is proffered by Ovid's epic six-book Latin poem *Fasti* in which the author recalls the rapes of both Omphale by Faunus and Lucretia by Sextus Tarquinius, in varying manners and with diverging consequences (Hejduk 2011). In the former myth, Ovid attempts to provide a sexual comedy of sorts when it is disclosed that Hercules, who has switched outfits with his girlfriend, tricks the attacker, Faunus (Fantham 1983). The descriptive language engaged, depicting the ludicrous extent to which Hercules, as the 'muscle-bound hero', bursts out of his sandals, and readily shatters his partner's bracelets (Fantham 1983, 194) makes for a supposedly good-natured farce in which violence is actually averted (Newlands 1995, 195). The latter story, however, is a far more brutal account, with the victim, Lucretia, being harrowingly described as a lamb attacked by a wolf in the form of the King of Rome's son Sextus, who is supposedly blindly spurred on by savage desire (Saunders 2001, 152). Although in this tale it would appear that a degree of significance is thus afforded by the author to the suffering of the woman, far greater attention is actually focused upon the public implications of the attack, and the ramifications for the government of Rome generally, and the historical significance of the event as a key driver for the establishment of the Roman Republic has instead been cited by authors as the focus of concern (Roynon 2013, 35).

It is evident throughout these examples, therefore, that rape has long been expressed in a somewhat flippant manner, with limited acknowledgement for the plight of the victim. Despite such apparent incongruence with our twenty-first-century definition of the action, and perhaps abhorrence with which these accounts are read, the influence of these early examples is nevertheless reflected in the foundations of British legal history. In particular, this early biblical concern for the protection of property rights appears in domestic common law, and the Saxon legal jurist Bracton stipulated in the tenth century that the punishment for a man who 'places himself upon her' was the loss of possessions, or if 'he lies with her', the consequences of death, with the caveat included that the raped virgin may accept the man in marriage, and their property consolidated (Bracton, quoted in Brownmiller 2013). It is with this sidenote that Brownmiller thus submits that such decision would inevitably take into consideration whether the arrangement of land would be beneficial, and leads to the conclusion that rape therefore entered the law through the back door, as a property crime against the man (2013) rather than the form of gender discrimination widely recognized today. By the seventeenth century, however, a more mature common law outlined the felony rape, and Lord Hale was remarking on the ease of making such allegations of a crime (Kaye 1977, 9). That said, consent was almost non-existent in these early manifestations and stringent requirements around a proven state of continued physical resistance, and assumed assent in cases of marital allegations (Plucknett 2001), were rife, a factor that did not escape the aforementioned jurist. Indeed, in perhaps one of the most enduring statements of the law on rape, Hale declared that 'it must be remembered . . . that it is an accusation easily to be made and hard to be proved, and harder to be defended by the party accused, tho never so innocent' (Hale 1734). Throughout the ages, the legitimacy of this statement has been considered, and the substantial barriers and difficulties faced by a complainant in alleged cases of sexual assault, and the inordinate likelihood of acquittals in this sphere in comparison to neighbouring prosecutions, has featured in the surrounding scholarship from the 1970s onwards (Geis 1978). It is with this seventeenth-century jurist that much of the knowledge around rape at common law can be derived, however, and the Helibron Report of 1975 stated that the traditional common law definition, still in use at the time of the committee's findings, was the authority of the law on rape (Geis 1978, 42), and remained the guiding principle in the implementation of the first statutory recognition of the offence.

As previously charted in the chapter on abortion, the series of Offences Against the Person Acts feature heavily in this history of the law on rape. Detailing the sentence of death for those convicted of rape, section 16 of the 1828 iteration of the statute outlined the common law formulation of forcible carnal knowledge of a woman, and onerously demanded proof of penetration on the part of the victim. This principle remained in place in the amended 1861 version and was the overarching guidance in cases of suspected rape until an overhaul of the law in the mid-nineteenth century. Indeed, indicating a greater acceptance of the magnitude of the crime, the handling of cases of such assault was assumed by an alternative strand of legislation in the 1950s entitled the Sexual Offences Act. Beginning in 1956, it adopted the preexisting definition of rape as 'the carnal knowledge of a woman, forcibly and against her will.' Following a landmark ruling in *DPP v. Morgan* [1976] AC 182, however, this construct was amended and statutory recognition given to the notion of consent in the Sexual Offences (Amendment) Act 1976. Concerning the case of a man who had invited three of his friends to his house to have sex with his wife, informing them that she was 'kinky' and therefore would submit a faux protest, they forcibly overcame her and had intercourse without her accord. Upon appeal to the House of Lords, the Court ruled in such an instance that honest belief in the woman's willing acquisition could provide a defence to rape, implementing a significant caveat to the former definition of such sexual assault. Interestingly, it is claimed among some authors that such reforms were indicative of elevated police reporting between 1945 and 2005 (Frank et al 2009), and looked to set in place the burden of proof on the woman. Certainly this tough line on the claimant remained in place until the current 2003 amended this sentiment to reasonable belief, a closer espousal of which will feature in the next sub-section.

Examination of the treatment of both the accused and the defendant over the centuries does indeed illustrate a continued lack of care of the victim as central to legislative concerns, and a significant responsibility upon the latter to materially prove an instance of rape, despite its statutory reclassification into a sexual offence in the mid-twentieth century. The tone around the offence of rape throughout history has long demonstrated caution and hesitancy towards the claims of the woman. And the seemingly antiquated declaration made by Hale that it is the woman on trial is actually evidenced in the recent past, most notably in the retention of the subjective test over honest belief. Contemporary legislation is now the culmination of a range of amendments that have occurred to the statutory field throughout the late twentieth century however, and, ostensibly, most notable changes have been evidenced in regard to the behaviour of the victim. The interpretation of consent is now afforded more space in the legislation and is the principal driver of jurisprudential concern, as will be explored further in the succeeding section.

4.2. THE SEXUAL OFFENCES ACT 2003

Irrespective of minor updates in the years subsequent to its passing, and overspill of regulation from bordering spheres, the Sexual Offences Act 2003 continues to reign as the seminal statute for prosecutions of rape in England and Wales. Almost completely replacing the 1956 Act, and the product of a consultation process of over three years, the instrument was hailed as one of the crowning glories of the Blair years, ushering in a modern and appropriate governing scheme, with the protection of victims at its very heart. Indeed, a key driver for its creation was articulated as the need to modernize the law in line with 'changes in society and social attitudes' (Home Office 2000). From the outset, however, procedural matters identified in its sections hampered the efficiency of the new law, and the wisdom of its wording in terms of expedient and effective judicial process were duly questioned. Beyond mere pragmatism, however, criticism soon became rife around the apparent disconnect between its supposed role as reflective of societal attitudes towards sexual offences, and its ability to afford appropriate protection to victims. This difficulty around implementation will be explored at great length later in the chapter, but it is of pertinence to explore the wording of the act.

Currently, section 74 Sexual Offences Act 2003 stipulates rape in England and Wales to be the intentional penetration of one person by another, without the consent of that second person. As a central theme to this chapter, it is this issue of consent that is again the focus of the regulation, and the statute importantly notes that a person gives this if they agree by choice, and have the freedom and capacity to make such a decision. The wording of this text is important, as it no longer requires positive dissent (Keating et al 2014), and no show of physical resistance is necessary to indicate a rape. In this sense, consent should be positively garnered by the instigator, and it is required by the legislation that they have taken all such steps to ascertain if this is the case. When determining if consent has been perceived by the defendant, this belief must be considered reasonable. Furthermore, section 75 details the evidential presumptions about consent, stating that factors such as unlawful detention or the unconscious state of the complainant, must be considered enough to believe that the victim did not consent. Although all of these factors are unsurprisingly subject to wider judicial interpretation, the effect of which will be examined below, this statutory recognition of the burden of proof as falling substantially upon the defendant, is a point of interest and marks a departure from the previous legal position.

Unlike the nuanced legislation around sexual offences in this jurisdiction, however, Scotland's legislative framework remained a complicated mix of common law and statute until the Sexual Offences (Scotland) Act 2009. Certainly Scotland adhered to a very different legal pathway, resting substantially on judicial activism in which the common law was heavily relied upon, with scant statutory reference to the parameters of the crime found in the Criminal Law (Consolidation) (Scotland) Act 1995, or Part 3 of the 2003 Draft Criminal Code for Scotland. Up until fairly recently, therefore, Scots law required that a woman's will was overcome by force, and that there was resistance 'to the last' (Cowan 2010). On the other hand, the Criminal Justice (Northern Ireland) Order 2003, and Sexual Offences (Northern Ireland) Order 2008 demonstrates significantly similar rubric to the offence as is evident England and Wales. On more peripheral notes, but certainly of importance for the ensuing analysis, 1999 additionally witnessed the introduction of section 41 of the Youth Justice and Criminal Evidence Act. This clause outlined the admissibility of sexual experience in court trials and stipulated restrictions on evidence or questions about a complainant's sexual history. More offensively referred to as rape shield legislation, in particular it states that no question may be asked to such effect in cross-examination. This statute in England and Wales was formulated later than in the other two legal jurisdictions, with section 36 of the Law Reform (Miscellaneous Provision) (Scotland) Act banning reference to the sexual character of the alleged victim in 1985, and in Northern Ireland, section 3 of the Criminal Law (Rape) Act in 1991. Again lagging behind its neighbours across the border, England and Wales removed the marital rape exemption clause in 1991, Scotland having done so in 1989.

Although an assessment of the wording of the statute would therefore suggest successful steps towards appropriate criminal justice, a robust assessment of the success of the act lies in conviction rates from across the UK's courts in which the rate of attrition for rape actually demonstrated to be relatively high in the succeeding discussion. This line of inquiry alone is further exasperated by stepping out of the courtroom, and the levels of 'no crime' at the implementation stage of policy, and the point of service delivery, are similarly concerning. Such factors, when conflated, suggest a culture in which the actions of the victim are heavily scrutinized, and the following sub-section is charged with investigating the reasons for this position. First suggesting that the containment of both action and intent all within the interpretation of consent arguably dictates a highly contentious legal process that places a significant burden on the victim from the outset, it is further suggested that a climate of scepticism is fostered by the police at all levels. Despite this chronological narrative of a series of antiquated laws that the state asserts have now been surpassed with more exacting principles of the actions of the defendant, therefore, it appears that discourse around the woman is never fully left behind.

4.3. A PROBABLE CRIMINAL OR A LIKELY VICTIM?

Despite the enactment of a series of measures aimed at protecting the victim, it often appears the reality that in accusations of sexual assault, it is not solely the conduct of the defendant on trial that falls under substantial scrutiny. Far more uncomfortably, and indeed challenging the black letter of the law uncovered above, it is the behaviour of the complainant in cases of rape that is frequently dissected. From the way that a woman is dressed, to the extent to which they knew their attackers, or even their intoxicated state, it takes little scanning of the popular press to stumble upon the attribution of responsibility to victims of sexual assault. The editor of Oxford University's 'The Oxford Student', for example, was removed from her position after publishing an article that branded an alleged victim of rape a 'conquest collector' with 'a reputation' (Young-Powell 2014). Furthermore, and even more startling is the inequitable level of responsibility attributed to women in examples of violent crimes more generally. In the course of investigation into the 2014 beach murders of British backpackers David Miller and Hannah Witheridge, for example, Prime Minister of Thailand Prayut Chan-o-cha made the startling suggestion that 'beautiful' women are not safe in bikinis in the country (Culzac 2014). Similar gender bias was reflected in the US Steubenville rape case concerning a teenage girl that was repeatedly sexually assaulted by male student peers. Surprisingly, despite video recordings of the attack, prevalent sympathetic framing of the assailants was continually evident in the rhetoric of news reporters. CNN's coverage of the events, in which the attackers were continually painted as 'promising students' and how, during their charge, 'literally watched as their lives fell apart', in particular fell foul of criticism from groups such as the Women's Media Center's Women Under Siege Project (2013). Although largely anecdotal, such examples suggest that the attribution of responsibility to female complainants for their own attack, albeit it to varying degrees, is an endemic practice, and this can arguably have a tangible impact on a woman's chance of successful prosecution. Indeed, across the spectrum of criminal activity in England and Wales, the rate of conviction for sexual offences has continually fallen lower than neighbouring crimes, and the levels have actually experienced a further dip of late from 61 percent in 2012 to 55 percent in 2013 (Ministry of Justice 2013). This is further reflected at another stage of the legal process and exasperated by the fact that of all the alleged attacks of this nature reported to the police, only a fraction of such complaints are officially recorded as suspected rape, the number of 'no crimes' standing at 26 percent in the same year

(HMIC 2014a). It consequently appears that in today's global climate, any discussion of policy around sexual offences, regardless of the forum in which it is conducted, inevitably incorporates consideration of those claiming to be the subject of assault, begging exploration of why this activity has become so entrenched in the UK.

Unlike neighbouring chapters in this book that seek to address apparent inconsistencies in the wording of the law, such as the criminal divide between activities concerning sex for sale evidenced in prostitution earlier, the discrepancy here is not endemic in the black letter of the legislation, and the current statutory scheme outlined above clearly prohibits the use of contextual information about the alleged victim. Rather, there appears to be a significant disconnect between this phrasing of the law and the reality for women both in the courtroom and the police station. The manner in which scrutiny of a woman's character and behaviour therefore manifests is of specific interest in this section, and engaging the aforementioned rate of attrition at trial and low police recording statistics in allegations of rape as two key drivers for research, the role of three layers of the criminal justice process in perpetuating the requirement of a 'proper victim' is considered. First, and somewhat intuitively, it is the stronghold of the legislature over the matter that must be explored, and the ability of successive governments to successfully set the tone on the matter considered. Marking a logical progression, however, the interpretative role adopted by the judiciary is obviously a fruitful area of study, and it is the analysis of courtroom debates, and the attitude of jurors, that provides a more accurate insight into legislative intentions. Third and finally, it is the conduct of the police force in their treatment of alleged victims that should additionally fall under deliberation. Beyond analysis of the procedural rules of parliament that have attributed to the black letter of the law on sexual offences, all three bodies display a propensity to fall back upon pre-determined assumptions; this is most heavily evident across the police and has already been publicly recognized through governmental review. By engaging the normative strain of new institutionalism, therefore, submitting that cultural conventions and cognitive frames of reference privilege a certain way of thinking (Lowndes and Roberts 2013), this section uncovers a 'logic of appropriateness', most significantly absorbed and perpetuated by SLBs (Lipsky 2010), that greatly impacts on the implementation of rape policy at the grassroots level. Although the UK is starting to challenge a perceived 'cop culture' (Myhill and Bradford 2013), suggestion of why officers in this institution wrongfully act as judge and jury specifically in cases of alleged rape are still scant. Here it is plausibly linked to the insular and patriarchal behaviour of such an organization, whose informal practices are able to flourish in light of the weak articulation of policy intentions in the very formulation of sexual offence legislation in the UK. Unsurprisingly, these routines have a negative consequence on the experience of the woman, but it can be additionally identified as overly burdensome to specific sections of the population.

To first address the notion of 'proper victim', it is the concept of rape myths, which have so heavily pervaded our discourse on sexual assault, and the array of qualities that can be garnered from these untruths, that first requires consideration. A host of inaccurate sentiments indeed prevail around the crime and can be readily identified in public discourse. Guidance on the Crown Prosecution Service's (CPS) website, for example, details a number of statements, from rape occurring between strangers in dark alleys, to women provoking attack by the way they dress and assertions that prostitutes cannot technically be attacked (CPS 2015). In reality, however, seldom do these assumptions around the violent crime ring true, and this is especially evident in the terms of the prejudicial idea of a scorned woman seeking revenge. According to a 2005 study, the level of false reporting of sexual assault rests at about 8 percent, with only 0.2 percent of individuals actually arrested for making a false allegation (Kelly et al 2005). Often these harmful assumptions are thus born from a misunderstanding about the very definition of rape; 40 percent of participants in a study conducted in 2011, for example, believed such 'attack' actually occurred as the result of overwhelming sexual desire (McGee et al 2011). Furthermore, the significance afforded to stranger rape is vastly misleading, with roughly 90 percent of assaults perpetrated by someone the victim already knows (MoJ 2013a). The study of these habits has long appeared in the scholarship, and first emanated from research around offenders, and specifically the level of victim responsibility perceived in intimate partner violence (Lila et al 2013). This is not a new trend in societal attitudes around sexual offences more generally, however, and psychological research dating back as far as the 1970s has noted the central place that the concept of victim responsibility has assumed in dialogues around the assault (Lea 2007). First beginning with her apparent respectability in terms of whether she was single, married or divorced (Jones and Aronson 1973), it later branched out to cover a range of factors such as her previous sexual history (Johnson et al 1995), consumption of alcohol (Stormo et al 1997) or even her clothing (Whatley 2005). Interestingly, these discussions are not always male dominated, however, and although women are generally likely to be more pro-victim than their male counterparts (Pollard 1992), a study borrowed from the same sphere of scholarship serves to highlight a significant trend of women attributing responsibility to female victims of sexual assault when they are viewed as dissimilar to themselves (Dexter and Penrod 1997). Two important notes of caution, however, should be extracted from this research; first, the studies collated display a somewhat US-centric approach, in which such matters of criminology have a greater academic tradition, and, secondly, much of the critique of victim-blaming in these examples is a comparatively dated exercise and thus perhaps does not appreciate the current legislative recognition of consent. It thus becomes necessary to assess if this adjudication of the woman is in fact a thing of the past.

Thus turning attention to an array of scholarship conducted in the UK in the wake of statutory amendments concerning reasonable belief in consent, an interesting facet is garnered. As in the studies of the 1960s and 1970s, there still appears a strong link between an array of entrenched inaccuracies around rape and the perceived credibility of the victim. Ranging from such assumptions that assault is a cry for vengeance, or women want to be raped, or even that the attack is impossible (Morris 1987), contemporary research still indicates the fervent nature of these prejudices. A study conducted in 2012, for example, drawing a clear distinction between male and female perceptions of victims, nevertheless indicated, as in the cases before, that intoxicated claimants, or those violating traditional gender roles, were all less likely to be believed by both men and women than those who did not (Grubb and Turner 2012). Furthermore, it appears that a perceived similarity to the alleged victim in an additional study correlated negatively with attribution of blame (Grubb and Harrower 2009), thus demonstrating an automatic division in the minds of the public between 'it wouldn't happen to me' and the question of how the victim 'attributed' to her own rape. Critiquing this research yet again, however, it must be challenged that although these trends are present in society at the point of contact with researchers, it is perhaps the case that such harmful assumptions have been abolished from the legal process through the improvements to the statutory field outlined above. Indeed, much of what we know about the attribution of responsibility in this sense comes from the field of psychology, and not the political, and therefore it is essential to question the rate of infiltration into the criminal justice process.

By addressing the high rate of attrition in cases of rape brought before the courts, extolling the notion that a degree of culpability rests with the victim is actually a criticism that can be both dismissed in terms of the formal actions taken by the legislature and judiciary, and equally levied at these two institutions. Upon examination of the entrenched values that appear to influence discussions and behaviour in these forums, it appears that both organizations have indeed failed to fully banish the practices intended by the contemporary legislation, and a wealth of evidence and examples corroborates this point. Immediately, this revelation runs contrary to legislative trends that have increasingly demanded that alleged attackers work harder for their defence; as discussed previously, the recategorization of rape as a sexual offence, rather than its previous status as a violent crime, removed the requirement for a continued state of physical resistance on the part of the woman, thereby rightfully recognizing the far more intricate and convoluted notion of consent. In addition, the subsequent 2003 Act replaced the antiquated and inappropriate clause of 'honest' belief in consent, to the more objective standard of reasonableness, and all of this should be viewed in the context of the introduction of 'rape shield legislation' by way of section 41 of the Youth Justice and Criminal Evidence Act in 1999 stating that in the course of trial of a sexual offence, no evidence concerning, or cross-examination pertaining to, the sexual behaviour of the complainant would be permitted. Granted, this later submission specifically is not without its difficulties, which will be discussed in due course, but the array of legislative interjection at least in part demonstrates an ongoing commitment to modernize the law.

In comparison to the legislation on prostitution, and furthermore abortion, therefore, infused as they are with assumptions and declarations on morality and public order, and inciting polarized societal opinion and a logically adopted position of 'inertia' by successive governments, the same radical, and potentially costly, push for reform is not evidenced in this policy domain. Adaptations to the law on rape can instead be viewed largely as the result of a contemporary demand for the proper workings of justice. Leaving aside the sections of prostitution legislation designed to protect women from direct exploitation in the form of trafficking or control by a pimp, the law prohibiting street solicitation, for example, is debatable in its intentions to prohibit a crime and protect a potential victim. Rather it can be suggested that it partially remains entrenched in statute because of a long-standing societal judgement concerning the morality of prostitution, and an enduring social order paradigm. A similar observation can be thrown at the retention of the criminal element of abortion legislation; any changes that have thus far been evidenced in this field were substantially driven by a mounting crisis in the 1960s and illustrated a rare punctuation to the equilibrium (Jones and Baumgartner 1999). Further changes to the termination of pregnancy, therefore, with the effect of fundamentally altering its status, and providing a rights-based statute, have not yet been calculated as beneficial or even logical for parliament. This first stage of casting aside the sentiment that history matters suggests that such legislative adaptations in the field of rape policy would therefore be created and met with an open mind, both reflecting and guiding societal attitude. To be sure, a responsive legislature should not be overlooked, and in as much as public opinion and the election cycle constrain amendments to the law on prostitution, the reverse can be said of this policy issue (Calvo 2007), and it is such factors that actually drive reform. In light of these modernizing measures, therefore, the conclusion could be garnered that an appropriate legislative scheme is in place, working for the protection of an array of victims.

Such a rapid conclusion, however, critically overlooks the disconnect between the wording of the law and its interpretation in the courts. Despite appearing to banish many victim-blaming practices across its institutions, the informal behaviour in the wider judiciary continues to award a degree of culpability to the female victim's actions. Returning to one of the principal drivers for this piece of research as the low conviction rates uncovered above, therefore, doubt must be cast as to whether these formal amendments have entirely diminished the attribution of responsibility to the victims of rape as evident in the literature since the 1970s. Although placing greater demands on the defendant during the course of trial in terms of a reasonable belief in consent, and removing the use of contextual evidence around the sexual behaviour of the victim, there is still a myriad of practices that point to an endemic routine of questioning the legitimacy of the victim. Comments made in regard to the state of dress of the female victim of assault, in addition to her usual conduct, previous sexual history and the possibility of her flirting with the suspected attacker prior to the alleged rape, for example, among others factors, were all provided space in the pre-2003 rhetoric of the court (Temkin 2000). Even after the introduction of reasonable belief in consent, however, the vocalization of victim blaming by judges is still evidenced in an array of cases. Mr Justice Males, for example, branded a student 'extremely foolish' for drinking too much minutes before her attack, despite a guilty verdict found in regard to her two attackers (*The Telegraph* 2015a). In the same year, the death of Glasgow student Karen Buckley was remarked upon by District Judge Nigel Cadbury when he sentenced another woman for an unrelated crime, in which he submitted his concern for women that get so drunk they 'don't know who they are with' (*The Telegraph* 2015b). As a result, the considerable unease about the conduct of rape trials (Temkin 2000), in which dirty tricks in cross-examination are rife (Brown et al 2007), and are further exasperated by the routine absence of physical evidence and frequent submission of 'neutral reports' by Forensic Medical Examiners (Rees 2010), appears to be as prevalent today as it ever was. Accepting that legislation alone cannot control subtle character attacks (Brown et al 1993) in terms of the perceived recklessness cited above, a further degree of acknowledgement by the legislature and the judiciary of the myth of the vengeful, lying woman (Clarkson and Keating 2013, 162) is arguably evidenced through a series of interrelated practices.

In the seminal instance of *Goodwin* (1989) 11 Cr. App. R. (S.), in which the Court of Appeal heard the case of a woman who has been imprisoned for three years upon being found to have made a false allegation of rape, one judge remarkably argued for the introduction of a register for such women (Rumney 2006). Since that time, and despite section 32 of the Criminal Justice and Public Order Act 1994 serving to remove the obligation on judges to warn the jury of the dangers associated with accepting a victim's uncorroborated story, there importantly remains in statute the discretion to do so. In practice, the uptake of this clause is significant, as in turn are higher conviction rates for cases clearly displaying physical violence (e.g., Taylor and Joudo 2005) and both of these trends partially erode the legislation put in place to combat the prevalent image of a scorned woman seeking revenge, and in reality illustrate that the demand for physical resistance, as seen in antiquity, is still true in contemporary judicial practice. Indeed, research collated from mock trials supports this further (Ellison and Munro 2009), despite a toxic inability to resist, highlighted in the literature (Marx et al. 2008). Such interpretation is perhaps not overly surprising given the context in which many of these measures are discussed in parliament. Providing somewhat of an aged example, debates in 1976 around the inclusion of marital rape into the Sexual Offences (Amendment) Act, incorporated acknowledgement that a woman would perhaps cry rape in order to ensure a better divorce settlement (Rumney 2006, 147) and spousal exemption was not abolished until 1991. In the same instrument, however, defendants were granted anonymity in the course of trial, a measure that has since been removed from the 2003 statute. Nevertheless the discussion on its reintroduction continues to wage, and the Ministry of Justice (MoJ) instigated a report into the matter in 2011, finding inconclusive evidence on which to assert the value of anonymity, but nevertheless garnering attention to the plight of the defendant (MoJ 2011), an issue that looks sets to continue to feature in debates in the current parliament (Parliament website 2015). This is also reinforced by several high-profile media cases and calls from the press for action, as in the instance of the television actor Michael Le Vell, in which he was cleared of all charges of sexual offences, and served to reignite this debate beyond solely the domain of the elite and arguably further exposed the issue to the wider public (Jackson 2013).

Engaging the normative strain (March and Olsen 1984) of the conceptual framework for this project, therefore, the embedded values exposed here appear to colour attitudes among judges and those working within the courts. Diverging from the rational choice model of institutionalism, this strain asserts that such actions are not necessarily a calculated choice, and in such sense may be 'intentional but not willful' (March and Olsen 1984, 161). Indeed, the judiciary is far from decisive in its action to attribute blame, and has outwardly had a discernible role to play in limiting the burden placed upon victims, with the courts long providing a forum for potential change to the legislation surrounding Sexual Offences in the UK. Certainly, the appreciation of the matter in the government's legislative agenda in 2002 can largely be seen as the result of the recognition of significantly low conviction rates in cases of rape. To cite this as indicative of the courts diminishing victim-blaming tendencies may appear odd, particularly in light of the aforementioned contentious nature of rape trials, but at this juncture it is appropriate to return to the previously discussed notion that the courts have a reputation for bringing to light, and keeping in the public eye, matters that other political institutions may wish to bury (Rosenburg 2008). In this sense, therefore, there have been examples of the courts' frustration with the inadequate workings of the law and in 2013, for example, a Croydon Crown Court judge remarked on the 'lamentable failures' of disclosure by the CPS (*The*

Law Society Gazette 2013). As a result, many of the right types of laws have undoubtedly been enacted across the jurisdictions of the UK, and updates to the burden of proof, in particular, have placed the victim back at the heart of matters. Irrespective of these formal measures, however, it appears that implementation is not always adequate (Stern 2010). This is not to say that this is a conscious activity across the judiciary, but a number of values nevertheless permeate the process, and this extends further into the pool of potential jurors in society more widely. Indeed, a number of hypothetical studies into the influence of rape myths in determining cases have been conducted, and a series of telephone interviews in 2011 indicated that 40.2 percent of the 3,210 participants perceived accusations of rape to often be false (McGee et al 2011). In addition, in 2009, researchers conducted a series of mini rape trial reconstructions, inferring lack of physical resistance, delayed reporting and calm emotional demeanor among other factors, and asked volunteers to deliberate the verdict as a group (Ellison and Munroe 2009) with results falling back upon these predetermined values. Consequently, legal proceedings continue to increasingly allow acknowledgement of the complainant's personality traits to creep into judgements, just as occurred prior to the 2003 Act (Williams 1987), and studies that demonstrated the vast significance afforded to the behaviour and actions of the victim, in addition to the defendant's characteristics, in the decision of jurors (Visher 1987) still appear to ring true to this day.

It should be acknowledged, therefore, that perhaps the larger burden of responsibility should fall upon the wording of the law and the dual stipulation housed in the legislation, and mirrored in the Sexual Offences (Scotland) Act 2009 and Sexual Offences (Northern Ireland) Order 2008, and an unusual blend of *actus reus* and *mens rea* that reates difficulties from the outset. Derived from Edward Coke's test for guilt, English law stipulates that a combination of actus reus—translated as guilty act—and mens rea—meaning guilty mind—amounts to criminal responsibility, or '*actus non facit reum nisi mens sit rea*', which, when translated, stipulates '*an act does not make a person guilty unless (their) mind is also guilty*' (Coke 1797, ch. 1 fo. 10). In practice, therefore, an unlawful act can be evidenced and evoke criminal responsibility on the part of the accused, such as the death of one caused by another, which would obviously fall within the act of homicide, but this will not always amount to the gravest of criminal offences, in this case murder, if a lack of intent can be shown. Rather, in this example, many legal systems across the world recognize the possibility of what is often termed manslaughter as a form of diminished responsibility, and the recent, highly publicized case of Oscar Pistorius in the South African courts illustrates this very point. Although the athlete was found to be liable for the death of his girlfriend Reeva Steenkamp by way of shooting, the jury found that there was no intent on the part of Pistorius to kill his young partner, and his sentencing of five years imprisonment was instead delivered for the judgement of culpable homicide (Smith 2014). Conversely, in the law on rape in the UK, however, and again mirrored in a variety of further legislative schemes across the world, both the recognition of the criminal act and the culpability of the defendant substantially rest on proving a lack of consent. True, in strictest definition the actus reus component of rape is intentional penetration, but in all instances before the courts in which the plaintiff is claiming rape, the sexual intercourse cited in the course of trial will only be transformed into an illegal act if this element of assent, both emanating from the complainant and in the mind of the alleged attacker, does not exist.

Specifically the statute requires that a defendant, A, will only be found guilty of rape if the claimant, B, does not consent to the act, and, in addition, if A does not reasonably believe that B consents. Undoubtedly its incorporation in the legislation is necessary, and no bone of contention with such amendment is proffered here, but such a staged process and the demand that, in addition to a lack of consent from B, it must be determined that A does not reasonably believe that B has given their consent, creates an unusual blend of the action and intent of a crime that is not often seen in statute and serves to initiate a notably litigious legal process. If it is determined by the jury, upon hearing submissions from all parties concerned, that A reasonably believed the sexual act to be voluntary, for example, despite persistent claims by B to the contrary, no criminal liability in any form is manifested. In other words, an 'all or nothing' situation is created in which an alleged attacker, if deemed to have plausibly supposed that they were participating in a consensual act, will not be convicted and the claimant will, in effect, be deemed a liar in the eyes of the law. Although not directly referencing the actions of the victim, therefore, it is hardly of surprise that the construction of the term 'consent' is of vast jurisprudential concern in courts to this day, across the three legal jurisdictions. To be sure, the debate regarding its presence, or lack of, forms the stark common feature that runs through the majority of rape trials, invariably seducing into consideration the supposed 'role' of the plaintiff, and subconsciously urging the evaluation of a proper victim in tandem with the image of a likely criminal as a result. Ironically, much of this discussion has manifested from the removal of bodily resistance as a statutory requirement in the UK. Although a development that was rightly heralded as an improvement in the quest for justice, the development has in fact exasperated the situation that, without this seemingly hard and tangible proof, the opinion of the jury is further aggrandized. Top-down studies of policy implementation have long emphasized this statutory language as the key starting point in the manner in which policy enters society, and its necessary deliberation by the courts certainly appears to corroborate this fact. Broadening the scope of this point, it is here that the critique of Matland (1995), and the notion that barriers to successful introduction can often manifest at the beginning formation stage, provide a fruitful line of investigation in regard to the role of the SLB.

Policymaking is rarely a purely linear exercise met with perfect implementation of rational intentions upon its introduction into society. Nakamura and Smallwood (1980), for example, submit that initial processes actually create important cues that set the tone of intensity for the legislative demands, that are later interpreted at the grassroots level. Moving beyond the role of the courts, therefore, and probing further down this line of inquiry uncovers that the insistence of these attributes is far more harmful at the beginning stages of the criminal justice process. In particular, the conduct of the police in the implementation of rape legislation actually demonstrates an even higher level of acknowledgement of a 'credible' victim than that exposed in the rhetoric of the courts. To be sure, explanation for this high rate of attrition in rape cases addresses only one aspect of the concerning trends around 'proper victim' in the UK, and the restriction on justice is further exacerbated by a low rate in which reported sexual assaults are actually recorded as crimes by the police. Thus, although it is certainly plausible that the legislature and judiciary can be considered integral in retaining and perpetuating a set of harmful myths, the submission that it is actually this third organization that is far guiltier of this behaviour holds even more weight. Briefly referring to the work of Hall and McGinty (1997), therefore, the transformation of legislative intentions, taken here as the terms of the 2003 Sexual Offences Act, is significantly affected by power, conventions and the organizational context in which they are formed and implemented; in this sense, policy is not merely a text, but is processual, constructed and emergent (Fudge and Barrett 1981), and thus can often diverge widely in its application on society. Taking much inspiration from Berman's (1978) stipulated need for analysis of both macro and micro level implementation, therefore, and adhering to the logic of Lipsky (2010), it is towards the target population, and those delivering the service, that attention must now be directed to really understand the effect of policy.

Top-down perspectives on implementation often house a misleading emphasis on statute framers as key actors (Matland 1995) and overlook the importance of service deliverers. Taken here to be the police, this law enforcement body is of crucial importance in a policy domain that, contrary to abortion and prostitution, has as its principal focus the regulation of criminal assault against women by a third party, and will thus incite vast interaction between the alleged victim and these SLBs. In this vein, in 2014, a groundbreaking HMIC report detailed the manner in which crime is recorded across all 43 police forces in England and Wales and, although appreciating a broad range of offences, it was actually statistics unearthed in regard to sex offences that caused much alarm. Referring to the 'no crime' generally, defined as an incident that is initially recorded as a crime, but subsequently found not to be notifiable on the basis of additional verifiable information, of the 3,246 such decisions, a significant 1,077 related to reports of rape (HMIC 2014a, 48). Granted, an additional study of crime statistics published around sexual assault indicates variation across regions, with Lincolnshire dismissing 33 percent and Cumbria only 3 percent (HMIC 2014b), and a postcode lottery of sorts is thus certainly apparent, but it is the fact that across the board, all regions are significantly low in their recording rates of such offences that is a point worthy of further investigation, and it can be claimed that the SLB is additionally attributing to inconsistency with a filter on all claims of rape. Asserting that victims of crime are being let down, therefore, the HMIC report stated the unacceptable process for victims of sexual assault (HMIC 2014a, 49), citing additional evidence to corroborate the negative experience endured by this grouping, such as the impact poor crime reporting can have on scandals such as the Jimmy Saville case and the sexual abuse of young girls in Rotherham (HMIC 2014a, 53). Although the experience of the victim is of crucial importance, and will correspondingly feature in the next sub-section, it is pertinent at this point of the study to explore the reasons that underpin this high rate of 'no crime' in rape, and to look for causal insight through the framework of normative institutionalism (March and Olsen 1984).

Indeed, even at a cursory glance, contextual assessment of the woman is frequently present in the process of reporting a crime, and negative experiences of police interaction have been articulated, both anecdotally and in formal reviews, on numerous occasions. Findings from a focus group brought together in the course of compiling a Home Office report, for example, made several references to a lack of support for women during the recounting of an offence; one contributor's opinion in particular was that the police invariably disclose their skepticism around an allegation of rape. In another more explicit recantation, a witness described a specific instance in which an officer suggested that the described attack was a one-night stand that the victim regretted (Payne 2009). Although it must be noted that the profiling of criminals is not a new trend and is certainly an activity that is undertaken across a myriad of countries and policy domains, including multiple homicides, online grooming and even fraud offences (Gresswell and Hollin 1994, Elliot et al 2012, Kapardis and Krambia-Karpardis 2004), the profiling of complainants in this manner is certainly atypical. The source and perpetuation of these assumptions and labels, therefore, is of vast concern, and the reasons for a sustained and aggrandized focus on the accountability of the victim in the additional arena of the police force demands a wider remit of exploration. In particular, both the acknowledgement of the limits of methodological individualism (Arrow 1994) and an emerging 'cop culture' (Myhill and Bradford 2013) are required to ascertain a more robust explanation for what appears to be established practice in this organization, and these points will be addressed in turn.

The initial stage in addressing these statistics is to question the deliberate intentions of the individuals involved. Amassing an array of insights from various studies, three factors about the conduct of police officers in response to rape appear important. First, due acknowledgement of the gravity of the crime is reflected in the matter of rape, with officers demonstrating a general acceptance of the seriousness of the offence and the negative consequences for the victim in the long term (Krahé 1991). As a simple normative question, with a clear ethical binary, and in recognition of their status as law enforcers, this is what should be expected from such individuals. When this factor is further mixed, however, with an additional recognition of credible victim, the definition of rape becomes fragmented, with studies citing that the interview process involves not only the search of truth, but also a process of establishing the veracity of the complainant (McMillan and Thomas 2009). Furthermore, the severity of the crime obtusely appears to be eroded by this process, as upon accepting a rape may have taken place, and thus recorded as such, it may later be adjudicated upon as not worthy enough to be taken to court (Stanko and Williams 2009). Indeed, in addition to the two stages of attrition identified in this chapter of reporting to the police and court trial, Gregory and Lees (1996) importantly highlight that both police referral to the CPS, and subsequent decision by that body to prosecute, forms two noteworthy filters. Finally, therefore, this fracturing of the definition of rape is carried out in a broadly similar fashion by police officers across the board; in other words, certain attributes or circumstances are deemed as standard indicators of a false allegation. In a study conducted in the South East of England, for example, there was a prevalence in which the terms 'unstable' or 'malicious' complainant were used by the police in justifications of acknowledging inaccurate claims (Lea et al 2003). Thus progressing through the literature from a point of a serious crime expounded by the individual, to a series of mitigating factors that appear to garner consensus across police officers, it becomes apparent that individual action alone does not reveal all facets of the causal narrative. Rather it can be supposed that a mechanism must be in place in order not only for such determinations of 'proper victim' to be made, but for these to represent a 'party line' of sorts across the organization. Just as was deliberated in the introduction of this book, therefore, an individual focus tells us little about the whole story here, and it is a wider culture that in fact harbours a more fruitful explanation.

If it can be consequently assumed that this process of assessing the credibility of a victim isn't entirely a purposeful action on the part of the individual police officer, appreciation of institutional constraints must come to the fore. Moving beyond a study of the individual, therefore, and stating that the process of institutionalization is one of perception rather than evaluation, normative institutionalism ascribes much importance to political bodies for the spread of ideas, norms and values (Lowndes and Roberts 2013). In this sense, the structure within which certain individuals operate can heavily influence their beliefs in a sub-conscious manner, to an extent that their ramifications can be felt across society more generally. Previous studies have attributed a general practice of 'victim blaming' across the police force as plausibly attributed to the patriarchal context in which they operate (Jan 2011). Expanding this sentiment, observation of an occupational culture across the organization is not a new endeavour, and was previously subject to an array of studies in the 1990s (Newburn et al. 1994). Granted, such body of literature does not match the nuanced and convoluted use of the term 'cop culture' in the United States, in which terms such as 'blue wall of silence' and 'blue code' are commonplace, and scholars were commenting two decades ago about the lack of definition of police culture in the UK (Chan 1996), a situation that can plausibly be assumed to be true to this day. Conflating an array of studies into smaller aspects of policing characteristics, however, a collective personality of the organization can be garnered and the 'macho' overtones of the police, although not a new revelation, come to the fore. Indeed much research has gone into the notion of ownership over 'the ground' they cover (Holdaway 1983) and the practice of telling exaggerated 'war stories' in a 'cult of masculinity' (Waddington 1999), and this sub-culture makes it difficult for officers to accept any form of non-conformist orientation (Burke 1994). Identity is a transient notion, however, and much of these studies, and indeed this perception generally, can perhaps be viewed as outdated and unsympathetic to the progression that has been made in the force. Greater recognition of cultural and gendered perspectives, however, still appears to be constrained, and amid a sea of diversity training, it appears more accurate that officers are resistant to change, and female, minority ethnic and gay and lesbian officers are more likely to absorb these standards rather than oppose them (Loftus 2008). This is further exacerbated by the barriers that women traditionally found within the organization in terms of access to higher rank and specialist roles (Brown 1998), often dictating that, in turn, such characteristics and values were also adopted by the gender as a way of getting ahead.

Allowing these values to become entrenched across the force, however, is the wider insular approach that is routine across the police, and it is actually the identification of informal behaviour during times of crises that provides the clearest indication of this. In the course of public inquiries, and the methodological individualism they favour (Arrow 1994), it is stark in the case of the police that scapegoating is often not as prevalent as it is within other sectors such as healthcare or social services. The example of the Independent Police Complaints Commission (IPCC) inquiry of the shooting of the innocent Jean Charles de Menezes at Stockwell tube station in 2007 following the London bombings demonstrates just the sort of 'cover-up' that has come to typify the force. The findings state that in the aftermath of his death, officers across rank set on a collective mission of projecting misinformation, presumably in an attempt to deflect blame from one to another, rather than to single out an individual in self-preserving mood (IPCC 2006). A similar occurrence arose after the death of Ian Tomlinson as he innocently walked home during the G-20 summits; struck by a police officer, he died from internal bleeding caused by blunt force trauma. Again mirroring the campaign of framing that accompanied de Menezes' shooting (Vaughan-Williams 2007), however, the police released a flurry of statements that at first failed to account for the officer's involvement in the incident, and instead heavily focused on those at the scene trying to save Tomlinson's life (Carey 2013). In times of crisis, therefore, the body can be characterized as one that 'closes ranks' rather than looking to scapegoat individuals, and this had strong ramifications for identifying unacceptable behaviour in regard to judging victims. The tight institutional bonds across this organization create an insular body (Herbert 1998) that permits much validation of behaviour among individuals rather than urging each officer to hold another to account. This is further compounded by the fact that many within the sector feel more relaxed in the company of officers who understand the 'backstage' role of their position (Waddington 1999), allowing further opportunity for a strong brotherhood to flourish. Beyond the express intentions of the police, therefore, and formal codes of conduct, a distinct 'cop culture' (Myhill and Bradford 2013) appears to be predicated on widespread patriarchal values that are diffused across the organization through a process of social learning (Béland 2005), and in which wrongful conduct is perpetuated by the insular structure of the police force that constantly reinforces a brotherhood. Following a 'logic of appropriateness' (March and Olsen 1984), therefore, the definition of rape, identified as increasingly fractured as contact with the victim grows, is subject to the same array of beliefs and practices, and individual police officers will contextualize their response in terms of the dominant image of a 'proper victim' with little critique or assessment from peers. Although as mentioned previously, the exact definition of this credibility desires yet more research into the construction of rape myths, it nevertheless appears that a gendered stereotype that can be identified in multiple arenas is happily endorsed and reinforced at the point of policy implementation.

The combination of muddy legislative intentions and a flourishing 'cop culture' (Myhill and Bradford 2013), therefore, heavily restricts the proper workings of the 2003 Act. In addition to the low conviction rates submitted by the criminal justice system, the recent HMIC report highlights that the greater hurdle exists for women in terms of ensuring the police officially record a reported crime. The wide regional variation, and comparatively low levels of this occurring in the area of sexual offences, indicates the crucial

SLB role engaged by the police, and the impact sub-conscious attitudes and engrained values can have on the proper implementation of policy. The 'logic of appropriateness' to adopt standard operating procedures underpins the actions of individual officers faced with her allegations, and so entrenched are these views that few police officers appear aware of their bias in reporting and instead, in a vast majority of cases legitimately feel they are adhering to a correct code of conduct for their establishment. This form of 'cop culture' (Myhill and Bradford 2013) is readily acknowledged in North American studies, and the harmful reluctance in UK scholarship to do the same appears dated. Furthermore, the dominance of these real victim traits also demands additional study through a gendered lens, incentive for which is substantially driven by the consequences of these dominant norms for the victim as unveiled below. Indeed, recognition of the impact of deeply embedded and regularly exercised cultural norms on society must be viewed not only from the perspective of influencing people in their attitudes of victims, but additionally the resulting behaviour of victims themselves requires examination. As a result, the ability to even speak up about a potential crime is highly constrained and indelibly coloured by perceptions of what a victim should look like and how they should behave, particularly in regard to spousal abuse.

4.4. NORMATIVE ORDER: THE FEAR OF COMING FORWARD AND MARITAL RAPE

A dominant image of the 'proper victim' formed on discriminatory undertones, and stereotyping of false allegations, arguably steers the behaviour of key institutions in the interpretation and implementation of rape legislation. To place the woman on trial, as mentioned previously in the remarks of Lord Hale, although archaic in its origins, appears to continue to ring true in contemporary judicial studies. Importantly, however, this is no longer confined to the courtroom, and the unveiling of the significant numbers in which alleged rapes are later classified as 'no crime' additionally suggests a troubling process in police stations across the UK. Although potentially indicating the aggrandized influence of the individual police officer, acting as judge and jury in the process, the analysis above moved beyond methodological individualism to highlight a deeply embedded 'cop culture' (Myhill and Bradford 2013) predicated on an insular, patriarchal brotherhood that is subconsciously adhered to by its agents through a 'logic of appropriateness' (March and Olsen 1984). The continued application of such values certainly has practical and harmful consequences for women entering the criminal justice system, but the effect of this behaviour extends further and serves to constrain even the initial stage of reporting. Indeed, an identifiable categorization of contestable victims, including those subject to marital rape, is now entrenched across society, with a cumulative effect of not only preventing the woman from coming forward, but additionally eroding the severity of the crime and impacting upon recidivism rates. Against a backdrop of a largely restorative UK, therefore, the demand of policymakers for a full public inquiry into the conduct of the police in the reporting of rape is strongly asserted.

A category of contestable victims in claims of rape, incorporating such broad members as prostitutes, students and wives, is clearly evidenced at the societal level across the globe. Street workers, as previously uncovered in chapter 3, continuously suffer from a higher than average amount of violent sexual assault than any other grouping, yet, as a collective, are substantially more inclined to choose not to report such an attack (e.g., Anderson 2001). Of importance, however, is the fact that a body of data has pointed towards the fact that this is not due to the wording of the law but rather is attributed to the experience they fear awaits them. Farley (2004), for example, readily submits that prostitutes could easily take legal action under existing law, but rarely choose to do so. Extracting from interview data that such rapes are systematically treated as if they do not matter, and has become somewhat normalized among prostitutes, a substantial 62 percent of the 854 prostitutes interviewed across nine countries had experienced rape (2004). Similarities can be drawn with another grouping of college-aged students in the United States who, according to Bureau of Justice statistics gathered between 1995 and 2013, are unlikely to report their rape to the authorities compared to their non-student counterparts, some stating that it was not important enough to report, that it constituted a personal matter and that they feared reprisal (Sinozich and Langton 2014). In the UK, a survey conducted by the parenting website Mumsnet found that of the 1,609 female respondents, 10 percent answered that they had been raped, and 35 percent sexually assaulted. Of those figures, 83 percent had in turn failed to report it to the police, and had not even confided in friends and family (Mumsnet 2012). Presumed to form part of this number are those that experience sexual assault at the hands of their husband. It is with this latter grouping that the forthcoming discussion is principally concerned as exemplifying the harm that can be caused by victim-blaming practices. Although it is difficult, if not impossible, to entirely extract societal influence from that of the police force, with marital gender roles continuing to play a large role across the wider public, and varying institutions offering a causal explanation for this 'raping licence' (Finkelhor and Yllo 1985), the reaction of the police force is key in the criminal neglect of marital rape, particularly as prosecution even for cases in which the suspect and the complainant have had prior acquaintance has long been of a far more problematic nature that instances of stranger rape (Gregory and Lees 1996, 12).

Although criminalized in Scotland in 1982, and later in England and Wales in 1991, the barriers in place for successful prosecution in the area of spousal rape are plagued with myths, inaccuracies and prejudicial reaction, arguably to a greater extent than the concept of 'proper victim' already extolled. As a result, the fear of coming forward that is experienced by this section of society is significant, and sheds further concerning light on the already low conviction rates, and police recording statistics, in terms of accurately portraying the level of sexual assault in the UK. Despite its surrounding stigma, colloquially termed 'wife rape' (e.g., Weingourt 1990) has been a frequently occurring atrocity throughout recorded history and in modern culture. Variation in these accounts, however, stems from the reaction to such an act, from its origins as the right and will of the husband to have sex with his spouse as and when he pleases (Ryan 2005), to a more nuanced field of rape in which Western debates, particularly in the United States, centre around its legitimacy as a subset of domestic violence, or a free-standing problem in marriage (Russell 1990). The matter was even treated originally with some frivolity, and Menandrian New Comedy of Roman times, for example, provided numerous plays in which a young man would rape and impregnate a female citizen in order for marriage to the girl to become acceptable to his family (Fantham 1975). As Lape notes, this served to normalize and resolve such action and is epitomized in Menander's *Epitrepontes*. Kharisios abandons his wife upon revelation that she has given birth to a child five months into their marriage, only to discover he indeed raped her at a religious festival earlier, thereby culminating in a 'happy ending' (Lape 2001, 80). From a contemporary US perspective, Whatley (1993) remarked on the dearth of literature available around marital rape, compared to stranger rape, and little development in the scholarship has been evidenced since. Indeed, regardless of the abolition of the marital rape exemption in the UK in 1991, there still exists much stigma around the topic, and unfortunately it reflects an under-researched field. The first academic appreciation for the subject only dates back as far as the 1970s in the work of Gelles (1977) and, furthermore, the current literature is hampered by a range of methodological problems, including definitional ambiguity, both in terms of the woman identifying the action as rape, and also across researchers, with unrepresentative sampling often gathered from battered women shelters and rape crisis centres (Martin et al 2007). One study conducted in 1990s, however, across a solid sample of 1,007 married women, revealed that 13 percent responded that they had, on at least one occasion, had sex with their husband against their will upon clear insistence that they did not want to. Furthermore, 5 percent submitted that a fear of violence had been used to elicit sex (Painter and Farrington 1998). A fear of coming forward, however, is not perpetuated solely by this elite ignorance of the problem at hand, and is evident in further forums.

A context of prejudice in determining probable victims of rape has already been posited and appears at multiple stages of the criminal justice process, and is most clearly expounded among the police force. Providing concern for the treatment of victims at the point of contact with these processes, this additionally serves to erode the objective severity of the crime, both in the eyes of the public and for offenders. Certainly in the previous subsection, the encroachment of rape myths into the rhetoric and minds of potential jurors was deliberated, and with a significant negative conclusion, but the infiltration of these victim-blaming practices can be extended further still and arguably serve to colour the perceptions of individuals in wider society. A study undertaken almost four decades ago at the University of Washington attempted to assess the extent to which social role and 'just world' considerations would affect people's perceptions of the personal responsibility of a rape victim in their own assault. Undergraduate students studying psychology at the university were asked to read descriptions of the same rape case during class sessions, but the work environment of the victim and the degree to which they knew their alleged attacker was continually altered. Occupations included a topless/bottomless dancer, a social worker, or a nun, and the complainant was said to be either acquainted or unacquainted with the assailant. A questionnaire was then completed by each student in which they were asked to score factors such as victim responsibility, victim carelessness, victim provocation and assailant responsibility on an 11-point scale. Among the vast set of results, the nun was attributed significantly less responsibility for her attack than her neighbouring dancer and social worker, and the dancer was rated as more likely than the nun to have done something to encourage her rape. Adding a further layer of analysis, men answering the questionnaire on average rated the victim as more careless and more likely to have done something to have provoked her rape across all three occupations than their female counterparts (Smith et al 1976). This harmful reduction in the perceived severity of the crime is not a thing of the past, however, and research in Germany exploring attitudes towards rape and robbery, for example, found greater attribution of blame to the victims of the former. In particular, the perpetrator blame was the same in instances of robbery, regardless of whether the victim was drunk or had in fact known the offender previously. The same was not true for victims of rape, that were held to greater account if, for example, they were too drunk to resist (Bieneck and Krahe 2011, 1794).

From this position, therefore, it is certainly not too far a leap to assert that the attribution of blame is manifested not only in the aftermath of attack, or even solely in the actions of the police force in the course of reporting the alleged crime, or throughout the legal proceedings in court, but can actually have long-lasting ramifications even after trial. In this sense, heavy scrutiny of the appellant's character does not always end after the delivery of a guilty verdict, and citing a much-reported case in the media, the circumstances around the release of former premiership footballer Ched Evans from prison in 2014 following his sentencing of rape is indicative of these circumstances. His return into society led many to enter into the argument of the appropriateness of his re-employment at Sheffield United Football Club (Pidd 2014). Of perhaps greater significance for this study, however, is that Evans himself continues to claim he is innocent, and a website to this effect has been set up, urging the public to view the woman in question entering the building in which the attack took place so as to 'judge for yourself' (*The Telegraph* 2014). Furthermore, this rumination over the circumstances in which the offence took place, and the consumption of alcohol as a reckless decision on the part of the victim, is frequently discussed. Comments made during a live television programme in 2014 that appeared to assimilate a woman's intoxicated state with mitigation in the case of her own rape were submitted, in which the presenter asserted 'It was unpleasant, in a hotel room I believe, and she [the victim] had far too much to drink', exemplifying this very point (BBC News 2014b). Similar circumstances were also evidenced in the US trial of former Vanderbilt University football players charged with the rape of a young woman in their collage dorm room. Although found guilty in 2015, and the repercussions still in their infancy, much interest has again been focused on the inebriated state of the victim, and rhetoric of the court has alluded to a campus culture of 'drunken sex' (Burns 2015). Arguably this is further reflected in the almost sympathetic tone for an array of convicted 'celebrity' rapists in the media, as in the example of Mike Tyson. Convicted in 1992 for the rape of the then 18-year-old Desiree Washington, his story reemerged in the British tabloids in 2013 when immigration rules dictated that the former heavyweight boxer was banned from entering the country (Meikle 2013) Since serving his time in prison, Tyson, who has continually claimed his innocence, has enjoyed somewhat of a resurgence in pop culture spheres, experiencing a comeback through a developing film career that is gamely noted in the press (*Day and Night* 2014). In a process akin to a feedback loop, in public policy however, such rhetoric serves to break down the severity of the crime and normalize its existence in society. This often manifests itself in the use of a language of rape, in which a man stating that he 'would like to rape her' can be judged as an everyday declaration of his attraction towards a woman, or can be seen as the correct punishment when a woman 'steps out of line'. In 2013, for example, Caroline Criado-Perez campaigned for Jane Austen's face to appear on British £10 notes. The response came from some angry Twitter uses that they would hunt her down and rape her (*Daily Express* 2013). The continual societal assessment of the woman, even after the attacker has completed a prison term, is therefore not unusual and is arguably the product of aggrandized institutional attention to the notion of a likely victim that serves to seep into multiple layers of society.

When the status of the alleged victim is further coupled with their role as a wife, this becomes even more concerning for those seeking justice.

The result of eroding the severity of the crime upon the offender is also discernible, and arguably has an impact upon rehabilitation; recidivism among sexual offenders, although comparatively low, is notable and of the 490,000 re-offences in England and Wales between July 2010 and June 2011, 3,300 were serious violent or sexual offences (Ministry of Justice 2013). A study conducted in the United States in the 1980s highlighted the continued propensity of rapists, even during incarceration, to find excuses and justifications to make their victim appear culpable (Scully and Marolla 1984). It thus becomes an interesting point to ponder if re-education during time spent in penal institutions as to the precise meaning of consent, and acceptance of responsibility of the part of the prisoner, would aid the reduction of re-offending. Of even greater significance in a study of this nature, however, is the knock-on effect this has in terms of the possibilities this leaves for serial offenders to go undetected, as in the case of 'the night bus stalker', 'the M25 rapist', and the 'black cab rapist' (*The Telegraph* 2009). When considering the attribution of responsibility to a woman in the instance of rape, therefore, it appears counter-intuitive to have a policy domain that discourages victims to act responsibly towards the next potential target by not reporting the crime.

Certainly, against the backdrop of a largely restorative UK this constraint on the reporting of crime appears obtuse. As a harm-centred approach to justice that has progressively evolved in Britain since the 1980s (Marshall 1996), it broadly concentrates on the centrality of victims, the obligations of offenders and the role of the community in creating a healing programme for all involved (Zehr and Mika 2003), and neighbouring areas of the criminal law have evidenced mounting appreciation for the position of the injured party, and the prevalence of such justice initiatives in the UK, and indeed across the globe, provide support for this (Galaway and Hudson 1996). In 2013, for example, the MOJ issued a Code of Practice for Victims of Crime, outlining the list of key entitlements and services at the disposal of those falling target of illegal activity, including the need to be referred to neighbouring supportive organizations (Ministry of Justice 2013a). Largely based on the idea of facilitating a meeting between victim and attacker, therefore, and thus often engaged only for minor crimes, and its appropriateness in the case of sexual assault rightly questioned, the emergence of such an ethos, and the impact of this approach, nevertheless reflects a developing legal system that is keenly attempting to best suit the needs of the people, rather than solely handing out arbitrary punishment (Daly 2002). When contrasted with the increasing acceptability of 'rape culture' in society, however, the positive steps taken by this approach are arguably limited in this domain, and this is particularly damaging in terms of women's readiness to speak out when experiencing sexual crimes. Certainly the subsequent chances of societal restoration for the women involved, which arguably can be causally linked to the cumulative effect of the institutional recognition given to the idea of a 'proper victim', are accepted as heavily restricted, particularly for those falling within clearly contestable groupings.

Again borrowing lessons from neighbouring policy fields (Dolowitz and Marsh 1996), therefore, the demand for a judicial public inquiry into this sphere of rape policy is long overdue. As the generic term used to describe various modes of investigation, the public inquiry in the UK can be both idealized as an opportunity for meaningful change, or discarded of as little more than the illusion of remedy until the disaster or incident in question is dulled in the minds of society (Elliot and McGuinness 2002). It is problems in terms of the latter that can be most readily seen in the course of examination into police matters and, despite the closely related Payne Report and Stern Review of 2009 and 2010 respectively, only marginal facets of the policing of rape have witnessed improvements. Indeed, doubt has been expressed in some quarters as to the practical utility of numerous reviews, reports and commissions of inquiry and, as Jan puts it, 'reviews come, reviews go, and women are still raped' (Jan 2011). Furthermore, this limited impact of change induced by such processes is a dominant trend in public policy generally, and was similarly replicated in the adjacent issue of institutional racism. In the wake of the Brixton riots in the 1980s, Scarman's report detailed the disproportionate and indiscriminate use of 'stop and search' powers against black people, but notably stated that institutional racism did not exist (Scarman 1981). More than a decade later, following the murder of Stephen Lawrence, a black British teenager murdered while waiting for a bus one evening, the treatment of race in the police force was again reignited, and a total number of 70 recommendations for reform were ordered. Of most significance in this second inquiry was the progressive step of highlighting a collective failure to provide appropriate services to persons based on colour, culture or ethnic origin (Macpherson 1999). Even in the immediate aftermath of this publication, however, the principal challenge was already mooted as the ability to actualize these recommendations (McLaughlin and Muriji 1999), particularly in light of the Scarman report's failure to stem the tide. Arguably, many of these failures to implement reform, however, stem from this messy status afforded to public inquiries, and the lack of constitutional or legal requirement that inquiries be judicial (Woodhouse 1995). The element that sets aside the likes of the Leveson inquiry, therefore, in which all the powers of the high court, including the authority to require witnesses to give evidence under oath, are deployed is suggested as necessary in regard to the police's treatment of the 'no crime' in circumstances of alleged rape is arguably called for in regard to proper victims.

The brutal physical and emotional impacts of rape are undeniably severe, but the consequences of regulation in many ways appear just as bad with not only the treatment of complainants failing to reach an acceptable standard, but the acceptance of women by society more generally constraining the justice process to an even greater degree. This bank of contestable victims face potential backlash from a multitude of sources in society, and may never be fully accepted as a credible source, even after a court process adjudicating on the veracity of their claim. Society instead appears much more lenient to the plight of offenders, during trial and even after their reintroduction into society. Although a restorative UK in this sense should be championed as a virtuous position, this cannot be effectively achieved if the gravity of the crime is eroded in such a way. Thus illustrating the failure of the black letter of law in this policy field in everyday practice, the example of marital rape, and the fear of coming forward palpably experienced by spousal victims, should be positioned as a key driver for investigation into the conduct of the police. Indeed, integral to society's reaction is the perpetuation of this 'proper victim' image and, short of scrutinizing all of society, which is of course impossible, this key law enforcement body is identified as a forerunner in setting these standards.

4.5. REACHING INTERNATIONAL STANDARDS OF REGULATION ACROSS THE EU

The merits of global governance schemes are debated copiously in the literature, but such benefits are not as easily garnered from the criminal law, with the array of matters falling within this remit often subject to a broad consideration of cultural traditions and normative values. As a result, therefore, multiple systems of regulations may exist over any one issue as was evidenced previously in the chapter on abortion. Importantly in the instance of rape, however, in which myths surrounding the behaviour of alleged victims are rife, definitional disparity across countries has the potential to further influence implementation of legislation at the domestic level in a negative fashion. In an age in which the line between state and international legal orders has become ever eroded, and central pillars dividing the two arenas are increasingly challenged (Krisch and Kingsbury 2006), the absence of a unified approach to the matter of sexual assault is indeed conspicuous, particularly across the states of the EU. This point is of even greater pertinence when it is acknowledged that a web of supranational guidance over the incidence of sexual assault is in fact collated from two significant interjections, and afforded support by deliberations of the European Court of Human Rights (ECtHR). Indeed, according to the doctrine around the supremacy of community law, and the principle of direct and indirect effect extolled in the case of *Costa v. ENEL* [1964] ECR 585, the EU prevails in conflicts with member states, thus making it an important area of inquiry. The text of the

EU treaties prescribes primary legislation in this regard and provides the most transparent form of supranational influence; similar to constitutional law at a national level, it details the distribution and exercise of the Community's power and the specific responsibilities of the various actors in the decision-making process (e.g., Richardson 1996). Although it is clear from the outset that rape is not afforded specific attention in such measures, this is not to say that the matter does fall under the close scrutiny of the EU's moral imperatives, and a fundamental sentiment of the Treaty of Lisbon is the promotion of rights and values, freedom, solidarity and security, and full legal status is afforded to the Charter on Fundamental Rights. Entering into force on 1 December 2009, the Charter builds upon, among others, the international agreement of the European Convention on Human Rights (ECHR) and provides assurance that no EU legislation, in the form of either regulations or directives, will contravene its provisions. Created under the auspices of the Council of Europe, the ECHR came into force in 1953 and is hailed as one of the most advanced and effective international regimes for the avocation of human rights (Henkin et al 1999). In pursuit of a guaranteed level of protection for EU citizens, a Commission was initially established to investigate potential conflicts and make referrals to a court if deemed necessary. Articles 25 and 46 of the ECHR were subsequently adopted by member states, however, aggrandizing the role of the ECHR by permitting individual and state-to-state petitions, and recognizing the compulsory jurisdiction of the Court (Janis et al 2008). By becoming party to the Convention and ratifying its provisions, nation-states therefore acquiesced a level of control to the EU, and it has been engaged as an interpretive tool by the EU ever since. The history of this relationship is characterized by growth, adaptation and reform (Greer 2006) and has provoked a supranational legal position across a range of issues; studies into the impact upon neighbouring rights-based debates, for example, have illustrated its presence in societal issues such as the death penalty (Manners 2002) and gender discrimination (Masselot 2007). A review of the case law and judicial activism of the ECtHR therefore provides important indication of the parameters of EU law. In addition, non-binding legislation, although not obligatory for member states, is important in the construction of normative power and should not be overlooked, its significance having previously been highlighted in neighbouring domains such as the development of asylum policies (Guild 1996).

First highlighting supranational guidance, therefore, and working in tandem to outline the global context in regard to rape and establish worldwide standards for corresponding legislation have been the complementary work of the UN's Handbook for Legislation on Violence Against Women (2010) and the Council of Europe's Istanbul Convention on Preventing and Combating Violence against Women and Domestic Violence (2011). Within a model framework of regulating for violence against women, it is submitted as a baseline principle that such action should be viewed as gender-based discrimination, but three significant conditions are further applied to this notion. These encourage the removal of any requirement that sexual violence be committed by force or violence, criminalize sexual assault within a relationship by stating that no marriage or other relationship will proffer a defence to a charge of sexual assault, and define sexual assault as the violation of bodily integrity and sexual autonomy (UN 2010 26). Mirroring this stance is the Council's submission that states should criminalize the engagement in non-consensual vaginal or oral penetration of another person with any bodily part or object (Council of Europe 2011 Article 36).

Providing further support for this web of legislative authority, this urge towards a positive obligation to punish rape was previously submitted in the jurisprudence of the ECtHR and the case of *MC v. Bulgaria* (Application no. 39272/98). Concerning the alleged violation of rights under Article 3, 8, 13 and 14 of the ECHR, the female applicant challenged the District Prosecutor's decision to dismiss her case on the basis that she was not coerced into having sex through the use of physical force or threats. Being aged 14 at the time, and having met a group of men in a disco, the girl agreed to accompany them to another bar if she could be home by 11 p.m. On route, however, the men stopped at a nearby reservoir. Deciding that she did not want to swim, the applicant waited in the parked car as the three others made their way to the water. A short time later, one of the men returned and forced her to have sexual intercourse with him, moving the seat back to a horizontal position and holding her hands behind her. One of the other males in the group was a brother of someone she attended school with and, feeling that would provide her with some protection, she accompanied him back to the third man's house. It was at this point a second rape occurred at the hands of the third man in one of the bedrooms; having not the strength to resist violently, she begged the man to stop. Upon vast deliberation on the necessity of absence of consent as a measure of rape, the court held a violation of Articles 3 and 8 in regard to Bulgaria's positive obligation to protect an individual's physical integrity and private life, and to implement effective remedies.

Although these international agreements and interpretive remit of the court therefore have the intention of developing co-operation and a consistent policy between member states, and illustrate a level of European normative power over a matter (Rosecrance 1998), these acknowledged standards have not been reached across all member states of the EU. In particular, and inciting great alarm, in a survey of legislation in all 28 member states is the lack of consensus as to whether it is the absence of consent or the use, or threat of the use, of force that is key to prosecution (EU). Austria, Germany and Hungary, for example, continue to require the use of force, with the latter further restricting the definition to purely penile-vaginal penetration. To be sure, the most significant variations in definitions of rape, however, emanate from considerations of the object penetrating the body, or the orifice which is being penetrated, and serve to draw the lines between rape and serious sexual assault in many countries.

The manifestation of a contestable crime can thus arguably originate from this fractious response to rape across domestic laws, and it begs the question if more adequate implementation, and appropriate response from society more generally, could be achieved if an integrated approach was assumed. It can certainly be contested that ill-defined legislative intentions in neighbouring countries that fail to reach appropriate minimum standards for rape legislation must shoulder some of the responsibility in creating a disproportionately debated offence. The legitimacy of allegations of rape or serious sexual assault faces vast attrition in individual cases, with deliberations over a proper victim proliferating at the police station and beyond in the criminal justice system and inevitably ordering the seriousness of such offences in comparison to each other. From a top-down perspective, however, the gravitas of the crime as a standalone occurrence is additionally challenged by an uneven system of global governance and failure in a number of EU member states to afford proper protection for fundamental human rights.

4.5. CONCLUSION

The statutory reframing of unlawful sexual intercourse from a violent crime to a sexual offence in the 1956 legislation marked a pivotal turning point in the legal landscape of the twentieth century and was swiftly followed by important events in 1976. Stipulating for the first time that rape amounted to a lack of consent, rather than sustained physical resistance, as was the previous position in early Offences Against the Person Acts, it appeared an important step towards increasing the level of legal recourse available to victims of sexual assault. Later followed by the replacement of an 'honest' belief in this assent, to that of 'reasonable' conviction on the part of the defendant, and accompanied by the implementation of rape shield legislation preventing reference to the complainant's previous sexual history, all of which have been mirrored in Scotland and Northern Ireland, objectively amounted to a far more robust and appropriate legal landscape. Such appraisal appears particularly convincing when compared to the origins of rape at common law, and throughout early history, as an offence merely against property, as opposed to infringement of a woman's bodily rights.

Instrumental in these developments, therefore, and not impinged by the same calculated constraints, and fear of costly changes to the underlying value of the law associated with abortion and prostitution, were the combined interjections of both the legislature and the judiciary, providing positive statutory improvements for victims, with the wording of the legislation undeni-

ably recognizing important nuances in the offence of rape that were previously overlooked. Relying solely upon this analysis of the black letter of the law,
however, overlooks the reality of the situation for many women reporting an
offence. As first flagged up by the comparatively low conviction rates in UK
courts for the offence in relation to adjacent serious crimes, these placating
legislative amendments actually belie a significant failure to dispel harmful
assumptions around credible victims in the eyes of those enforcing the law.
Certainly, the language engaged in the course of trial, and the surrounding
parliamentary discussions, consistently extol a degree of culpability on the
part of the woman, and, by widening the theoretical framework to engage the
insights of normative institutionalism, the deep-rooted and long-standing acceptance of contextual factors underpinning the behaviour of this institution
is revealed. As a result, the actual implementation of this policy field far
from mirrors statutory wording, and adjudication on a likely victim is deeply
entrenched in the courts.

It is at the micro level of implementation, however, that a specific institutional stronghold demanding a 'proper victim' is really uncovered. Adopting
a bottom-up perspective of the policy process, and acknowledging the significant influence possessed by SLBs, an exploration of the police force across
the UK indicates a key role for this institution over the mater of rape in the
criminal justice system. Due in large part to the absence of clearly defined
intentions in the legislation at the governmental level, and mismatched dialogue and attribution of blame in the language used by the courts and the
legislature, these service providers have significant room for manoeuvre in
the application of the law. Adopting the approach of methodological individualism (Arrow 1994), it could readily be assumed that this lack of explicit
principles at the elite level would allow for wide regional variation in the
usage of the statute. Although, to an extent, there is certainly fluctuation
between the regions, a more important trend of high levels of 'no crime'
across all regions can be extracted. The power of SLBs alone to apply a
policy domain as they see fit does not provide sufficient explanation for this
situation, and it is instead the 'logic of appropriateness', and a deep-seated
set of norms and conventions in dealing with alleged victims of rape that is of
significance. Fostered within an overarching 'cop culture' predicated on an
insular, patriarchal brotherhood, these practices combine to sub-consciously
influence the assessment of a likely victim, as opposed to probable criminal,
in the eyes of individual agents at the point of contact with a woman. In
addition to this sub-standard running of the criminal justice system, however,
the societal ramifications of sustaining an image of a 'proper victim' are
multiple and enduring in their effects, and can have an acute impact on
certain groups such as spouses, in addition to placing further women in
danger.

Further fueling the contestable crime debate, however, is the failure of some member states across the EU to reach minimum appropriate standards set by the UN in regard to the nature of consent, the list of body parts vulnerable to such an offence and the removal of marital exception in the legislation. In conjunction with the countries that far surpass these requirements, therefore, a broad spectrum of what really amounts to rape is created at a supranational level, restricting a unified approach to the matter and incidentally endorsing the debate on 'proper victims'. This persistent disparity reengages the suggestion made previously in the chapter that it is in fact ill-defined legislative intentions, this time at a comparative, international level, that necessarily entail greater decision making on the part of the SLB and significantly contribute to a varied approach at the implementation stage, in addition to catalysing societal debate over the gravity of the offence. Rather than solely a sub-conscious normative bias on the part of police officers when approaching victims, therefore, it can instead be challenged that it is top-down implementation from elites that is additionally found lacking in this context, and the absence of exacting measures housed in domestic statutes, coupled with the juxtapositions in global criminal schemes, should shoulder some of the responsibility of the extent to which victims receive a varying experience of the criminal justice system across the UK. It is troublesome, however, to completely dispose of the idea that the behaviour of SLBs creates an inconsistent approach to women and the sub-conscious influence of the aforementioned rape myths and 'cop culture,' remains steadfast in its valid causal insighs. In summation, therefore, it appears just to claim that rape can be evidenced in many instances as a poorly defined concept both formally and informally, because of the combined influences and actions of the legislature, judiciary and SLBs.

Although perhaps the murkiest stereotype uncovered in the course of this book, the product of varying judgements over clothes, intoxication and profession to name a few, the notion of the 'proper victim' is also one of the most concerning. It was remarked in the introduction of the book that the labels of 'criminal' and 'victim' are oscillated between in the legislation, and this has certainly been the case, for example, in prostitution regulation. It is in this domain, however, that it could be assumed that such a label is easily asserted, without problem, as the female victim is not partaking in criminal conduct in any manner, yet it has quickly become apparent upon investigation through the lenses of NI that the victim title is contestable in this field. Although running contrary to the inflexibility with which other domains have created stereotypes, therefore, the negative impact on women's issues more generally, as pondered in greater detail in the closing chapter, is actually of great significance here, threatening to impact upon any woman who experiences sexual assault.

Chapter Five

Welcoming Public Debate: Developing the Regulation of Pornography through Open Discussion

The distribution of pornography in the UK far from attracts the stigma of decades previous, and the prevalence of adult material in conventional culture is more widespread than ever before, seeping into various aspects of the media and arguably becoming increasingly unchallenged by society. It was recorded in 2006 that sales of such material has reached $2.5 billion and comprises 12 percent of all websites, with this number constantly expanding (Family Safe Media 2008). No longer confined to peep shows and clandestine viewing, therefore, the consumption of erotic material is often not shied away from, and a survey in the UK in 2014 indicated that 60 percent of respondents from 2,500 school and university students openly admitted to watching porn (NUS 2014). This progressive attitude is similarly mirrored in the cinematic world, and *Rolling Stone* reported in 2014 on 30 films that had 'pushed the envelope and still played in multiplexes' (*Rolling Stone* 2014). In particular, the avant-garde Danish film director and screenwriter Lars von Trier is largely held responsible for introducing unsimulated sex into mainstream movies starring long-established Hollywood names such as the epic, two-volume *Nymphomaniac* (Child 2013). Furthermore, it is now not uncommon for many of those working within the sector to themselves experience a celebrity-like status, and the American-born Jenna Jameson, for example, heralded as the 'world's most famous adult entertainer' (*Forbes* 2005), has not only starred in numerous adult films over the last two decades but has successfully crossed into everyday pop culture, with her 2004 autobiography spending six weeks on the *New York Times* best-seller list (*New York Times* 2004). It is also of importance to note that this encroachment into conventional society has not gone undetected in the world of academia, with Routledge similarly recognizing this growing subject by launching the first peer-reviewed journal on the subject, entitled *Porn Studies*, in 2014 (Taylor and Francis Group 2014). Irrespective of this expansion, however, the regulation of the field is far from one-dimensional, and the UK has experienced some tightening of the statutory field of late through the successive introduction of section 63 of the Criminal Justice and Immigration Act 2008 and the Audiovisual Media Services Regulations 2014, even amid claims that these instruments significantly curtail freedom of speech.

In contrast to the domains previously studied, therefore, in which inertia and entrenched norms prevail, policy adaptation in the regulation of pornography is conspicuous. Indeed, in a landscape that has seemingly been shaped by increasingly liberal values towards sexuality, and fosters what appears to be a growing societal acceptance, this creeping normalization of pornography in global culture (McRobbie 2004) has curiously been accompanied by statutory intervention in recent times. This sort of policy dynamism is of central concern to discursive institutionalism (Schmidt 2000), and it is with this strain of NI, rather than the element of continuity typifying the three 'traditional' strains (Hall and Taylor 1996) previously studied, that this chapter is most concerned. Although the power of ideas in policy is not a new observation, with much literature produced on the concept of framing to name just one body of work (e.g., Rein and Schön 1993, Jacoby 2000, Daviter 2007), it is with the more specific interactive process of discourse, and a 'logic of communication' (Schmidt 2008), that a causal account for the success of new concepts in adapting institutions can be provided. Placing much emphasis on the role of the individual, it is therefore David Cameron's tough line on child protection in regard to pornography that provides an interesting point of focus here. While seizing political advantage of key events, such as the death of Baby P and the convictions of Stuart Hazel and Mark Bridger, the analysis suggests successful amendments can largely be attributed to a pre-existing agenda on the part of the Prime Minister (PM) that subsequently embodied the problem of pornography. Crucial for allowing the creation of new solutions however, was the coordinative and communicative discourse engaged across the Conservative Party and the media respectively and adaptations to the concept of harm in this manner consequently leave the door open for ongoing innovative discussion around the ramifications of such material for women more generally.

The chapter progresses as follows. The history of the regulation and sale of pornography, having a far less direct legislative framework than the issues of abortion, prostitution and rape, is initially tracked from the Obscene Publications Act 1857 to the current statutory position for hardcore publications under the 2008 Criminal Justice and Immigration Act. Second, the contemporary regulatory debate is outlined, and Cameron's perceived 'hard line' on protecting the vulnerable during his time as PM, specifically in regard to Internet pornography, and his innovations in regulating specific acts, outlined. This is viewed as particularly surprising in view of the vastly different approaches to pornography, and the relative ease of access, in countries such as Denmark, but these diverging UK developments actually serve to set the scene for the prevalent debate currently waged in this area: the question of 'who needs protecting?'. In addressing why the issue of safeguarding has been adapted in this domain, and resulted in the introduction of Internet porn filters, the discursive arm of NI is applied to the actions of David Cameron and his rhetoric with both the Conservative Party and the mass media. Appreciating that success can be attributed to varying use of coordinative and communicative discourse, the fourth section suggests a blueprint for future policy change by linking explicit content to violent crimes, although the chances of success in this domain are last considered in the context of supra-national law, and the EU's concern for freedom of speech and an open Internet. To conclude, therefore, the chapter asserts that Cameron's long-standing concern for child protection followed a 'logic of communication' (Schmidt 2008) to frame Internet pornography as a grave harm for children. The triumphant manner by which this has been achieved, adjudicated here as tangible policy change, rather than the comparatively low levels of uptake across households, points towards the possibility of a larger shift in the level of protection afforded to women, and, in particular, recently recognized 're-venge porn'.

5.1. REGULATING THE SALE AND DISTRIBUTION OF PORNOGRAPHY

The legislative landscape encompassing the law on sexually explicit material in the three legal jurisdictions of the UK lacks a primary source of authority and instead derives from a number of principles, including a body of obscenity legislation and a criminal statute. Due in large part to the vast and subjective degree of interpretation it invites, and to a lesser extent its relative infancy as a term in common usage, the labelling of material as pornographic has long been problematic for policymakers and is consequently a subject matter that is ill defined across these measures. Much of what we do know of the regulatory field is born from the law around censorship, a quick survey of which readily demonstrates the rate at which the domain has matured. Taken here to comprise a fictional drama designed to elicit sexual arousal (Mosher 1988), but diverging from some recantations to include both moving and still images, pornography throughout this chapter is viewed in terms of its revenues; namely magazines, Internet websites, cable television and in-room hotel movies (Williams 2004). From the early Victorian period, to the post-

1960s liberalization, therefore, two specific waves of legislation are identified; a series of Obscene Publications Acts in 1857, 1959 and 1964 respectively and, in reaction to the development of the Internet, an extension of
liability from publication to possession in section 63 of the Criminal Justice
Act 2008. Notable across both streams, however, is the failure to explicitly
engage with the subordination of women in such material, and the harm this
poses for the gender more broadly.

Sexually charged images date back centuries and are far from a modern-
day construct. The Turin Erotic Papyrus on display in Italy, for example, a
scroll painting comprising a series of vignettes of various sexual acts among
Ancient Egyptians, is just one instance of such visual representations. Interestingly, however, a history on pornography specifically is difficult to elicit,
and this has not gone unnoticed in the surrounding literature. What we do
know to be true is the derivation of the word itself, from the Greek 'pornd'
meaning 'whore', and 'graphos' meaning writing, thereby indicating its gendered origins, but this in itself can be misleading (Kerr 1991). Indeed, if one
is to subscribe to the Foucaultian notion of sexuality and its invention, such
pornographic material only really came into being in the nineteenth century,
when sexuality became problematic by society and certainly the Middle Ages
did not recognize or even engage with such a term (Trinks 2013, 162). Thus,
although even ecclesiastical buildings of the twelfth century depict such
images, such as San Pedro de Cervatos in Northern Spain that clearly dis-
plays an orgy of a copulating couple (Trinks 2013, 162), this lack of consensus over the precise meaning of the term constrained discussion, a theme that
has certainly bled into later statutory law on the matter, and, up until the
latter half of the twentieth century, it was only unanalytical descriptions of
erotic practices that really crowded the scholarship in this field (Hoff 1989,
17). A more accurate and fruitful line of inquiry in this sense is therefore
proffered by the appearance of the term 'obscene' in legal history. Although
the parameters of the word, and the content it covers, have been eroded by
temporal interpretation, the focus of the material has largely remained constant, and it is women that have been the dominant subject in a series of
interventions.

Indeed, official statutory restrictions around material deemed inappropriate in the UK, including pictures, images and stills, is deemed the logical
starting point in mapping the policy field around pornography. Although
previously a common law misdemeanour, the first legislative attempt to govern this domain came in 1857 through a series of Obscene Publications Acts.
Sparked principally by a desire to address the proliferation of cheap literature
on the subject, and specifically the sale of penny newspapers to the working
classes (Roberts 1985), Lord Campbell's Act marked an important political
acceptance of the need to regulate this field (Manchester 1988). Following
his presiding over two court trials in which he was reportedly shocked at the

horrors that were being disseminated on the streets, he engaged the metaphor of obscenity as a cultural poison, and manipulated a debate on the regulation of chemical poisons to comment on indecent publications. Favourably received by press reports, the law soon passed its third reading (Manchester 1988). Interestingly, however, scholarship from neighbouring disciplines has noted the desire of the act to regulate not only publication, but also the visibility of such material (Nead 1997, 178), a situation drawing clear comparisons with the governance of prostitution covered earlier in the book.

Further clarifying the interpretation of the law, therefore, was the colloquially termed Hicklin test, a case law ruling that served as the leading principle in determining the definition of obscenity from its delivery in 1868, to statutory overhaul in 1957 (*R v. Hicklin* [1868] 3 QB 360). The facts of the case concerned Henry Scott, who had resold an anti-Catholic pamphlet detailing the nature of confessionals and, specifically, the questions put to females during those times. The article was deemed obscene for this very reason and correspondingly ordered to be destroyed. Upon appeal to the Quarter Sessions, however, Scott found support from the Recorder in charge of such order, Benjamin Hicklin, who agreed that his purpose with the dissemination of such material was not to corrupt but to expose problems in the Church. Judge Cockburn, upon appeal to the Court of the Queen's Bench, stipulated that the intention was immaterial, however, and that the test of obscenity was in fact whether there was a *tendency* of the matter to deprave and corrupt (Alpert 1938, 53). In other words, obscenity was an adjudicated fact rather than an action. Substantially restricting artistic merit as a result, however, this Hicklin test was always controversial but came under substantial fire in the 1950s alongside society's increasing appreciation for liberal interpretations of art, and much impetus for an amendment to the law was provided (Hilliard 2013). Repealed by the Obscene Publications Act 1959, therefore, a further judicial interpretation of this new act was delivered in the case of *DPP v. Whyte* [1972]. Submitting that the test of obscenity should not rest exclusively on the corruption of an individual, but the corruption of a significant number of people who were likely to read it, a new standard was born. Most recently manifesting in an 1964 iteration, therefore, this principle remains the cornerstone of obscenity legislation in England and Wales.

Supposedly reflecting this contemporary response to harm, and the expansion of pornographic mediums, however, a second phase of pornography legislation in the UK resulted from digital advances and 'big bang' popularity of the Internet. Certainly, running parallel to this increasing acceptance has been the mounting problem of access to hardcore material and, in light of media attention to cases such as that of Jane Longhurst, a special-needs teacher who died through a non-consensual act of asphyxiation at the hands of Graham Coutts, pressure was heaped upon the government to provide more copious regulation. During the trial of Coutts, it was made clear that the attacker had frequented a number of hardcore pornographic sites, and calls for the shutting down of these outlets were heard from both the family of Longhurst and also MPs. Leading that charge was David Blunkett, at the time Home Secretary, who met with the US deputy Attorney General to discuss the matter and continued to work closely with the family's campaign to shut down such sites (BBC News 2004). The nature of Internet regulation, however, made such a task insurmountable, a fact that was not ignored by the government and, following consultation in 2005, proposals for criminalizing the possession of such material was mooted. Citing that such material had no place in society, the paper made clear links between pornography and its effects on attitudes, beliefs and behaviour (HO 2005, 16). Marking a sharp division with the more recent approach of risk to children by the Conservative Party, as explored in detail later, the consultation process continually alluded to the status of the woman and even discussed depictions of rape, particularly citing those that appear in 'real time' (5). Of the 397 responses garnered, however, opinions appeared sharply divided with many of those opposed to strict provisions, drawing on arguments of freedom of speech (HO 2006). As a result, the government was urged to draw the line at those acts that were life threatening, or likely to result in serious or disabling injuries, culminating in a new governance scheme in 2008.

The result of a three-year consultation period, therefore, the Labour government purported to be addressing a mounting societal concern for material that was increasingly accessed by consumers, but fell outside the reaches of the existing Obscene Publications Act. Unlike this preceding instrument, however, in which regulation did not relate to the consumer, section 63 of the Criminal Justice Act 2008 stipulates the offence of possessing an extreme pornographic image, liability for which extends to Northern Ireland. In reference to the word pornographic, the act stipulates this to mean anything that is assumed to have been produced purely for the purposes of sexual arousal. In regard to the possibility of harm, however, an image is determined extreme by the legislation if, as aforementioned, it threatens a person's life, if it is likely to cause serious injury to a person's breast, anus or genital, or if it involves sexual interference with either a corpse or an animal. No explicit reference was made to depictions of rape or neighbouring forms of sexual violence against women. Once again, as in previous chapters, the diverging legal jurisdiction of Scotland demands attention, however, and an important extension has been submitted by Hollyrood. Formerly similar to England and Wales in its regulation of pornographic material through section 51 of the Civic Government (Scotland) Act 1982, which largely fulfills the same functions as the Obscene Publications Act detailed above, 2010 saw the introduction of section 42 of the Criminal Justice and Licensing (Scotland) Act, explicitly outlawing the possession of all depictions of rape or non-consensual penetrative sexual activity. Such interjection is intriguing, particularly in light of the consultation process, for the 2008 process formed a joint initiative between the Home Office and the Scottish Executive, and clearly has ramifications for the notion of protection, not just in this host region, but for England and Wales in terms of the potential for future change for women; a point that will be returned to later in the chapter.

An outline of the statutory field consequently uncovers that despite the patchwork of policies, an undertone of attrition between libertarian individual responsibility, and paternalist governmental concern, similarly evidenced in the women's issues previously discussed, is nevertheless prevalent in the status of pornography in the UK. In contrast to the expansive history of abortion, rape, and to a lesser extent prostitution, in the statute book, however, the law on pornography is far less nuanced and rests heavily on the ongoing censorship debate. Indeed the chronological development of the law over the centuries illustrates that the adjudication of material, pertaining significantly to the context in which imagery is displayed, has been notoriously complex (Mosher 1988). That which is on the periphery, however, is still subjected to strict regulation, as exemplified by the Labour government, and this development interestingly marks a clear statutory break between censorship and protection. The governance of such content in this timeframe, however, cannot automatically be characterized as one of a protracted setting of an agenda, in the manner evidenced in the Conservative Party's approach below, but rather was largely reactionary to societal and technological developments over the decades that have provided new and alternative platforms for the dissemination of pornographic material, and the possibility of harm to citizens that they then in turn incite. The classification of pornography in this sense, therefore, embodying as it does a standard of sexual conduct deemed obscene, is a transient activity that changes with the demands of contemporary society. Recently introduced measures, with the view to protecting children, are indicative of this very point.

5.2. CAMERON'S CRACKDOWN

In contrast to the range of developments in the field of pornography that suggest it now fills a credible role in society, the legislative approach to such material is not wholly permissive, and the reach for prosecution has certainly been increased from publication to possession. In addition to the criminalization of extreme pornography in 2008, however, successful amendments to this regulatory field have featured in David Cameron's time as Prime Minister, the reasons for which will be analysed through the conceptual framework of discursive institutionalism in the succeeding section. Prior to this analysis, however, it is necessary to stipulate precisely what has been introduced by the current government and, in addition, the chronological context of these instruments. Indeed, the harmful impact of explicit material has frequently dominated debate at Downing Street over the last election cycle and is set to continue into the next Tory term. Although this is most tangibly evident in the coming into force of the Audio Media Regulations 2014, which criminalize a range of specific activities perceived as providing potential harm for those involved in, and viewing, such activities, of perhaps even greater innovation in this policy domain has been government endorsement of Internet porn filters, aimed at addressing the associated harm to children. Within this burgeoning field of new legislation, however, and contrary to the developments in Scotland explored above, the depictions of rape in pornographic material, and a growing body of 'revenge porn', have only recently been criminalized in England and Wales.

In 2013, a groundbreaking agreement was reached between the government and four key Internet service providers (ISPs) over access to online content of an adult nature. Writing in the *Daily Mail* in December 2012, in response to a tough campaign long fought by the newspaper, and significantly driven by the murders of Tia Sharp and April Jones, Cameron announced proposals for a 'default on' system of so-called 'porn filters', in which households would have to opt out of these child protection measures (Chapman 2012). In an address of the harm posed to children from the Internet, both directly, in terms of violent and sexual crimes, and also indirectly, through exposure to such material at a young age, these plans were later endorsed by key ISPs both at a public Wi-Fi level and within households. In a speech to the NSPCC in 2013, therefore, Cameron announced that an agreement had been reached with TalkTalk, Sky, Virgin and BT to introduce the measures as standard for any new customers, with family-friendly filters automatically selected (CO 2013).

Adding a further layer of regulation to this field of Internet pornography, the Audio Media Regulations came into force in 2014, stipulating the banning of a range of extreme activities. The reasons for increasing the scope of measures which arguably have their roots in the 2008 Criminal Justice and Immigration Act was deliberated in the explanatory memorandum and referenced again the growing popularity of online viewing, and the associated risks of harmful material that runs alongside such expansion. In particular, the sufficient nature of child safeguards was questioned, and the need for more nuanced restrictions stipulated. As a result, the regulation set in place that the current restrictions enforced by the British Board of Film Classification (BBFC) for home video would apply to online content, including sadomasochistic acts and asphyxiation. This range of banned activities, however, has again been the source of much conflict among different groupings due to the very ethos they embody. Indeed, conspicuously absent in the explanatory note, and indeed the reach of the regulations, was the concept of protection for those taking part in the acts, and although it was later announced by the government that life-threatening activities were a secondary driver for the reforms, this claim must be viewed with scepticism. Not only did the dialogue feature a heavy propensity towards child protection, sustained analysis of which will follow later in the chapter, but the acts listed comprise a messy mix between dangerous and non-dangerous activities, while also leaving out notable potential harms such as rape and other forms of sexual assault. Of particular disdain for the lesbian, gay, bisexual and transgender (LGBT) community was the incorporation of female ejaculation, far from a dangerous activity and instead seemingly looking to curtail certain practices prevalent among such groupings (Razavi 2014). This perception of prejudice sparked a substantial body of feminist opposition and a sea of protests, extending to also cover those who feared the evils of censorship more generally, and received support from the Liberal Democrats and, specifically, Nick Clegg (Grice 2014). Far from addressing principles of harm, therefore, the regulations appeared, in part, to cast moral objection over certain consensual activities.

Addressing the absence of sexual assault, however, the Criminal Justice and Courts Act 2015 further added to the regulations to additionally incorporate depictions of rape into the list of banned activities by virtue of Section 37. In addition, following deliberations in a House of Lords Committee report into social media crimes, the same Act equally recognizes colloquially termed 'revenge porn'. Defined as the electronic publication or distribution of sexually explicit material, usually following the break-up of a couple, originally intended for consensual private use, the offence was posited beside crimes such as cyberbullying and trolling. Making wide reference to human rights, and the private remedies at the disposal of such victims, the Communication Committee pushed for clarification of the law in this regard (HoL 2014). By virtue of section 33, therefore, the offence of disclosing private sexual photographs and films with intent to cause distress carries with it the possibility of two years imprisonment. The incorporation of both of these provisions is undeniably important for women, and their ramifications for the gender, in addition to their key drivers, will be explored in the final subsection.

Scrutiny of hardcore pornography has thus undeniably been undertaken in earnest by Cameron's government over the last four years. Arguably, this reflects an adapted understanding of protection, and the continual demands of an expanding society as reference above. Heralded by some as a poor example of technological governance, however, and others as the worrying start of censorship, the success of these measures requires evaluation, particularly in regard to the ramifications for future regulation protecting women. Indeed, it appears that the incidental harm to children threatened by pornography has been the Conservative Party's primary focus ahead of concerns around sexual violence, and marks a divergence from Labour's efforts around cases such as that of Jane Longhurst, thereby questioning the future direction of the policy domain. First, however, the successful agreement with ISPs over 'porn filters', regardless of the subsequent uptake, is nevertheless important and uncovers how discursive institutionalism (Schmidt 2002) can have a significant impact upon policy outcomes. Irrespective of its target audience, the idea of protection has thus indelibly influenced the formulation of this regulatory field, but policy change against the grain of creeping liberalization importantly questions how this has been achieved.

5.3. WHO NEEDS PROTECTING?

The paradox of increasingly pervasive pornographic material in society, against progressively tighter regulatory restrictions, questions the protective intentions of the law. As highlighted previously, the level of acceptance of matters of an erotic nature has undoubtedly expanded in the twenty-first century, and the adult entertainment business has a thriving economy. Despite Foucault (1978) rejecting such a 'repressive hypothesis' in the nineteenth century in favour of the perception that discussion around sex was always rife among the dominant bourgeois social class, it is nevertheless difficult to rebut the observation that pornography now permeates mainstream practice in more ways than it has ever done before, and studies have certainly asserted the momentum at which a variety of such material has appeared in the last 20 years (Attwood 2002). Although the popular press in the United States has a tendency to haggle over precise figures, with the often quoted $10 billion estimate proffered by Forrester Research all the way back in 1998, and later deliberated by the *New York Times* (Rich 2001), counteracted by *Forbes* magazine's insistence that a number closer to $3.9 billion, the industry is undoubtedly sizeable (Ackman 2001). Regardless of this apparent erosion to a Victorian stigma, however, recent interjections into the statutory field additionally indicate the perception of risk in this policy domain. Diverging from the long-standing claim that sections of sexually orientated speech serve to subordinate women and demand stricter controls as a result (Dworkin 1985), however, the association of an alternative group of citizens with an incidental 'harm' caused by pornography has in contrast ensured a fruitful contemporary challenge to the regulation.

The success experienced by a new form of anti-pornography discourse, however, prevailing within the Conservative Party's child protection agenda, is the focus of this section. Stating that institutions are continually defined and redefined by ideas, simultaneously shaping them and shaped by them, discursive institutionalism optimistically embodies the possibility of an innovative process. According to the theory, effective policy change can be achieved through a dual process of coordinative discourse within institutions, and the communicative dissemination of these ideas to the wider public (Schmidt 2008). Although uncharacteristic for NI studies generally, the theory therefore allows for the marriage of pre-existing thoughts to new and alternative modes of regulatory practice through an imaginative rhetoric. In contrast to the governance of other women's issues studied in the course of this book, therefore, an analysis of this domain through such conceptual lenses uncovers a progressive approach to regulation that allows agents to think, speak and act outside their institutions (Schmidt 2008). Underpinned by a 'logic of communication' in this sense, the process allows for the challenging of existing institutions and the deliberation of new structures. In the study of Cameron's crackdown on pornography, therefore, the coordinative discourse across the Conservative Party, flourishing within the agenda on child protection, allowed for the mooting of a novel response in regard to Internet pornography. Further capitalizing on certain media outlets, the PM has long been able to effectively communicate new policy ideas in this domain to the wider public largely through the framing of issues in terms of 'Broken Britain', as readily demonstrated through the events surrounding the inquiry into the death of Baby P. Specifically in the cases of Stuart Hazell and Mark Bridger, the PM was able to garner further support for a successful agreement on online 'porn filters' with four ISPs; more than a point of interest, the successful introduction of these measures, and tighter controls in the recent 2014 regulations, suggests the possibility of further change for women in the future in regard to the subordinate treatment of the gender in pornographic material and the link to violent crimes. Importantly, however, the analysis reveals that the identifiable issue for the government is the idea of child protection, not the problem of pornography generally.

The Conservative Party's concern for child protection is manifested in an array of examples. Clearly linking these instances into an overarching agenda, however, is David Cameron's dedicated attention to this vulnerable grouping, instrumental in his role as leader of the party, and later as PM. Introduction of the short-lived Independent Safeguarding Authority (ISA) in 2010, in particular, now replaced by the Disclosure and Barring Services (DBS), brought with it the introduction of a standard vetting process for anyone in a role that required weekly contact with children through a school or other known organization. In another example, during a televised interview, he discussed in detail the concept of giving children their childhood back, and tackling what he termed the 'inappropriate sexualisation' of youths (BBC News 2010). Furthermore, in 2014, he voiced strong support for a proposed ban on smoking in cars carrying young persons. Looking to the future, therefore, such broad focus looks set to continue and, in 2015, an additional plan concerning protection for children was presented by the PM to a Downing Street summit, in which professionals turning a blind eye to abuse would be held accountable for their actions, and could face possible prison time (Holehouse 2015). Although its success is yet to be determined, fruitful discourse on the matter has already been entered into. From just a snapshot of suggested interventions, therefore, it appears that the party has long articulated the rights of the child, and the need for protection that ensues, and this continual expansion of such an agenda has organically become of consequence to the regulation of pornography. Diverging from normative institutionalism, therefore, and the continuity inducing legitimization of ideas and action through a 'logic of appropriateness' (March and Olsen 1989), discursive institutionalism approaches the possibility of change through the discussion of new ideas, and the successful manner in which they are then conveyed to the wider public. Acknowledging that ideas alone indeed cannot have an impact on policy formulation, however, Schmidt (2008) proffers that it is in fact the interactive process of dialogue that determines why some succeed and some fail.

In this sense, the presentation of definitions and solutions to the problem of child protection have arguably led to innovative statutory measures for the Conservative Party, such as the implementation of colloquially termed 'porn filters'. The introduction of these ideas, however, can largely be traced to an initial framing stage of the issue at hand in terms of a broader, mounting societal crisis. Indeed, across the interventions discussed above, a clear cognitive deliverance can be observed, with Cameron proposing a move away from a non-interventionist approach and towards a concerted attack on social justice (Dodds and Elden 2008) through the specific notion of 'Broken Britain'. Citing a range of perceived failures on the part of the Labour Party, for example, statistical information from Cameron's time in opposition was often primed (McCombs et al 1997) in a fashion that highlighted concerning trends such as one-parent families, or corrupt policing. It should be pointed out, however, that the use of the term 'prime' itself can come under fire here as, on several well-publicized occasions, wholly inaccurate figures were quoted by the Conservative Party, an important matter that will be returned to shortly in regard to Baby P but was additionally evident in the infamous move of a decimal point. Referring to teen pregnancy in disadvantaged areas in England and Wales, the Tories produced a dossier that inaccurately reported the rate to be 54 percent rather than 5.4 percent. Whether unintentional, or the product of a smear campaign (Walker 2010), these ideas nevertheless entered the political arena through the background ideational abilities of the PM, and his perception that failures in regard to the safeguarding of children demanded immediate attention. Such a tactic is certainly not novel in policy discussions and has previously been evidenced in the actions of the National Farmers Union (NFU) during the foot and mouth disease in 2001 (Hindmoor 2009), and its prevalence in the run-up to the 2010 election made good campaigning sense. Of perhaps greater significance, however, is that the frame has since reemerged in government to aid the uptake of a range of new social policies with far-reaching consequences (Hawkins 2011) and the movement between the two stages of ideas and discourse is exemplified in the case of Baby P.

A clear stipulation of 'what is and what to do' (Schmidt 2008) is readily evident in the wake of the death of Peter Connelly in 2007 and provides early indication for the future handling of pornography regulation by Cameron. Concerning the case of a toddler brutally murdered by his mother and her partner when under the eye of Haringey Council as a child at risk, the discussion surrounding the tragedy quickly descended into a farce of finger-pointing (Butler 2014). Involving multi-agency failure, from NHS professionals, to social care workers, and even the police, it was readily pounced upon by Cameron, and a series of ferocious framing wars (Boin et al. 2009) with Gordon Brown ensued during the PM's questions in 2008. Of particular note during this time was the manner in which the subject was broached by the then leader of the opposition in which he challenged the independence of the inquiry into the events. When accused of playing party politics on the back of such a statement, Cameron was quick to lose his temper (Treneman 2008) but nevertheless indulged in a theme that has come to characterize much of his agenda on child protection (Parton 2013). When commenting on the defendant in the case, for example, he made clear attempts to link the incident to the Conservative Party's perceived problem of 'Broken Britain' and a rise in teenage mothers. Although inaccurately stating Peter Connelly's mother to be 17, when in fact she was 27 at the time of the offence (Robinson 2008), his tactics illustrated the marriage of background ideational abilities with the crisis at hand and a first step towards presenting a policy proposal. Although Schmidt (2000) herself recognizes the importance of the substantive content of dialogue, taken here as cognitive ideas around child protection, to achieve a broad consensus across policy elites, however, it is additionally asserted that an effective process of communicative discourse must be entered into.

Consequently, Cameron set about garnering elite support through two interrelated tactics: a coalition-building exercise and an emotive interaction with the public. Tackling first this idea of coordinative discourse within the child protection agenda, the nature of political discourse dictates that it often occurs in private and away from the eyes of the public, and thus poses substantial difficulties in terms of research. Taken here to be indicative of this dialogue, however, was a letter submitted to *The Guardian* signed by 19 individuals, comprising politicians, child experts and family organizations, who all urged Gordon Brown to launch a long-term, cross-party inquiry into the events that surrounded Peter Connelly's tragic death. Of particular pertinence, however, was the assertion by the Labour MP Graham Allen that it should have at its forefront the need to tackle the problem of today's abused children becoming tomorrow's abusers (*The Guardian* 2008). Reflecting what had long been part of Cameron's strategy, the letter clearly articulated the need for proactive measures and attached to the idea of harm a positive solution. With such political attention, however, came the necessary support from the wider public, and the process for Cameron's second tactic demanded an alternative stream of rhetoric. Indeed, discourse matters not just to whom you say it, but how you say it (Schmidt 2008), and an amendment to the language used is evidenced through his engagement with the media. Indeed, following the debate in the House of Commons, therefore, an editorial piece simultaneously appeared in the *Evening Standard* that further corroborated his claims, but this time with the addition of vastly more emotive phrasing, incorporating questions designed to reflect the frustrated and appalled mood of the country such as 'How on earth was this allowed to happen?' (Cameron 2008).

In light of these actions, however, much criticism has been afforded to the PM for his behaviour during this period, but the marriage of crises with his overarching agenda has surfaced again in the years since. Drawing lessons from this approach, and applying this process to the more recent cases of the murders of Tia Sharp and April Jones, support for the relatively distinct programmes on child protection and the philosophy around harm caused by pornography can again accurately be attributed to this dual process of communication. Certainly, institutions according to the discursive approach are not external-rule-following structures, but are instead internal structures and constructs in agents (Schmidt 2008), and it is this very interactive process that sets discursive institutionalism apart from other promulgations and allows for a wider remit of institutional change. Beginning with the facts of the two cases, therefore,Tia Sharp was a 12-year-old schoolgirl who was sexually assaulted and murdered by her grandmother's partner, Stuart Hazell. It was revealed to jurors during the trial that two memory cards containing extreme pornography had been found in his home (Marsden and Ward 2013). In equally harrowing circumstances, April Jones was snatched while playing outside her parents' home and murdered by Mark Bridger; her remains have not been found to this day. Again, child pornography was located on his computer (Bentley 2013). The open dialogue across members of the Conservative Party in the wake of these instances that occurred within a matter of months of each other allowed for new ideas within this child protection policy to flourish. The Tory MP Claire Perry, advisor on the sexualization and commercialization of children, for example, compiled oral evidence in an Independent Parliamentary Inquiry into Online Child Protection (Perry 2012). Adopting the same pragmatism that has characterized Cameron's social programme in the years preceding, the report acknowledged the economic benefits garnered from the Internet, and its revolutionizing effect on the global climate, but still remarked that with such advantages came risks, specifically in regard to the absence of central control over the matter (3). Although such obstacles to effective regulation had similarly been cited by the Home Office in consultations surrounding the Criminal Justice Act back in 2005 (HO 2005), the bulk of deliberations in this new iteration concerned the threat of exposure for the child, and technical discussion on the level of filtering warranted. Simultaneously, the government requested research into the matter to be conducted by Mother's Union, an international Christian membership charity, the result of which reflected similar terminology; highlighting such features as the need for emotional adjustment and what is desirable for children to see and hear (Bailey 2011), the potential harm of pornography was continually posited as towards the young person rather than the woman.

Rather than constrained by the past, rules of the game, or even deeply embedded cultural values, all underpinning the traditional variants of NI previously studied (March and Olsen 1984), therefore, political actors in this sphere could instead be identified as embracing a broad-minded approach to the construction of 'victims' and 'harm' and engaged in a productive interactive process of exchanging ideas. Throughout these talks, however, a clear definition of the problem at hand has been supplied, and it is important to identify Cameron's approach as not specifically aimed at the problem of pornography, but the necessity of child protection. Needless to say, this is a worthy objective, but it does have implications for women more generally, as will be explored below. What is significant to extrapolate at this point, however, is that the marriage of a programme of Internet porn filters discussed previously, with the philosophy of harm to children, can only partially be attributed to this political process. Entering into a productive coordinative discourse with his colleagues in the Conservative Party allowed for both the discussion of innovative measures, such as the aforementioned porn filters, and elite-level support for action, but an effective process of communicative discourse across media outlets, as previously analysed, to draw public support for the proposal was additionally required. In the second stage of consolidating this new approach, therefore, the harrowing events of Tia Sharp and April Jones underpinned the rhetoric featured in Cameron's speech to the NSPCC (Cabinet Office 2013). Interestingly, the PM alluded to a long conversation with the parents of the two murdered children, but was cautious not to divulge anything of a private nature. Rather his empathetic tone called for everyone to be involved in tackling this problem, and was accompanied by an earlier remark concerning his belief in a need for action as a father himself. Of central concern to this study, however, was his explicit support for Internet service provider (ISP) filters in regard to porn, stating that households would have access to certain websites blocked unless they actively opted out of such a scheme. Again linking the need for such measures to child protection, he stated that the Internet provides two problems in this regard: the proliferation in accessibility of child abuse images and the viewing of pornographic material by children (Cabinet Office 2013). Reflecting his long-standing approach of 'what is and what can be done', the balance was struck here with a language palatable for the general public.

The efficacy of this emotive frame, therefore, must be acknowledged at this juncture, particularly in comparison to growing societal acceptance of pornography more generally. Indeed, acknowledgement of the corrupting effect of such material is not a new revelation, and the reach of this fad has increasingly pervaded popular culture targeted at youngsters over the last two decades. Areas of gaming, for example, in which technological advances have allowed for the proliferation of graphically intense and sexually explicit video games (Martinez and Manolovitz 2010) has encompassed the launch of material such as the PlayStation game *Playboy: The Mansion* in 2005. With sex clearly assuming the central theme, this is just one such instance of mature content that is now commonplace in teen-orientated activities (*New York Times* 2005). In far less sensationalized examples, even the entrenched regulatory demand of the nine o'clock 'watershed' in UK television pro-gramming has arguably been diluted with the number of breaches of Ofcom's Broadcasting Codes steadily increasing; music videos containing depictions of bondage, in particular, have been among the complaints heard from view-ers (BBC News 2011). Although these examples are of course not the form of hardcore pornography referred to in the regulation, it still provides further context as to the magnitude of change induced by Cameron and highlights that normative claims alone provide little traction in amending entrenched policy. This is not, however, to throw the baby out with the bath water, and further stipulate that an emotional response is not required. Rather the elites in this example have created a master discourse on the matter that joins up the coordinative and communicative discourse through a 'logic of communi-cation' (Schmidt 2000), and a value-based approach has been tactically avoided, with Cameron largely resisting the urge to moralize or scaremonger (Cabinet Office 2013). Instead personalizing the need for practical action in terms of being a father, a move that was similarly successfully engaged by Obama and the institution of gay marriage (CNN 2012), the utility of a cognitive underpinning is extolled. Of even greater significance, however, is the extension of this argument to the banning of a series of sexual acts from online material in the recent regulations. Although challenged in some quar-ters as a curtailment of freedom of speech, and an anti-feminist judgement on the conduct of women, the rationale of child protection has nevertheless successfully supported the introduction of these measures.

The rate of liberalization as directly contrasted with the implementation of more exacting regulatory measures therefore demonstrates an unusual dynamism in policy formulation that cannot be accounted for in a manner evidenced previously in this book. Indeed, the policy stagnation in abortion and prostitution, the former characterized by only one critical juncture in 1967 and the latter with an enduring public/private divide, is plausibly accounted for by a range of insights from both historical and rational choice variants of new institutionalism (March and Olsen 1984). Furthermore, the implementation gap in UK rape policy can be critically explored through elements of normative institutionalism, and a 'cop culture' (Myhill and Bradford 2013), that serve to inequitably distort insufficiently defined legislative intentions. Neither policy inertia, however, nor significant micro-level inequalities, underpin this policy domain, but it is instead innovations in this field that have required explanation. By engaging the theoretical capabilities of discursive institutionalism (Schmidt 2002), therefore, extensions and amendments to Cameron's child protection agenda can be identified as the result of an effective process of communicative and coordinative discourse. Long identifying a cognitive understanding of the harm caused to this grouping, the additional risks of pornography, brought to light in high-profile cases, was easily absorbed into this programme and, through a 'logic of communication', allowed for the introduction of Internet porn filters. In this sense a clear divide can be asserted between the Labour Party's concern for pornography and its effect on violent behaviour more generally, recognizing cases such as that of Jane Longhurst, to the Conservative's concern for child protection and the incidental regulation of hardcore material that this has led to, its rationale resting more heavily on instances such as Tia Sharp and April Jones. Importantly, this provides a possible course of action for those seeking change in pornography regulation in the future, but simultaneously casts heavy doubt that this will be achieved through a normative approach to the status of the woman. Although a significant amendment to the law concerning depictions of rape has been introduced, it appears to again be sustainably driven by this child protection programme, and the problem of pornography arguably fails to be submitted as a problem in isolation. In this vein, it is actually the recently recognized revenge porn in social media crimes that draws greater parallels with the discussion above.

5.4. ALTERING THE DOMINANT DISCOURSE: LINKING VIOLENT CRIME AND PORNOGRAPHY

Encompassing the regulation of Internet pornography within an agenda on child protection rests heavily on a cognitive approach, and an open dialogue that allowed for the creation of novel solutions to the harm posed to this vulnerable group. Such measures have come as a sharp shock to a system that, prior to the 2008 and 2014 measures, had continually fended off assaults to provide stricter controls. Most notable in these campaigns has been the voice of anti-porn radical feminists who have long promoted the corrosive effect of such material on the gender. Central to their movement, however, has been a value claim for its removal from society, as juxtaposed to the

empirical manner in which child protection was approached by the government. Although recent amendments to the law to ban depictions of rape
would allude to some success for this battle, such statutory changes appear to
again fall within this young persons at risk frame, signaling that a victory for
women should not yet be asserted. Instead, the reality of an ever-expanding
and increasingly popular field of pornography constrains any argument that
appears to pertain to the social cost (Layden undated) of such material. This
is made even starker in light of the low uptake of Cameron's porn filters,
with some ISPs reporting only 4 percent of households have kept the measures activated (Ofcom 2014). Rather, for pornography to be removed from
the clutches of freedom of speech, and solely redefined as a problem, the
costs to an individual's civil liberties require staunch rationale. It is deliberated in this section that this is unlikely to be proffered by linking pornography
and violent crimes against women and requires a broader human rights
framework as was utilized in the recent criminalization of revenge porn.

The status of pornography in UK culture has indeed experienced a protracted evolution from its earliest conceptions as a fleeting, ephemeral issue
of only trivial importance (Sigel and Cocks 2001), to it status as a symbol of
depravity, through the liberalized climate of the 1960s and the feminist backlash of the 1970s and 1980s. As uncovered in Cameron's crackdown above,
the stated intention of contemporary regulation around pornography is to
control a range of harmful consequences, but conspicuously absent in the list
until an amendment in 2015 were depictions of rape and, even now, many
activities that demonstrate the subordination of women, both directly in
terms of those engaging in such acts, and indirectly for the treatment of the
gender more broadly, continue to be permitted. The rationale for such absence is thus certainly not straightforward, but it is with much conviction, on
the basis of the analysis conducted above, that justification for these instruments finds much more veracity in the child protection frame, rather than
concern for the status of the woman. This hypothesis is indeed strengthened
when particular regard is paid to the substantial anti-porn, radical feminist
movement that has voiced concern for protection, and mobilized support for
stronger regulatory controls since the 1980s. Although statutory amendments
of significant consequence have undeniably been introduced in recent years,
these have not addressed such objections, and certainly cannot be attributed
to the success of this section. Rather, those championing the problems for
equality posed by pornography, long pitted against the faction supporting the
perceived evils of censorship, have experienced a protracted period of limited impact upon the regulatory field, and the normative critique of such material has long failed to achieve traction.

Specifically, this feminist critique of pornography is built on the overarching conviction that such material reproduces and enforces gender inequalities, citing subordination, silencing and objectification as key themes

perpetuated by the material. The mounting normalization of explicit content in popular culture has indeed run alongside important changes in the status of women, homosexuals and other sexually defined groups since the sexual revolution of the 1960s and 1970s, creating much concern for the status of the woman. Certainly, a movement to this effect has long been in existence, with infamous US campaigners, such as Andrea Dworkin and Catherine Mackinnon, long waging a war against such material (McNair 2009), and a resurgence of a new generation of feminists as recounted by Long (2012) having taken on the baton of activism. Describing everyday tales of grass-roots protests, the author highlights a local gathering of activists outside a supermarket in central London. In reference to the store's 'no pyjamas' policy, the group arrived clad in nightwear and set about making their point that 'porn is more offensive than pyjamas' by covering lads' mags throughout the shop in brown paper bags (Long 2012). Such events are bountiful in their number, and are largely forged on notions of harm to the woman, be it in terms of supporting a culture of rape or the portrayal of women as anonymous beings, there to be exploited by men for their sexual gratification (Zillmann and Bryant 1982). Irrespective of these activities, however, little change has tangibly been created by this movement and, according to Rich, even in the early days of the much-referenced US wave of activism, it was probably correct to be seen as largely ineffectual and unlikely to erode the commercial-sex industry it challenged (1983). Thus the lengthy road to the introduction of new measures banning depictions of rape should be assessed within this context; despite radical feminist perspectives often appearing in the surrounding discourse, limited effort to tackle concrete harms to women arguably occurred in the wording of the 2014 legislation, with the position of pornography as a contemporary and acceptable societal norm instead appearing dominant.

Certainly restriction of even the semi-nude body in public was previously of grave importance, and by-laws affecting the 1850s seaside resort, for example, heavily controlled the use of bathing machines and costumes, and insisted upon segregated bathing (Smith 1996, 15). In contemporary society, however, the same level of constraint is clearly not apparent with daily newspapers regularly printing topless images of women, and 'lad mags' continually advertised in accessible forums such as mainstream television. A similar development is also evident in works of literature, with a series of books throughout history subject to strict censorship in the UK, from the Marquis de Sade's *120 Days of Sodom* to Nabokov's *Lolita* (*The Independent* 2010). Fast-forward the years, however, and *Fifty Shades of Grey*, a novel openly abound with bondage sex scenes, is the biggest-selling book in Britain since records began, with its publishers claiming it is now more popular than the highway code (Singh 2012). That said, all of these examples, regardless of their corresponding regulation, indicate that a gender-specific genre (Gubar 1987), focusing upon the erotic tales of women, has long been in existence and has correspondingly posed a significant conundrum for policymakers.

Unlike these Victorian roots, therefore, in which such material was largely viewed as the underside of culture, and the naked body an 'unnatural' sight (Smith 1996, 15), we have arguably lived through a series of changes to moral temper, reflected in both our sexual behaviour, and our reaction and attitudes to the actions of others (Marcus 1966), which challenges this anti-porn movement. Although to pinpoint a moment of acceptance for this form of entertainment is not yet possible, or indeed appropriate for a term that is ill-defined and constantly adapting, it appears of pertinence to acknowledge the juncture of public transformation and sexual revolution (Radner and Luckett 1999) provided in the 1960s. As previously mentioned in the course of this book, Britain experienced wide cultural change during this period, and a wave of permissive reforms swept through the country, including the decriminalization of homosexuality and abortion. Coupled with the growing notion of freedom of sexually orientated expression (Strossen 2000), therefore, this social revolution (Roszak 1970) allowed for many of the previous values that constrained public reference to explicit content to be eroded and those laws perceived as overly conservative similarly challenged. Assaults have been periodically reignited as the reach of print media has increased throughout the twentieth century, and correspondingly, despite the enduring presence of these acts, court rulings, assuming a position as a key vehicle for change as similarly evidenced in rape legislation, have placed pressure on the government throughout the years to recognize this new outlook.

In particular, two prosecutions under such reaches have provided not only empirical colour to the meaning of the law, but demonstrate a shift in concern for the publication of such material. In the first case, involving the banned publication of D. H. Lawrence's *Lady Chatterley's Lover*, Penguin Books was unsuccessfully prosecuted under the Obscene Publications Act 1959, and the novel instead gained widespread popularity (*R v. Penguin Books Ltd* [1961] Crim L R 176). Reflecting a more liberal and sexually explorative climate, little offence can now be taken from such a judgement, and many would view the deliberations in court as putting right anachronistic notions of acceptable behaviour. In the second example, the Court of Appeal overturned the conviction of the editors of the underground magazine *Oz* who were prosecuted for publishing, among other images, a sexually excited Rupert the Bear (Palmer 1971). Again demonstrating the appropriate broadening of the term obscene in line with contemporary favour, a clear shift in the acceptance of such material is evidenced.

By way of contrast to the aforementioned cases, however, a notable example in 2009 concerned the first prosecution against written pornography online and demonstrates a worrying blend of sexual liberalization and threat of danger to women. Submitted by a blogger, the tale titled 'Girls (Scream) Aloud' was an explicit story about the rape, torture and killing of the pop band Girls Aloud. Of importance in the discourse on harm to be explored in the succeeding section, however, it was presented to the court that the CPS' initial spur for seeking prosecution against Darryn Walker was born from the notion that the site could easily be accessed by young fans of the pop group. Although upon specialist evidence from an IT expert demonstrating the unfeasibility of the story being found on the web without a purposeful search, the CPS consequently submitted the unlikely prospect of successful prosecution and the trial was abandoned on the first day, this rationale is of note (Davenport 2009). Certainly an exploration of this body of jurisprudence does not display only a linear move towards liberalisation, but this recent push by Scotland Yard's Obscene Publications Unit affords recognition of the growing problem of hardcore and nascent pornography, a principle that is now directly addressed in the Criminal Justice Act 2008. Of significance, however, was the framing of such risk in terms of the harm posed to children.

In spite of an ostensibly liberalized climate that demonstrates significant acceptance of pornography in mainstream entertainment, therefore, a paradigm shift has occurred that responds to the associated harms of such explicit material for vulnerable groups, as revealed above. Diverging from the other strains of NI, the dynamic approach to institutional change offered by discursive institutionalism (Schmidt 2008) indeed provides hope for a change in policy if new ideas and alternative discourse can be linked. The aforementioned transient definition of protection therefore brings into focus the newly introduced ban on depictions of rape in online material. Drawing inspiration from the blueprint for policy change demonstrated by Cameron's child protection agenda, linking explicit content to violent crimes submits the potential for amendments in regard to the protection of women. Certainly, the direct destruction caused to the gender, heralded by the anti-porn movement of years past, has so far been unsuccessful. Legislating on morality is not a new concept and has certainly been carried out throughout antiquity, and even looking beyond the example of abortion, already copiously covered in this book, problems of ethics are infused in an array of matters from suicide and euthanasia, to the declarations of war (Glover 1990). Such issues throw up vast dilemmas and require principled reactions from policymakers and the public alike, and varying, and often binary, value judgements are displayed in these spheres. Different justifications are engaged for acts of combat (Halverscheid and Witte 2008), for example, and such was seen in the UK's participation in the Iraq war which, despite comprising a range of technical and scientific points of debate, did not avoid sustained reference to the ethics of war. As further illustration of this point, the moral significance of euthanasia is inextricably connected with our construction of the value of life, and we deem it necessary to protect that principle (Harris 1997). The debates around these types of issues will therefore continue to wage regardless of a landscape characterized by either policy change or policy continuity, but what is instead unlikely to occur is the complete re-moralization of a debate; once an issue has experienced radical social transformation, and has been welcomed into civilization, it is difficult to see a path back to its original position. Take the example of homosexuality, for instance; once regarded as depicting deviant behaviour and an evil that demanded punishment, the Wolfenden Committee largely put paid to that position, and the removal of the issue from the criminal law was witnessed in the 1960s. Jump forwards five decades, and further legislation has been introduced by the Marriage Equality Act to permit homosexual couples to legally marry. The point here is not to draw offensive comparisons with the long-awaited rights justly afforded to the LGBT community in the UK, and the creeping pornification of Western culture, but to highlight that once collective barriers have been removed, it is difficult to stem the tide of cultural development. Perhaps a more helpful example is the removal of capital punishment from the UK. Although an issue that sporadically frequents the issue attention cycle (Downs 1972), it is difficult to imagine hangings being welcomed back into everyday life, and the cultural shock that would ensue in the witness of live executions would be vast in its ramifications. To seek to remove pornography from everyday life, therefore, is a mountain of Everest proportions, with a summit that is unlikely to be reached. Certainly, even in more pragmatic terms, stricter regulation of the material on the basis of a degrading representation of women as subordinate to men, in a state committed to the furtherance of gender equality, alone appears a challenge too far. Rather it is the indirect consequences of the industry that provide an additional platform for action, and linking to violent crimes goes beyond children.

Setting aside the more normative ideals of anti-porn feminists, therefore, and looking beyond those women directly engaged in the policy sector, the empirical realities of such material for the gender demand examination. In this sense, it is with the infamous adage that 'pornography is the theory—rape is the practice' (Morgan 1980), that an evidential approach needs to be assumed. To an even greater extent than was revealed in the chapter on prostitution previously, the impact of pornography cannot be viewed in isolation at the moment of production or consumption, and instead has a tangible influence upon gendered relationships within society. To this end, the link between pornography and violent crimes has been the focus of some limited research across the globe, but extrapolated from this body of data is a confusing mix of insights for the negative effects of pornography. Although some studies point towards a link, such as Marshall's report in 1988, in which 23 rapists and 51 child molesters evidenced significantly greater use of pornographic materials than was indicated by either incest offenders or non-offender controls (1988), such results are questioned by crime statistics. Indeed the majority of industrial nations are experiencing a decline in sexual assaults despite the increasing availability of such material (Ferguson and Hartley 2009), and this 'porn up, rape down' (D'Amato 2006) frame is gradually garnering support. In a study conducted across the four countries of the United States, Denmark, Sweden and Germany, for example, little correlation was found between the move from scarcity in terms of pornography, to relative abundance in everyday life, and an increase in rape statistics (Kutchinsky 1991). As previously studied in the course of chapter 4, however, these statistics can be misleading on a variety of levels; the first and most obvious being the levels of attrition in reported rapes at various points of the criminal justice system. This does indeed provide us with a clear and plausible justification. A more nuanced, and empirically accurate approach, however, would additionally incorporate the substantial lack of identification with rape or harmful conduct towards women; drawing the lines between that which is lawful in pornography and what is not permissible towards women in reality can become blurred. Furthermore, this does not completely negate the growing work done within the behavioral sciences in the United States, which links aggressive behaviour with overexposure to extreme content. To this end, elite discourse itself still acknowledges that a link does exist, as exemplified in Lord Thomas' evidence to MPs concerning the conviction of Jamie Reynolds for the murder of Georgia Williams, whom he hanged immediately after watching extreme pornography (Daubney 2015). Prosecutors revealed that he had a vast 16,800 images and 72 videos of an extreme nature on his computer (BBC News 2013). If the Conservative government is actively promoting that overexposure to adolescents can have negative impacts, then the same can surely be true for adults in varying degrees dependent upon their disposition and general character.

That said, the true test of the influence of this research must still rest upon tangible policy change. Granted, depictions of rape are now classified under 'extreme pornography', and it is thus a criminal offence to both publish and possess material of this nature. Largely remedying a legal loophole that was created by the wording of Labour's 2008 Act, however, its introduction must again be viewed in the context of Cameron's child protection agenda more generally, with frequent reference to the need to shield children from exposure to such harms. When rape itself is perceived to be so contestable, as rates of attrition in chapter 4 uncovered, it is perhaps not a shocking submission that harm to women alone provides a weak cognitive definition of a problem and solution, and is unlikely to punctuate (Jones and Baumgartner 1999) singlehandedly. Indeed, according to Sabatier (1988), problem perception is of critical importance and thus debate may be rife in the academic community around the habitual use of pornography by sex offenders, but it must still go to war against the freedom of movement that has clearly strengthened with the rate of liberalization. The range of harms to women do not end at the physical, for example, and the reinforcing of damaging gender roles, now operated through the significant medium of the Internet, can extend to the recent trends of revenge porn, slut shaming and even cyberbullying (Shah 2015). Interestingly again, however, it is not such danger that formed the substantive content of deliberations around criminalizing the sharing of private sexual content in Section 33 of the Criminal Justice and Courts Act of 2015. Of greater significance was its status as one of a range of social media crimes that run the risk of breaching a range of human rights. In particular, the House of Lords made specific reference to a ruling in the European Court of Justice in which it was determined that data subjects have the right to ask search engines to remove links to that data subject (HoL 2014, para 42). For reasons of pragmatism, therefore, and staying abreast of supranational jurisprudence, it appears that achieving this amendment again needed a more substantial vehicle for change.

The successful linking of child protection with the harm posed by online material has created a new paradigm on pornography regulation. The success of this approach has now been demonstrated both in the introduction of Internet porn filters and, more recently, the banning of depictions of rape. The introduction of this latter intervention curiously suggests, however, that the protection of women can have little impact in this regulatory field in favour of freedom of speech, and the social evils of censorship. Such a statement may seem obtuse and, undeniably, the new clause is a step forward to the protection of women, but the fact that it is again attributed to the protection of children by David Cameron suggests that, at its heart, are not concerns for the subordination of the gender. Although this section therefore set about proffering potential policy change through linking violent crimes against women and hardcore material, it appears that such rhetoric, granted still in its infancy in comparison to the moralist anti-porn feminist wave of the 1980s, is meeting with little success in terms of its impact on regulation. Although a clear link between these two facets can be submitted on an evidential platform, the framing of the issue is unable to fully shake the association of costs to civil liberties.

5.5. SUPRANATIONAL LAW AND THE OPEN INTERNET

Despite a promulgated web of child protection policies developed by the UK government, the principle of net neutrality at the supranational level of the EU threatens the legitimacy of these measures. The creation of the European Union has undeniably changed the nature of the nation-state and, in the decades since its inception, has considerably altered subnational processes across a broad range of political and economic functions (Goldsmith 2003). The European Coal and Steel Community (ECSC) in 1952, for example, was born primarily from requirements for resource interdependence in post-war Europe, and the original supranational remit represented these structural imperatives (Moravcsik 1998). Subscribing to a neo-functionalist interpretation, however, this initial delegation of power from nation-states gradually commanded the development of new projects and coalitions, extending out to create the broader European Economic Community (EEC) in 1958 and eventually the European Union (Haas 1958). The inevitable 'spill-overs' and 'unintended consequences' resulting from these activities have progressively encroached upon national affairs, and this aggrandizement is readily apparent in recent deliberations concerning the regulation of the Internet in the Single Telecoms Market Law. Stipulating information and communications technology (ICT) as the source of smart, sustainable and inclusive growth, the Union's fragmentation into distinct national markets has fallen under scrutiny, and the demand for a single market for electronic communications was asserted in the 2013 Spring European Council (European Commission 2015). The legislative package titled 'Connected Continent', due to be voted on in the European parliament in the autumn of 2015, looks to scrap mobile phone roaming charges from 2017 onwards, enshrine the concept of net neutrality and grant all Europeans the same access to content regardless of their region. In regard to the latter, the Bill details that EU consumers often encounter the situation that they are unable to purchase from online shops due to territorial restrictions. As a consequence, however, the removal of this blocking directly challenges the current enforcement of the previously discussed porn filters in the UK. As explained by patent attorney Denis Kesseris, "if you're a German customer who wants specific content, you should be able to access it in the UK as well" (Lanktree 2015).

The regulation of porn across the EU's member states to date certainly reflects a varied scheme of measures that house competing ideals. Many of the member states host some form of regulation in regard to hardcore pornography, with conditions such as the banning of sale to minors in France, to complete prohibition in the Ukraine. Italy, by way of contrast, permits the sale of such material in spaces such as video stores and even vending machines, and, in the case of soft porn, German television allows the showing of such programmes in the evening. Overarching this disparate collection of rules, however, is nevertheless a coordinated attempt to reduce child pornography with 19 countries providing citizens the ability to report illegal content through a network of EU-established hotlines (Delbert 2010). Furthermore, a positive obligation upon member states to protect the vulnerable has been posited by the ECtHR in the case *MC v. Bulgaria*, discussed previously in regard to legislation concerning rape, and this has been extended to freely accessible pornographic content on the Internet (Council of Europe 2011b). The extent to which these proposed supranational measures will therefore threaten child protection appears limited, and it can alternatively be suggested that the UK will instead have to look to new ways to continue to enshrine the concept. In this vein, future research into online pornography legislation will be a fruitful area of study.

5.6. CONCLUSION

The regulation around pornography is largely indirect, amounting to a legislative landscape that is cobbled together across various statutes. Generally speaking, most of its facets do not fall under any form of governance and, since the amendments to the 1857 Obscene Publications Act, a growing societal acceptance of such material has been evidenced. The analysis housed above reveals that this trend has only really been broken in statutory terms by the Criminal Justice and Immigration Act 2008; in reaction to the death of Jane Longhurst, and other violent incidents, and despite of an unfavourable consultation process, it stipulates that the possession of hardcore pornography is illegal in England, Wales and Northern Ireland, and is mirrored through similar legal sanctions in Scotland in a measure enacted in 2010. In light of the backlash incited by the introduction of this Act, Cameron's recent crackdown on Internet pornography, and his success in forging an agreement with key providers on this matter, is of vast significance and evidences a surprising move towards greater censorship. Further compounded by the list of activities now banned under the 2014 regulations, it would appear on the surface that important steps have been taken to address the level of protection afforded to women. On closer examination, however, the instruments are largely the product of a successful marriage by the PM of his long-standing child protection agenda with the proliferation of Internet pornography. Clearly demonstrated in the examples of the debates surrounding the harrowing crises of April Jones and Tia Sharp, and a 2013 speech to the NSPCC, a coordinative and communicative discourse has encouraged support for such measures from the Conservative Party and the media respectively.

The unveiling of this 'logic of communication' (Schmidt 2008) brings with it the possibility of future amendments to the level of protection for women. Suggesting the limited success of anti-porn feminist movement can be attributed to the normative framing of such material as a matter of morality, the cognitive presentation of an evidential link between violent crimes and pornography could provide solid ammunition for the demand to add depictions of rape to the list of banned activities. Unlike the benefits of a liberalizing trend in abortion legislation, however, the erosion of the reaction of that perceived to be obscene is actually problematic for those seeking amendments to the law, and it is contended that harm to children may always be viewed as a distinct category of regulation. Conversely, it is mooted that the consequences of failing to recognize harm to women as a legitimate problem in its own right will impinge upon conviction rates in regard to the newly introduced crime of 'revenge porn'. Garnering insights from the attrition rate in rape, it is suggested that the contestable victim notion will once again raise its head, and this is unlikely to be stamped out by supranational law. Indeed the EU has long evidenced a concern for freedom of speech, and this has been readily recognized by a host of liberal approaches to pornography in neighbouring member states. In addition, however, debates currently prevail concerning the enforcement of a unified approach to regulating the Internet, creating an open field across the EU, and substantially challenging the existence of porn filters in the UK. Not only does this challenge the acknowledgement of harm to women in such material, but it also has the potential to undo many of Cameron's measures designed to protect children from the perceived dangers of the Internet.

Returning to the idea of stereotyping perpetuated in the legislation around women's issues, and the implementation of its terms, the dominant imagery of women in this domain marks an additional break from the other policy fields. Contrary to the troubling behaviour of seeking an abortion, or the hardened street hooker, or indeed the 'proper victim' of rape, it is in fact the absence of copious regulation around harm to women in this domain that creates a perception of those engaging in the activity. Much of the chapter on prostitution, for example, deliberated the respective benefits of abolitionism, prohibition and regulation, for example, indicating that prohibition centres on concern for the public and heavily labels the street prostitute as a criminal. The deeper appreciation of the protection of children in policy around pornography, however, supports the widely held assumption of a liberated woman partaking in this form of sex for sale. Just as in the example of celebrity porn stars referenced previously, therefore, such a stereotype does not carry the burden of stigma the way the drunken woman alleging rape does, to provide just one instance. It cannot be easily assumed, however, that this is automatically helpful for the agenda, and the section above has illustrated that harm can be posed to women by the production and proliferation of this material. It thus must be suggested that in order to truly forward gender equality, further measures to eradicate problematic practices in this domain should be considered.

Chapter Six

Conclusion: Harmful Stereotyping and Institutional Stronghold in the Regulation of Women's Issues

Throughout history much has been forbidden to women, and the battle for gender equality has been long fought, debated and studied. Even the long road to achieving the vote in 1919 came at the expense of decades of protesting, lobbying and, in some more tragic circumstances, the death of women dedicated to the cause (Kay 2008). Although such victories were far from heralded as the end for the empowerment of women, the successes experienced by the suffragettes in the UK in the early part of the twentieth century nevertheless went some way towards levelling the playing field and, in the decades following the recognition of a woman's voice in parliament, a series of legal measures were enacted with the intention of creating greater gender equality across aspects of education, employment and entrepreneurship (OECD Gender Initiative 2011). Despite these developments, however, a number of issues with an inequitable level of female burden continue to be heavily regulated in the UK, and peculiar legislation persists with the direct effect of prohibiting certain activity, and housing a series of warring stances, in which an arbitrary determination of either 'criminal' or 'victim' is made. A simple explanation for determining these statutory statements of appropriate and inappropriate conduct was assumed from the outset as largely the product of the classic good/bad binary that underpins the perception of female behaviour, in which an entrenched duality serves to sanction, and conversely prohibit, different behaviour upon assertion of the gender to be either this or that. Significantly driving this project, however, was the conviction that this alone provides insufficient explanation as to how these decisions are reached, and it was instead towards the role of institutions, as opposed to an observation of individual action, that this project turned.

Throughout the course of the last four chapters, therefore, it has been observed that diverging organizational structures and varying institutions in the domains of abortion, prostitution, rape and pornography have shaped each of these novel policy fields in a somewhat insular fashion. Recognition of the problems associated with this disparate practice in the UK opened chapter 1; that issues largely pertaining to women often house conflicting and arguably hypocritical positions, such as the illegality of sex for sale on the street contrasted with the lawful production of adult movies, or the absence of an explicit recourse to abortion in pregnancies resulting from rape, regardless of their clear common tie. These dichotomies were loosely defined and largely anecdotal, however, and certainly had little backing in the scholarship, thereby serving as the key empirical rationale for this entire project, urging a more sustained evaluation of why such seemingly similar actions are governed in an apparently incongruent manner across the UK. The first stage of this undertaking has already been presented, and comprised the individual case studies just submitted. Now bringing together this range of insights under the umbrella of rules, practices and narratives, defined by the third phase of NI as how 'institutions do their work' (Lowndes and Roberts 2013, 45), a collective evaluation of the regulation of women can be conducted. In this second, final stage, it is revealed that the problems posed by a solitary approach to each policy domain is further exasperated by the manner in which many practices across institutions serve to distort an array of formal rules. Although the proliferation of narratives and open dialogue could mitigate this effect, this is an underdeveloped aspect of women's issues.

The following will therefore offer a threefold appraisal on the insights gained throughout the course of the book. Beginning with shedding light on the black box of policymaking, the rich insights garnered through the variants of NI will be presented, and the manner in which traditional women's issues are approached in the UK, highlighting the importance of institutions that often persist under the radar of public scrutiny, will be amalgamated. Directly engaging the principal objective of this venture, and mirroring the project's opening gambit, the UK's rules, practices and narratives, that together uncover how institutions regulate the many facets of women, will then be deliberated through attention to this multi-variant approach. In the course of doing so, the sub-section will address both the empirical and theoretical benefits of maintaining such a fledgling method. Finally, it has always been hoped that this endeavour proffers more than just a point of interest, or indeed a purely pessimistic critique of the state of female-orientated legislation. Indeed, much of what has been uncovered demonstrates positive steps for the gender, but to accompany that which has not, and in order to dispel harmful myths, suggestions of future research and lessons that can be learned for practitioners is last considered. Simultaneously promoting a gendered research agenda for further studies, and urging action for policymakers along three interrelated trajectories—evidence-based policymaking, multi-agency work and increased victim awareness—the book draws to a close.

6.1. SHEDDING LIGHT ON THE 'BLACK BOX'

Confusion, definitional ambiguities and contradictions are all rife across the legislation on women's issues in the UK. As each chapter began to chart the history of regulation in that specific policy domain, it quickly became apparent that oddities from antiquity to modern day are commonplace in abortion, prostitution, rape and pornography. To be sure, there was a certain inevitability that with such ethically infused and morally charged subject matters, this was bound to be uncovered, and the shock factor that may have occurred if the studies pertained to tax law, or electoral reform, for example, would have been far more acute. The governance of these issues is naturally complex, and all serve to create novel policy problems that require creative, and sometimes unique, regulatory and legal responses. Even with recognition of this fact, however, the process of mapping the reasons for these irregularities uncovered a range of institutional constraints, barriers and strongholds that are not often spoken about, or indeed researched, and ironically the individual policy domains, regardless of the myriad of value judgements they traverse, actually appear to largely boil down to overly simplistic stereotypes of female conduct.

Take as a starting point the crime of abortion. Chapter 2 detailed how assumptions around access to treatment in the UK, both at a domestic level and in a global context, amounted to a negative perception of free and easy terminations on demand. Yet every woman seeking an abortion in all three legal jurisdictions, for whatever reason, still has to navigate the criminal law, and, specifically in England, Wales and Northern Ireland, the Offences Against the Person Act 1861; the same statute that continues to govern grave crimes such as murder and assault. The element of wrongdoing in the termination of pregnancy, therefore, has been preserved in statute, and, as exposed by the analytical value of historical institutionalism, has become a deep-rooted convention that is followed by successive governments and the medical profession alike. In turn, this continues to affect the possibility of beneficial clinical developments and constrains the legitimate status of the pregnant woman as a patient. Indeed, the high level of medical hegemony infused in the 1967 statute creates a far more subjective process than alternative schemes, leaving women vulnerable to the vagaries of clinical discretion. Still operating under the incorrect perception of the UK as the European capital for abortion, however, this important norm is largely overlooked, and the detrimental impact on activism in this domain has been evidenced in a discernible manner. It is indeed apparent that society is increasingly alienated from elite debates in comparison to their EU neighbours; believing the simple binary question of pro-life and pro-choice to have been settled, many no longer engage with the issue and perceive little demand for a more comprehensive standard of care. As a result, this seeps into patriarchal notions of needing to protect the hasty woman that, at the drop of a hat, has decided upon an abortion and may later regret her flippant actions. This of course is the far milder interpretation of the need for criminal liability, and the more offensive rationale based around the female who uses abortion as a contraceptive method can also be readily found in society. Conversely, sympathy for the woman making such a difficult choice, or indeed recognition of her bodily autonomy, is far more constrained, underpinned as it is by this enduring value of termination as wrong.

Moving away from this path-dependent (Krasner 1988) approach, the 'logic of calculation' laid down by rational choice institutionalism (March and Olsen 1984) provides much insight into the stagnant status quo that typifies prostitution policy. Looking to the influences on parliamentarians' preferences as emanating both from the procedural constraints of the legislature (Norton 2001) and the electoral arena (Denzau et al 1985), the costly nature of morality policy, and the long-standing social order and decency framework, dictates that this legislative field has thus far refused to fully consider an alternative policy typology, regardless of Northern Ireland's recent neo-abolitionist reform. In light of limited incentive to change, particularly in terms of affording recognition to an array of labour rights, therefore, street prostitution is still anachronistically viewed as a public evil and, as a result, the hardened street hooker is perhaps the clearest criminal label evident across these women's issues in the UK. Civil society further compounds this position by focusing on ridding this undesirable behaviour from their own backyard, rather than addressing the troubling circumstances of the individual women who may have been forced into such activity by means that fall outside the formal bracket of trafficking. In this sense, parliamentary response, or the lack there of, can be most easily correlated to that of crisis management, removing the problem of the prostitute when necessary, and returning to a default position of inertia when possible. Although a paradigm shift (Baumgartner et al. 2008) in regard to the nature of harm from a societal to an individual perspective, and the potential introduction of further abolitionist measures, is mooted in light of the cases such as the 'Bradford Murders', this is yet to materialize and would likely require a broader range of exogenous pressures to really allure the career politician (Fenno 1978) to further the plight in parliament through a PMB. Throwing a further spanner in the works in regard to the criminalization of purchasing sex in England, Wales and Scotland, however, are the insights collated from alternative schemes across the EU, and specifically the Swedish model's ability to tackle levels of sex trafficking have been countered by widespread deficiencies in the level of protection afforded by the scheme to those that continue to practice prostitution.

Chapter 4 shifted organizational focus slightly, however, to appreciate the influence of cultural norms (March and Olsen 1984) in implementing policy. Whether born from a lack of clarity around legislative intentions, and adopting the wider language of the courts, or a more grassroots product of 'cop culture' (Myhill and Bradford 2013) predicated on an impervious and patriarchal bond, the requirement of a 'proper victim' in cases of suspected rape exacerbates the pigeonholing; a woman must often conform to a certain image in order to be taken seriously in her report and a crime recorded, allowing the police to worryingly act as judge and jury. This not only fails many victims at the point of contact with this SLB, but also has a further devastating effect on women coming forward in the first instance, particularly in cases of spousal abuse. Of wider interest in this analysis, however, was the circular effect this has on attribution of responsibility by society more generally; indeed drawing a line between public opinion and organizational culture in this sense is messy. Take the police officer that mulls over a media story around sexual assault in the company of friends. If contextual factors are discussed, such as how drunk the girl was or what she was wearing, it becomes difficult to delineate the importance of this cultural setting in comparison to the police force. What is of significance in regard to the latter organizational culture, however, is the stronger desire to follow a 'logic of appropriateness' (DiMaggio and Powell 1991) in a workplace environment, and it is here, therefore, that the lines between normative institutionalism and rational choice institutionalism start to blend. Accepting an array of contexts in which these values can flourish, however, additionally unveils the broad contestation that surrounds victims of rape generally, and the likelihood of change in this regulatory domain is correspondingly limited. The irony in this issue, therefore, is that the good/bad binary is even infused in the concept of victim and is further exacerbated by the supranational context. Indeed, wide variation in legislation across EU member states further contributes to the notion that sexual assault is a contestable crime at varying stages of the UK's criminal justice system and in the eyes of the public more generally.

Finally, and diverging from the analysis of policy inertia, and institutional continuity, evidenced in the three preceding domains, the regulation of pornography provided much more of a blueprint for successful change, albeit not necessarily for women. Demonstrating that an open dialogue can foster the adaptation of existing institutions, the expansion of the agenda on harm to children, to additionally incorporate protection from pornography, has been achieved largely by the actions of David Cameron. Engaging in two levels of discourse, catering both to the coordination of members of the Conservative

Party, and communicating these new ideas in palatable manner to the general public through the media, the harrowing cases of Baby P, Tia Sharp and April Jones all provided meaningful contexts for this new approach. Underpinning this account, however, is the relative importance of women within this paradigm of protection. Granted, depictions of rape have now been banned from online material under new regulations, but this move can again be attributed to a matter of child protection, thereby failing to fully address the subordination of the gender in pornography more generally. Although it is important to recognize that further dialogue could open up in this regard, the counterfactual should also be appreciated that deeply embedded cultural norms now exist around the acceptability of pornography. The infiltration of this material in everyday life dictates that restrictions on its content and publication are strongly defended with principles of freedom of speech; although these can be eroded by a child protection paradigm, it is unlikely that a feminist movement can do the same, and undeniably bolstering these obstacles are principles of supranational law that endorsed a more liberal approach to neighbouring European countries. Interestingly, however, the EU's legislative scheme does look set to challenge the UK's porn filters, restricting the potential recognition of harm to women, but additionally eroding the measures implemented by Cameron in regard to pornography and risk to children. Thus despite the merits of discursive institutionalism (Schmidt 2000) in explaining amendments to date in this domain, it appears more accurate to suggest that these insights have greater ramifications for explaining policy change more generally, rather than dictating future innovation in pornography regulation. At present, the inaccurate stereotype that persists in this policy domain, therefore, is the liberated woman indulging in pornographic work by virtue of her own free choice, duly protected from all harms, both to herself and others.

To confirm from this comparative study, therefore, that institutions do indeed matter, and can have a significant impact on shaping the regulation of abortion, prostitution, rape and pornography, appears almost trite at this stage. Indeed, upon investigation, their significance is undeniable and, in fact, the assumption that they would be key in the explanation of such political outcomes was always a safe bet. It is actually the uncovering of inequitable stronghold or influence over the formulation and implementation of particular aspects of these issues, however, that is of greater empirical value when these studies are brought together. Referring back to the various assaults on the conceptual framework detailed in chapter 1, therefore, it appears just to declare at this stage that such rich insights could not have been uncovered if methodological individualism (Arrow 1994) alone had been adhered to. Certainly varying organizational structures and institutions have perpetuated and, in some circumstances even created, a dominant and potentially harmful image of a woman that has been importantly uncovered. These have worryingly included the thoughtless pregnant woman, rather than the patient in need of care, and the hardened street hooker, as opposed to the socially acceptable high-class escort. The proper victim of rape, sober, layered in clothes and with the absence of any form of sexual history, with a legitimate claim to make in comparison to her promiscuous, scorned friend who is crying sexual assault in a pit of rage is equally concerning. And finally, the liberated porn star who is free to go about her business with no fear of harm, or contributing to the harm of other women.

Disturbingly, these are not just throw-away myths that populate jokes in pubs, or 'water-cooler' gossip and playground jibes. Throughout the course of this book, these labels have been unveiled at varying elite levels, as well as in society more generally, and serve to colour a range of individual case studies. It must be remarked, however, that the source of this concern is not the morality of these labels. Indeed it is not the aim of this endeavour to deliberate the meaning of freedom of choice, or the rights of the foetus, or even the ethical interpretation of 'sex for sale'—all of which are, needless to say, worthy subjects of additional research in neighbouring spheres. Rather it is the one-dimensional nature of the stereotypes fostered by the regulation that is of countenance. Endemic in the behaviour and actions of key actors in the public policy domain, the failure to remove prevailing typecasts of women in these matters serves to constrain a more beneficial governance scheme. It is thus not that all policy in this arena is flawed, but that a more nuanced and inclusive approach is lacking, and the sum total of these policy domains for women, as uncovered below, demonstrates this very remark.

6.2. BENEFITTING FROM A MULTI-VARIANT APPROACH

The blinkered and often incongruous positions endemic to each specific policy domain is further complicated when the issues of abortion, prostitution, rape and pornography are drawn together, and it becomes clear that many women fall between the gaps created by the contradictory regulation. Although it is acknowledged that even in their earliest conceptualization, the strains of NI were always generous in sharing aspects of their logics, it is actually their differences, in addition to these commonalities, that together provide a valuable theoretical framework (Lowndes and Roberts 2013), the virtues of which have been submitted right from the outset. The significant methodological challenge that has accompanied this project, however, was the potential to apply these various arms in an arbitrary and premeditated manner to individual policy domains, thereby restricting the value and legitimacy of a comparative account of the regulation of women. To reiterate the response to this hurdle, however, it was never intended that these four studies would alone provide an exhaustive explanation for the reasoning behind regulation, but would instead serve to investigate the parameters of causality. In this sense, the union of a specific variant of NI with a policy domain is not of seminal importance; rather it is the suitability of the strain in addressing the inference that could be gained for women more generally that has remained the decisive factor in selection. Interestingly, therefore, this range of plausible insights can now be brought together in this section under the broader framework of rules, practices and narratives that are promoted by third phase institutionalists (Lowndes and Roberts 2013, 46). Through this consolidation and convergence, both inference and contradiction respectively are revealed, and the question of how women are regulated in the UK is explicitly addressed.

Most closely akin to the foundations of the old, descriptive institutionalism, the role of formal rules in structuring political behaviour remains of great significance despite heavy criticism from some quarters. Rules in this sense, therefore, adopt somewhat of an official tone, and are formally constructed and written down (Lowndes and Roberts 2013), typically positioned as the tools of the historian and the lawyer (Rhodes 1997). Having studied the black letter of various statutes in each chapter, it is clear that not one of the four issues covered evades the full glare of the legal system. Taken on face value, the terms of such legislation could be seen as purely beneficial, such as the amendment of reasonable consent in the 2003 Sexual Offences Act or the ban on depictions of rape in pornography by section 37 of the Criminal Justice and Courts Act. However, some aspects of the statutory landscape have provided a point of countenance and deliberation, such as the continued criminal status of abortion and prostitution. Regardless of arguments centered around good or bad law, however, and leaving aside the innovation in pornography regulation in recent times, these findings are largely typified by policy inertia, with few changes, and even fewer radical overhauls. Throughout the course of the analysis, this can be attributed to two factors. First, a 'path-dependent' (Krasner 1988) approach, as extolled by historical institutionalism, highlights the importance of ideas at the initial formation stage of policy as setting in place a certain trajectory until enough exogenous pressure is manifested for change (Skocpal 2002). In the case studies presented, this was typified by abortion regulation. Second, a range of procedural rules in parliament constrain the legislature from acting on policy that cuts across the traditional left/right divide (Norton 2001), as alternatively exemplified in the instance of prostitution policy. This latter remark can span most pieces of morality policy and is not particularly novel.

Collating these two broad rules here, however, an even more robust institutional account can be proffered around the regulation of abortion and prostitution. The nature of such topics dictates that all must work against the reluctance for statutory amendments on such ethically infused matters. Future legislative change in regard to abortion, for example, is unlikely when viewed in terms of this aforementioned incentive structure; the 1967 Act largely works for its prescribed purposes, and thus little reward is offered for those looking to incite change. Although previously accounted for in terms of the evolutionary underpinning of historical institutionalism, in which the absence of pressure will dictate that a path-dependent approach (Krasner 1988) will remain largely unchallenged, the causality drawn from rational choice institutionalism provides an additional, as opposed to alternative, version of events. Similarly, the absence of formal rules in this manner, therefore, may contribute significantly to the disaggregate approach to women witnessed across all four topics and should be a point of note for policymakers. Due to this large resistance to change, however, as attributed to either strain of NI, these stagnating rules permit institutional practices to flourish, often with detrimental effects.

This second form of institutional constraint diverges from formally recorded rules, and refers to conduct and patterns of behaviour most readily assimilated with the normative strain of institutionalism (Lowndes and Roberts 2013, 59). Bringing together the informal rules present across the four studies, therefore, an array of practices is evident at various stages of the policy process. In policy creation, a seminal principle for the gender is the determination that the criminal law remains the primary referee over access to abortion, a code that has spanned many reformulations of the legislation. Although some may argue that the term 'law' here would automatically conflate to the rules outlined above, it is argued that this instrument assumes a hierarchy, and this form of rule goes beyond the status of a statute and is adopted as a convention in the UK. As such, it is deeply entrenched at all policy levels, including implementation by the medical profession, as readily exemplified by the prohibited home administration of misoprostol. The Secretary of State's refusal to adapt the law to permit the use of this tablet away from clinical settings demonstrates the hold such a framework has over the workings of the law. Furthermore, this instrument infers additional insight for the preservation of the status quo in prostitution. Underpinned by a historical convention that separates indoor and outdoor activities in the minds of the public, as discussed previously in chapter 3 in regard to Victorian standards of social order and decency, this practice colours political innovation in the field.

Alternatively, the informal routine of questioning the appropriateness of a victim is heavily prevalent in the reporting stage of rape. Emanating from a 'cop culture' (Myhill and Bradford 2013) established as routine in the police force, it serves to erode the attempts of the Sexual Offences Act to place the burden of proof on the defendant not the claimant. Furthermore, this 'logic of appropriateness' (March and Olsen 1984) has implications for the other case studies in terms of the level of protection for the criminal street prostitute. Previous studies have highlighted that these practices can prevent intervention, and urge actors on the ground to match situations to rules (Lowndes and Roberts 2013), but it is contended here that it is actually the opposite that can be detrimental to the proper workings of the criminal justice system. In acknowledgement of the largely stagnant legislation on women's issues generally, and now these deep-seated practices, this allows a disconnection between earlier statutory intentions and the present realities of the regulatory field. With abortion, for example, the matter was intended to cater to a public health requirement, and, as mentioned before, an important element of this is evidence-based policymaking. Yet in light of evidence to suggest developments are safe and beneficial to the patient, the law has not been interpreted to permit these new measures. In this sense it is possible to suggest that informal practices, often falling away from public view, warp legislation put in place by democratically elected officials.

A final mode of institutional constraint posited by Lowndes and Roberts' (2013) innovative text is labelled as narratives. Discursive institutionalism, and the work of Schmidt (2008) in particular, is of course most comfortable in these surroundings, and the use of coordinative and communicative discourse in marrying the demand for protection for children with pornography regulation has been clearly expounded in chapter 5. In addition to the obvious, however, a narrative can tie together a series of events into a meaningful whole (Feldman et al 2004) and, in this sense, can be suggested to encapsulate the debates in parliament that surrounded the passage of the 1967 Act. Attributed in chapter 2 to the conflation of Kingdon's political, policy and problem streams (1995), the information that was contained in this model was additionally the content of official debates. Thus demonstrating that a chain of events, including rising maternal mortality and the thalidomide tragedy, should be married with the increasing liberalization evidenced in society to create policy change in line with a public health frame, was an accessible dialogue to accompany David Steel's PMB. Both of these practices can again be inferred across other domains, however, and the restricted dialogue on street prostitution, frequently bypassed in parliamentary debates, and the causal narrative around the need to investigate the conduct of police yet to be articulated, all provide both helpful causal explanations for the regulation of women, but also the potential for change. Indeed, if the definition of protection in prostitution is successfully widened to incorporate harms to the individual prostitute, the inducement for political action may be great. This is only likely to be achieved, however, through lengthy dialogue, and a reframing of the debate.

Connecting these three modes of institutional constraints (Lowndes and Roberts 2013) unveils a detailed account of the collection of rules, practices and narratives that converge to regulate the woman. From a general survey of this collection, it appears that the body of constraints fall within rules and practices, with little narrative around women's issues uncovered. In terms of the former two, however, a distinct trend across these categories was limited statutory change and flourishing informal practices. It is here, therefore, that it is contended that many deficiencies in the regulation of women are born and a potential disconnect between the intentions of the law and the implementation of policy is evident. In the opening chapter, the anecdotal points largely assumed that the black letter of the law failed the gender, such as the disparate collection of 'sex for sale' legislation. Upon investigation of each field, however, and referring to the 'black box' above, it appears that it is the informal routines that are perhaps of even greater significance. This contributes to a disparate collection of domains in three ways: they allow unofficial stereotyping to flourish, because they are often organically created from within the institution, they are manifested in an insular fashion that pays little regard to neighbouring issues, and finally they are largely set aside from the public glare. So, in the example of the abortion pill, this should serve as a key point of debate across women in the UK, yet a survey of opinion polls conducted in chapter 2 largely illustrated the alienation of the general public from such scientific debates. It can be suggested that apathy in this field, therefore, is born from this outward perspective of female empowerment, but concealed constraints on the empirical status of the woman. This oversight is classic in gender studies.

Drawing again on the stereotypes uncovered in the 'black box', this disproportionate appearance of institutional practices, as opposed to formally recorded rules, or innovative narratives, perpetuates these depictions and creates harmful contradictions across policy domains. Indeed, many women can fall between the gap of protection because of these very images, and a number of media stories highlight this problem. In 2013, for example, just such an incident took place in which a young woman, soliciting sex on the street, willingly got into a car with a man but was later forced to perform sexual acts that she did not consent to. Interestingly, in the emergency call that followed her ordeal she readily felt the need to disclose that she was a prostitute, perhaps for fear that she might not be believed (*Luton on Sunday* 2014). From a more theoretical standpoint, when a woman partakes in pornographic material within a relationship, with the express intention of it remaining in the possession of her and her partner, what happens if those images are later released or stolen? The question of the rights of women in cases of what has been colloquially coined 'revenge porn' has come under vast legislative scrutiny in the UK in recent times (BBC News 2014) but, regardless of statutory statements, may not be treated with such severity by the wider public due to prevailing stereotypes of the woman free in her choice to produce "harmless" pornography. Furthermore, from the same logical perspective as previously cited, this does not have relevance solely for the extreme of cases, but can unwittingly impact upon any woman. The hacking of a range of celebrities' personal material on their computers, for example, saw a series of compromising photos of female film stars stolen from the iCloud. In addition to the criminal investigation that shrouds this event, the popular public reaction is of interest, particularly those who have laid blame at the door of those women who took the photo in the first instance. British comedian Ricky Gervais, for example, suggested on social media that celebrities 'should make it harder for hackers' by 'not putting nude pictures of yourself on the computer' (*Huffington Post* 2014). Debatably such an attack on human rights is somewhat mitigated by the fact that pornography in the UK, for example, is widely, and often publicly consumed, and thus it appears of less consequence whether or not the person acquiesced to the release of such images.

Concern for contradictory regulation is additionally perpetuated by these stereotypes, and in situations other than what is sometimes viewed as the exception, and turning attention to the incompatibility of less sensational cases, the impact of diverging governance decisions upon daily life can also be demonstrated. Restating a central theme discussed previously in the book, as an activity that directly engages the work of more women than men, the solicitation of sex in public, for example, as previously discussed, is an indictable offence under the Street Offences Act 1959, and carries the possibility of an anti-social behaviour order being issued on conviction. It is of note, however, that prostitution is but one activity within what has become termed the sex industry; a title which additionally, but not conclusively, encompasses the working or running of brothels and strip clubs, human trafficking for sexual purposes, phone sex, pornography, mail-order brides and sex tourism (Andersson et al 2013). Far from an umbrella issue of 'sex for sale', therefore, these various actions are keenly extrapolated from each other and are regulated in widely varying manners by the appropriate governing bodies, one result of which is that street solicitation is banned and attracts the possibility of criminal sentencing, but the making and distribution of pornography is deemed lawful if conducted within certain parameters.

Not all legalistic distinctions are shocking; however, it could be suggested that these activities are rightly considered differently in the eyes of the law for reasons of severity. The issue of human trafficking as a form of transnational organized crime, for example, has escalated in recent decades in line with increasing globalization and the decline of border controls (Shelley 2007, 116), and its victims are vast and continually growing. To be sure, even the lucky that survive experience multiple health problems of both a physical and mental nature with HIV and post-traumatic stress disorder (PTSD), in particular, being displayed in high levels among this grouping (Tsutsumi et al. 2008). There is an argument to be proffered, therefore, and indeed entered into previously, that street prostitution should remain distinct in many ways from the choosing of work within the sex industry in the form of lap dancing, pornography or even prostitution. The voluntary versus forced dichotomy of sex worker experience (Doezema 1998) provides an overly simplistic view, however, and to take the situation at face value appears to be a somewhat immature response. A cautionary note must therefore be sounded at this juncture that even this classification of willing acquisition should itself not be treated lightly, as the reasons underpinning a woman's choice to enter such an arena are numerous and can be driven by multiple influences, and thus even a seemingly independent decision to undertake sex work can be misleading.

Again, however, for many, legislating on matters such as prostitution and pornography can appear far removed from their own lives and, although an argument can easily be forwarded that even regulation in the seemingly distinct world of sex work has a tangible impact on the treatment of women generally, societal concern for finding justification for this type of discrepancy is arguably limited to the activities of specific sex worker collectives concerned with seeking full decriminalization, or the recognition of employment rights (West 106). It is important to note, therefore, that similar abrasion between stereotypes occurs in the more everyday issues of rape and abortion. These two matters, on average, are thought to directly involve a larger proportion of the UK population than sexual services, with the police recording 20,725 rapes in 2013, and the number of abortions totalling 185,331 in the same year (Office for National Statistics 2014, Department of Health 2014). Despite the government's recent affirmation of the Geneva Convention concerning a woman or girl's absolute right to an abortion when medically necessary in circumstances of war rape (*Hansard* 9 January 2013, col 210), a woman falling pregnant as the result of an attack in the UK has no explicit statutory right to a termination upon those grounds alone, despite the possibility of criminal proceedings affirming that she has suffered a violent criminal act, and therefore a breach of her own rights, by another. Although such a court ruling is highly unlikely, if not impossible, to be delivered in the short nine-month period of gestation, the average duration from offence to completion in criminal courts averaging 496 days in 2011 (Ministry of Justice, Home Office and the Office for National Statistics 2013, 45), this is still a notable theoretical point. No explicit remedy is provided for the fact that a woman can be medically examined and signs of sexual assault recorded, yet this alone will not be admissible if she is later found to be pregnant and seeks an abortion.

Unlike the more taboo matters of prostitution and pornography, therefore, such figures cannot be as readily discarded of in the everyday conscience of women for reason that 'it simply does not affect me', and disquiet for the various juxtapositions in the law on these matters are the concern of national grassroots campaigns, such as Abortion Rights and Rape Crisis, which boast a comparatively larger and more diverse level of membership. The regulation of these topics therefore has the potential to affect all women during their lifetime, either in a direct manner by those who have sadly been the victim of rape, or have sought to end an unwanted or potentially harmful pregnancy, or indirectly, by influencing a woman's decision to walk home alone late at night, or in the sense that abortion cannot easily be isolated from wider contraceptive issues such as easy access to the morning-after pill. To be sure, these warring legislative stances can have a damaging impact upon perceptions of sexual assault, and comments made in regard to 'legitimate rape' by US Senate candidate Todd Aiken in the run-up to the Missouri election in 2012 illustrate this very point. Submitting that pregnancy cannot result from sexual assault if such an attack is truly against the woman's will because 'the female body has ways to try to shut that whole thing down' (*New York Times* 2012), Aiken vocalized a long-standing and harmful myth around rape, one that is far from supported by medical fact, with clinical studies previously highlighting the significant frequency with which rape-related pregnancies can occur (Holmes et al 1996).

From the outset, a convergence of NI strains has been a risky theoretical approach, and one that finds both support and criticism from neighbouring projects. Upon completion of this analysis, however, it can be proposed that adopting a multi-variant approach in the study of key women's issues has provided two specific benefits. First, the engagement of each policy domain with a separate variant of NI demonstrates the insular approach of policymakers to issues that have the clear unifying feature of an inequitable level of female burden. Granted, by adopting this staged approach, the account does run the risk of over-stating this segregation, and the dividing lines becoming a product of the division already inherent in the methodological approaches of each strain. It is asserted with much conviction, however, that this threat was warded off by the continual reference and appreciation to the commonalities and blurred lines across the variants, both in each chapter, but also in the course of this sub-section under the umbrella terms of rules, practices and narratives. Furthermore, this final assimilation has allowed for a collective response to how women are regulated in the UK, and clearly brings into focus the problem of dimensionality. A woman is not just one label, and certainly does not fall left or right of a binary at all moments in her life. This truth, however, is difficult for the regulation to cope with, and results in failures in regard to protection and respect for human rights. Second, this project has taken not only great lead and inspiration from the development in the scholarship on NI in recent years, but has also attempted, through rigorous application and comparison, to add to the growing pool of third phase institutionalists. Observations made throughout the project are clearly a point of countenance for many, including this author, but it is what can be extracted by policymakers from these revelations that must be tackled and, in line with theoretical developments, the need for a more gendered approach is suggested.

6.3. DISPELLING THE MYTHS: LESSONS FOR PRACTITIONERS AND TOWARDS A GENDERED LENS

In a contemporary world it feels almost ridiculous to need to reassert that a woman is the summation of her different attitudes and qualities and can be many things, across a range of scenarios. Yet it appears that the pertinence of this point has been repeatedly extolled as the book has moved though its chapters. From the outset, the common tie across these policy domains has been women, and the arbitrary labelling of criminal and victim, or the 'Madonna/whore duality'. Of great alarm, recognition of this dual typology has also increasingly manifested across society, to the worrying extent that it is now claimed to have formed central significance in the representation of women in Western culture (McDonald 1995). To be sure, women have, for far longer than men, been divided into the 'good' and the 'bad' girls (Easteel), but the classic Rizzo/Sandy divide, as portrayed in the popular Hollywood musical *Grease* (1978), oddly appears to continue to resonate in the contemporary world, and studies from sociology indicate that such bipolar labelling remains the familiar and typical cultural account of women's sexuality (Conrad 2006). Upon thorough analysis of UK policymaking, however, the irony becomes apparent that the second key feature binding these matters is the significant number of women that fall between the gaps of these overlapping fields. Indeed competing institutional constraints have obscured this failure, and as a result, organizations have often overlooked the fact that they are not just women's issues in name, but in practice a single woman can come into contact with each piece of disparate, and often contradictory, legislation. Before this point is jumped upon, however, it is important to note that all women should not be treated the same, as this is just as repugnant a thought. Rather the use of the term here is engaged in an attempt to humanize the approach, and refer to a physiological connection that dictates the inequitable level of burden in specific matters. It is certainly not asserted at any point in the course of this book that all women are saintly and treated poorly; one woman in prostitution can indeed be a criminal, while the other is a victim, and there are recorded cases of false allegations of rape, and all of these distinctions should be recognized by the law. What should not be overlooked, however, is that the criminal in one domain can be the legitimate victim in another, a fact that, through the stereotyping practices of institutions unveiled above, pervades some of the regulation.

Indeed, as we have already seen, the problem arises when the criminal is also raped, or the victim falls pregnant, and it is at this very point that the label of woman is needed. At this juncture, it is posited that if this is the overarching term engaged at the macro level, this will place her at the heart of micro-level deliberations, and the question becomes 'was the woman raped?' or 'is it this woman's choice to take part in pornography?' As it stands, however, the UK's scheme arguably reflects a piecemeal collection of stagnating regulatory measures that seldom give consideration to the woman in her entirety, and play second fiddle to an array of informal practices that enable antiquated images to flourish. This is not to say that all policy domains are entirely flawed, and improvements in some form have arguably been made across the board, but it is when a comparative analysis is undertaken that their incompatibility with each other appears problematic. With the ever-increasing encroachment of the EU into health and social affairs at the member state level (e.g., Greer 2006, Martinsen and Vrangbaek 2008), however, it appears inevitable that in the years to come, a greater appreciation of the rights and responsibilities housed in these legislative stances must come under the spotlight of investigation.

It is here that the first suggestion for future research can be made. Greater work must be dedicated towards discovering exactly why these dominant images have emerged, and attempt to dispel some of the myths. In this sense, a gendered lens needs to be applied to the issues discussed in the course of this book, and with it the developments recently seen in terms of feminist institutionalism (Krook and Mackay 2010) that the results of this project point towards. Indeed, a query that could quite easily come to mind when reflecting on this project is the absence of a gendered approach to the study from the outset, particularly in light of the recent developments producing a strong and credible marriage of feminist theory with the new institutionalism. The response to this is straightforward; the focus of empirical study has indeed been concerned with issues that bear inequitably upon women, but not necessarily about gender inequality. Granted, these two are far from mutually exclusive, but the premise of this book was to explore issues of particular societal concern, housing strong value-laden directives, and pertaining substantially to human rights. It just so happens, that in the midst of all of this, the unifying factor is women. This is not to say that each chapter has not endeavoured to highlight the constraints on female behaviour in society, and harmful stereotyping that can manifest from institutional stronghold over a matter, and that even by collating this evidence, the narrative has encroached upon feminist dialogue, but the overarching objective was to explain what the regulation of these issues are, why they are created in such a manner, and how they are of consequence. The result of this comparative case study analysis, however, in addition to these policy-specific problems, such as the constraints on evidence-based policymaking in abortion, has been to highlight that women should not be treated as the coincidental unifying theme. What can be seen across the matters of abortion, prostitution, rape and pornography is a fragmented and insular approach that relies substantially on labels such as criminal or proper victim, but ignores the fact that a woman can be all of these.

Progressing to the practical steps that can now be suggested in light of this study, three key lessons can be drawn for policymakers. The duality present in the labeling of women has been perpetuated by a disparate development of the law in the different policy domains, and a blinkered approach to the perceived crime or necessary protection in that field. Theoretically, therefore, this extols the virtues of using the strains of NI in an aggregate fashion in a complex policy field to uncover such deficiencies, as has been asserted above, in addition to proposing a more gendered research agenda in the future to further investigate these dominant stereotypes. Practically, however, this suggests the need for an integrated approach across these policy domains, but this of itself is a rather broad and somewhat vague conclusion to be drawn, that proffers little tangible utility to the practitioner. Unpacking this sentiment, therefore, it can be suggested that a more holistic approach to the woman could be achieved through three interrelated practices; greater adherence to evidence-based policymaking, multi-agency work and wider awareness of victims. Interestingly, these have all been mooted in varying degrees in potential reforms to the individual policy domains; here it is posited that their application to 'women's issues' is key.

It is often claimed in a frustrated manner that policy cannot be made in a vacuum, immune from exogenous pressures, and this, as a fundamental principle, the author takes no issue with. Indeed, a nuanced approach of the type suggested here will never be achieved if all contextual factors are abandoned. It must be suggested, however, that in some instances the scales have in fact been tipped too far in the other direction, and this is a distinct problem. Although presented as an issue of healthcare and a matter of public harm respectively, the regulation of abortion and prostitution are still heavily entrenched in a moral statement on the activity. As revealed throughout the analysis of the workings of these schemes, however, the criminal and lawful divide is not enough, and after radical overhaul of the system must come the necessary questions of how to then keep this abreast of societal developments. Interestingly, it appears that this has been achieved in terms of pornography; the proliferation of the Internet has made hardcore pornography more widely available. This is a fact. As such, it has been addressed with a relevant solution by David Cameron, and the same must happen with the other policy domains. Of perhaps greatest pertinence here, therefore, are the closing sentiments in the chapter on rape of the need for a public inquiry. The 2014 HMIC report revealed substantial failings, and these need to be acted upon in order to produce effective and appropriate policy responses. These should not just address the issues at hand, however, but the woman in her entirety, adopting a cross-sector approach that additionally appreciates the treatment of prostitutes who are sexually assaulted, or prejudicial attitudes across the healthcare sector in regard to the pregnant porn star seeking a termination. Although there is considerable doubt on how to handle the variegated and contested evidence base that typifies most sectors (Pawson 2002), improvements can nevertheless be made within the boundaries of existing regulation if reports and inquiries are listened to.

Interrelated to this submission, therefore, is the need for a multi-agency approach to fortify a women's sector. It was previously submitted in the introduction that much of the literature fails to provide a comparative analysis of the four subject matters featured in this book, often operating under the assumption that each issue entails its own specific set of policymakers. True, abortion heavily rests in the healthcare sector, as juxtaposed to rape and prostitution as possessed by the criminal law, and pornography largely a matter for the media. This is not to say, however, that such policymakers cannot have a seat at more than one table, and in practice they often do. What is suggested here, therefore, is that this could be expanded upon under the ethos of a 'joined-up' approach to allow a fuller spectrum of policymakers, be it government officials or practitioners, to enter into a more sustained and open dialogue across matters. Former PM Tony Blair's endorsement of a 'joined-up' approach to government in the 1990s arguably failed to find synthesis in the underlying ethos of certain fields, which let to a stilted approach to issues, but there are certainly benefits that can be derived from these attempts. In particular, it is with the work of Pollitt (2003), bravely proffering a working definition for JUG when the programme itself was in its infancy, that considers both horizontal and vertical coordination. A more inclusive activity, therefore, would allow for crucial information sharing to be undertaken across the domains.

Finally, incorporated in this open approach should be the voice of victims. The meaning of protection, and especially who needs protecting, has featured throughout the case studies; of course, most notably in the chapter concerning pornography. Frequently underpinning the construction of the term, however, whether explicitly recognized or not, has been a value judgement about the morality of street prostitution, or the right to freedom of speech in pornography. It is not solely a move towards a more evidenced-based approach, therefore, that is required, but that the construction of the term protection needs to be considered. This principle of harm, as previously explained, rests on tangible indicators, but some of these drivers should be garnered from the victims themselves that can only be achieved effectively through the aforementioned process of multi-agency work. Curiously, however, the majority of positive discussion on the plight of the victim currently emanates from an offender-centric approach. In line with restorative justice practices, for example, a series of police forces across England and Wales have produced information and courses to address rehabilitation in terms of all the victims touched by a crime (e.g., Cheshire and Greater Manchester Community Rehabilitation Company). In 2009, for example, South West Scotland Community Justice Authority (SWSCJA) hosted a multi-agency victim awareness day, the result of which was the publication of a handbook titled 'The Ripple Effect' (SWSCJA 2009). These endeavors are worthy and, as discussed previously in chapter 4, they too would benefit from greater acknowledgement of the female victim, in all her possible manifestations. Falling in line with this, it can be additionally suggested that a greater presence of women in the policy process may aid the perception of the female victim. Representative democracy has long been mooted as a progressive step towards gender equality in the parliamentary stage of law formulation (Lovenduski and Norris 2003), but additional studies have increasingly highlighted the need for the positive results that can be gained from similar action at a bureaucratic level. In regards to the police, for example, it has previously been observed that the rate of arrest for domestic violence varies in relation to the authority and discretion afforded to female police officers (Andrews and Miler 2013) and similar patterns in regard to the treatment of claimants of rape must be considered. Although already charted from a US perspective (Meir and Nicholson-Crotty 2006), this has yet to take place in a rigorous manner in England and Wales in light of the HMIC insights discussed previously.

Thus in acknowledgement that solutions are not easy to find, it is with these suggestions, and the overarching sentiment that an integrated and holistic approach to the woman is required in matters boasting an inequitable level of female bias, that this project draws to a close. Unfortunately, it would be unrealistic to expect that it is only a matter of time before these harmful informal practices are dispelled; stereotypes are constantly changing and reshaping to contemporary society, but rarely do they depart for good. This in itself is not particularly a matter of gender, but one of human nature. What can be hoped, however, is that with increased research and practitioner awareness of those that fall between the gaps, the regulation will also demonstrate a greater level of flexibility and an ability to adapt. For all the debates and research that flourishes around the intricacies of the policymaking process, sometimes it is, as originally intended, the black letter of the law that counts, and it is thus vital that these statutes strike the correct balance between prosecution and protection. Of course, all of this rests, however, on full acknowledgement of 'women's issues'.

Bibliography

Ackman, Dan. 2001. 'How Big Is Porn?" *Forbes* http://www.forbes.com/2001/05/25/0524porn.html

Adler, Freda. 1977. "Interaction between Women's Emancipation and Criminality—A Cross-Cultural Perspective." *International Journal of Criminology and Penology* 5(3): 101–12.

Akbor, Ruhubia. 2010. "Crackdown on 'red light district' to be relaunched." *Manchester Evening News*, 19 April. Accessed 12 August 2014. http://www.manchestereveningnews.co.uk/news/local-news/crackdown-on-red-light-district-to-be-relaunched-941562

Allen, Graham. 2008. "We need to think a generation ahead to prevent these tragedies." *The Guardian*, 1 December. Accessed 23 June 2015. http://www.theguardian.com/society/2008/dec/01/child-protection

Allison, Graham T., and Philip Zelikow. Essence of decision: Explaining the Cuban missile crisis. Vol. 2. New York: Longman, 1999.

Alpert, Leo M. "Judicial Censorship of Obscene Literature." Harvard Law Review (1938): 40-76.

Alston, Richard. 2001. "Urban Population in Late Roman Egypt and the End of the Ancient World." In *Debating Roman Demography*, edited by Walter Scheidel, 161–204. The Netherlands: Kominklyke Brill, NV.

Anderson, Michelle J. "Women Do Not Report the Violence They Suffer: Violence Against Women and the State Action Doctrine." Vill. L. Rev. 46 (2001): 907.

Andersson, Bettan, Gerdan Christenson, Asa Christenson, Annina Claesson, Kim Eldinadotter, Fonti Gerani, Sara Ström, Amin Wikman and Lisa Akesson. 2013. "Speaking of Prostitution." *The Women's Front*. http://prostitutionresearch.com/wp-content/uploads/2013/12/Speaking-of-Prostitution-2013-Sweden1.pdf

Andrews, Rhys and Karen Miller. 2013. "Representative Democracy, Gender and Policing: The Case of Domestic Violence Arrests in England." *Public Administration* 4(91): 998-1014.

Arrow, Kenneth. 1951. *Social Choice and Individual Values*. New York: Wiley.

Atkinson, Anthony, Eric Marlier, and Brian Nolan. 2004. "Indicators and Targets for Social Inclusion in the European Union." *Journal of Common Market Studies* 42(1): 47–75.

Attwood, Feona. 2002. "Reading Porn: The Paradigm Shift in Pornography Research." *Sexualities* 5(1): 91–105.

Bailey, Reg. 2011. "Letting Children be Children: Report of an Independent Review of the Commercialisation and Sexualisation of Childhood." June 2011, Department for Education. https://www.gov.uk/government/uploads/system/uploads/attachment_data/file/175418/Bailey_Review.pdf

Barnard, Marina. 1993. "Violence and Vulnerability: Conditions of Work for Street Working Prostitutes." *Sociology of Health and Illness* 15(5): 683–705.

Baumgartner, Frank and Bryan Jones. 2003. *Agendas and Instability in American Politics.* Chicago, Chicago University Press.

Baumgartner, Frank, Suzanna De Boef and Amber Boydstun. 2008. *The Decline of the Death Penalty and the Discovery of Innocence.* Cambridge: Cambridge University Press.

BBC News. 2004. "Blunkett to urge US web porn curb." 24 February. Accessed 23 April 2015. http://news.bbc.co.uk/1/hi/england/3515797.stm

BBC News. 2008. "No deals on 42 days, says Brown" http://news.bbc.co.uk/1/hi/uk_politics/7449678.stm Accessed 15 December 2015.

BBC News. 2010a. "Stop sexualising children, says David Cameron." 18 February. Accessed 23 November 2014. http://news.bbc.co.uk/1/hi/uk_politics/8521403.stm.

BBC News. 2010b. "Tories criticized over teenage pregnancy figure error." 25 February. Accessed 2 July 2015. http://news.bbc.co.uk/1/hi/uk_politics/8515798.stm

BBC News. 2011a. "England riots: Broken Society is top priority—Cameron." 15 August. Accessed 15 January 2015. http://www.bbc.co.uk/news/uk-politics-14524834

BBC News. 2011b. "Ofcom issues TV watershed warning." 30 September. Accessed 20 March 2015. http://www.bbc.co.uk/news/entertainment-arts-15123049

BBC News. 2014a. "Arrests for rape and kerb crawling in Bristol crackdown." 19 March. Accessed 26 April 2015. http://www.bbc.co.uk/news/uk-england-bristol-26643374

BBC News. 2014b. "Judy Finnegan apologises for loose women rape comments." 14 October. Accessed 17 December 2014. http://www.bbc.co.uk/news/entertainment-arts-29598732

BBC News. 2014c. "'Revenge porn' illegal under new UK law." 13 October. Accessed 6 June 2015. http://www.bbc.co.uk/news/29596583

Béland, Daniel. 2005. "Ideas and Social Policy: An Institutionalist Perspective." *Social Policy & Administration*, 39: 1–18.

Bentham, Jeremy. Reprinted 2005. *An Introduction to the Principles of Morals and Legislation.* Montana: Kessinger Publishing Ltd.

Berman, Robert. 1978. "The Study of Macro and Micro Implementation." *Public Policy* 26(2): 157–84.

Bieneck, Steffan and Barbara Krahe. 2011. "Blaming the Victim and Exonerating the Perpetrator in Cases of Rape and Robbery: Is There a Double Standard?" *Journal of Interpersonal Violence* 26(9): 1785–97.

Bindel, Julie. 2010. "Iceland: The World's Most Feminist Country." *The Guardian*, 25 March. Accessed 6 July 2015. http://www.theguardian.com/lifeandstyle/2010/mar/25/iceland-most-feminist-country

Bingham, John. 2009. "Night stalker: from Jack the Ripper to the black cab rapist, Britain's criminal reigns of terror." *The Telegraph*, 16 November. Accessed 13 January 2015. http://www.telegraph.co.uk/news/uknews/crime/6579199/Night-stalker-from-Jack-the-Ripper-to-the-black-cab-rapist-Britains-criminal-reigns-of-terror.html

Bland, Lucy. 1992. "'Purifying' the Public World: Feminist Vigilantes in Late Victorian England." *Women's History Review* 1(3): 397–412.

Boin, Arjen, Paul t'Hart and Alan McConnell. 2009. "Crisis Exploitation: Political and Policy Impacts of Framing Contests." *Journal of European Public Policy* 16(1): 81–106.

Bradshaw, Peter. 2002. "Managers, Blame Culture and Highly Ambitious Policies in the British National Health Service (NHS)." *Journal of Nursing Management* 19(2): 1–4.

Brents, Barbara and Kathryn Hausbeck. 2005. "Violence and Legalized Brothel Prostitution in Nevada: Examining Safety, Risk and Prostitution Policy." *Journal of Interpersonal Violence* 20(3): 270–95.

Brents, Barbara and Teela Sanders. 2010. "Mainstreaming the Sex Industry: Economic Inclusion and Social Ambivalence." *Journal of Law and Society* 37(1): 40–60.

British Pregnancy Advisory Service. 2014. "Back Off: Call for buffer zones around clinics as anti-abortion activity intensifies," 28 November. Accessed 24 April 2015. https://www.bpas.org/about-our-charity/press-office/press-releases/bpas-release-abortion-clinics-need-buffer-zones/

Brooks-Gordon, Belinda, and Loraine Gelsthorpe. 2003a. "What Men Say When Apprehended for Kerb Crawling: A Model of Prostitutes Clients' Talk." *Psychology, Crime and Law* 9(2): 145–71.

Brooks-Gordon, Belinda, and Loraine Gelsthorpe. 2003b. "Prostitutes' Clients, Ken Livingstone and a New Trojan Horse." *Howard Journal* 42(5): 437–51.

Brown, Beverly, Michelle Burman and Lynn Jamieson. 1993. *Sex Crimes on Trial: The Use of Sexual Evidence in Scottish Courts*. Edinburgh: Edinburgh University Press.

Brown, Beverly, Carys Hamilton and Darragh O'Neill. 2007. "Characteristics Associated with Rape Attrition and the Role Played by Skepticism or Legal Rationality by Investigators and Prosecutors." *Psychology, Crime and Law* 13(4): 355–70.

Brown, Jennifer. 1998. "Aspects of Discriminatory Treatment of Women Police Officers Serving in Forces in England and Wales." *British Journal of Criminology* 38(2): 265–82.

Brownmiller, Susan. 2013. *Against Our Will: Men, Women and Rape*. New York: Simon and Schuster.

Brundage, James. 2009. *Law, Sex and Christian Society in Medieval Europe*. Chicago: University of Chicago Press.

Burke, Shelia. 2015. 'Vanderbilt Rape Case Defendant: No Memory Of Alleged Assault.' Huffington post http://www.huffingtonpost.com/2015/01/26/vanderbilt-rape-defendant_n_6550328.html.

Burnett, Dean. 2014. "The UK Pornography Law: A Scientific Perspective." *The Guardian*, 5 December. Accessed 26 April 2015. http://www.theguardian.com/science/brain-flapping/2014/dec/05/uk-pornography-law-scientific-perspective-children-safety

Burton, Antoinette. 1990. "The White Woman's Burden: British Feminists and the Indian Woman, 1865-1915." *Women's Studies International Forum* 13(4), 295–308.

Buse, Kent, Adriane Martin-Hilber, Ninuk Widyantoro and Sarah Hawkes. 2006. "Management of the Politics of Evidence-Based Sexual and Reproductive Health Policy." *Lancet* 368: 2101–3.

Butler, Patrick. 2014. "Baby P: The untold story is the anatomy of an establishemtn cover up." 27 October, *The Guardian*. Accessed 3 November 2014. http://www.theguardian.com/commentisfree/2014/oct/27/baby-p-untold-story-cover-up-bbc

Buxton, R. (1973) "Criminal Law Reform: England." *American Journal of Comparative Law* 21(2): 242.

Cabinet Office. 2013. "The Internet and Pornography: Prime Minister Calls for Action." Accessed 3 May 2015. https://www.gov.uk/government/speeches/the-internet-and-pornography-prime-minister-calls-for-action

Cairney, Paul. 2009. "The Role of Ideas in Policy Transfer: The Case of UK Smoking Bans since Devolution." *Journal of European Public Policy* 16(3): 471–88.

Caldwell, John. 2004. "Fertility Control in the Classical World: Was There an Ancient Fertility Transition?" *Journal of Population Research* 21(1): 1–17.

Caldwell, Simon. 2014. "Scandal of the doctors who were let off after approving abortions for women they'd never even met." *Mail Online*, 22 April. Accessed 14 October 2014. http://www.dailymail.co.uk/news/article-2609950/Scandal-doctors-let-approving-abortions-women-theyd-never-met.html

Calvert, Randall. 1995. "Rational Actors, Equilibrium, and Social Institutions." In *Explaining Social Institutions*, edited by Jack Knight and Itai Sened, 57–95. Ann Arbor: University of Michigan Press.

Calvo, Ernesto. 2007. "The Responsive Legislature: Public Opinion and Law Making in a Highly Disciplined Legislature." *British Journal of Political Science* 37(2): 263–80.

Cameron, David. 2008. "We've had a raft of excuses and no apology." *London Evening Standard*, 12 November. Accessed 23 June 2015. http://www.standard.co.uk/news/weve-had-a-raft-of-excuses-and-no-apology-6886449.html

Cameron, Samuel and Alan Collins. 2003. "Estimates of a Model of Male Participation in the Market for Female Heterosexual Prostitution Services." *European Journal of Law and Economics* 16(3): 371–88.

Cammack, Paul. 1992. "The New Institutionalism: Predatory Rule, Institutional Persistence, and Macro-Social Change." *Economy and Society* 21: 397–429.

Canter, David, Maria Ioannou and Donna Youngs. 2009. *Safer Sex in the City: The Experience and Management of Street Prostitution*. Surrey: Ashgate Publishing Limited.

Care. 2014. "78% favour criminalising sex buyers in NI." 17 October. Accessed 3 June 2015. http://www.care.org.uk/news/latest-news/78-favour-criminalising-sex-buyers-ni-0

Carey, Jules. 2013. "The Ian Tomlinson case shows why the police cannot investigate themselves." 12 August, *The Guardian*. Accessed 13 January 2015. http://www.theguardian.com/commentisfree/2013/aug/12/ian-tomlinson-police-apology.

Carline, Anna. 2011. "Criminal Justice, Extreme Pornography and Prostitution: Protecting Women or Promoting Morality?' *Sexualities* 14(3): 312–33.

Carroll, Jason, Laura Padilla-Walker, Larry Nelson, Chad Olson, Carolyn McNamara Barry and Stephanie Madsen. 2008. "Generation XXX: Pornography Acceptance and Use Among Emerging Adults." *Journal of Adolescent Research* 23(1): 6–30.

Carter, Daniel, Robert Prentky, Raymond Knight, Penny Vanderveer and Richard Boucher. 1987. "Use of Pornography in the Criminal and Developmental Histories of Sexual Offenders." *Journal of Interpersonal Violence* 2(2): 196–211.

Cavadino, Paul. 1976. "Illegal Abortions and the Abortion Act 1967." *British Journal of Criminology* 16(1): 63–67.

Chalabi, Mona. 2013. "Pornography: what we know, what we don't." *The Guardian*, 24 May. Accessed 13 September 2015. http://www.theguardian.com/news/datablog/2013/may/24/missing-statistics-pornography

Chamallas, Martha. 1988. "Consent, Equality and the Legal Control of Sexual Conduct." *Southern California Law Review* 61: 777–862.

Chan, Janet. 1996. "Changing Police Culture." *British Journal of Criminology* 36(1): 109–34.

Chapman, James. 2012. "Victory for the Mail! Children WILL be protected from online porn after Cameron orders automatic block on sites." *Daily Mail*, 19 December. Accessed 3 September 2014. http://www.dailymail.co.uk/news/article-2250809/Victory-Mail-Children-WILL-protected-online-porn-Cameron-orders-sites-blocked-automatically.html

Child, Ben. 2013. "Lars von Trier used body doubles to shoot Nymphomaniac." *The Guardian*, 21 May. Accessed 14 October 2014. http://www.theguardian.com/film/2013/may/21/lars-von-trier-nymphomaniac-body-doubles

Church, Stephanie, Marion Henderson, Marina Barnard and Graham Hart. 2001. "Violence by Clients towards Female Prostitutes in Different Work Settings: Questionnaire Survey." *British Medical Journal* 322: 524–25.

Clark, Tim. 2002. "New Labour's Big Idea: Joined-Up Government." *Social Policy and Society* 1(2): 107–17.

Clark, Tom. 1969. "Religion, Morality, and Abortion: A Constitutional Appraisal." *Loyola of Los Angeles Law Review* 2: 1–16.

Cmnd. 5668. 2002. *Protecting the Public: Strengthening Protection Against Sex Offenders and Reforming the Law on Sexual Offences.* London: The Stationery Office.

CNN. 2012. "Obama announces he supports same-sex marriage." May 10. Accessed 24 April 2015. http://edition.cnn.com/2012/05/09/politics/obama-same-sex-marriage/index.html

Coke, Edwardo. 1797. *The Third Part of the Institutes of the Laws of England: Concerning High treason and Other Pleas of the Crown and Criminal Causes.* London: E. and R. Brooke.

Committee on Homosexual Offences and Prostitution. 1957. *Report of the Committee on Homosexual Offences and Prostitution.* London: Her Majesty's Stationery Office.

Committee on the Working of the Abortion Act. 1974. *Report of the Committee on the Working of the Abortion Act.* London: Her Majesty's Stationery Office.

Conrad, Browyn. 2006. "Neo-Institutionalism, Social Movements, and the Cultural Reproduction of a Mentalité: Promise Keepers Reproduce the Madonna-Whore Complex." *Sociological Quarterly* 47(2): 305–31.

Conway, Edmund. 2004. "Westminster wages war on vice cards." *The Telegraph*, 27 August. Accessed 15 September 2014. http://www.telegraph.co.uk/finance/2893592/Westminster-wages-war-on-vice-cards.html

Cook, Nancy. 2007. *Gender Relations in Global Perspective: Essential Reading.* Ontario: Canadian Scholars Press Inc.

Cook, Rebecca J., and Bernard M. Dickens. "Human rights dynamics of abortion law reform." Human Rights Quarterly 25, no. 1 (2003): 1-59.

Cooper, Joseph. 1977. "Congress in Organizational Perspective." In *Congress Reconsidered,* edited by Lawrence Dodd and Bruce Oppenheimer, 307–68. Washington: Congressional Quarterly Press.

Council of Europe. 2011a. "Convention on Combating Violence Against Women and Domestic Violence." Accessed 6 July 2015. http://www.conventions.coe.int/Treaty/Commun/QueVoulezVous.asp?CL=ENG&NT=210

Council of Europe. 2011b. "Internet: Case-Law of the European Court of Human Rights." Accessed 14 July 2015. http://www.echr.coe.int/Documents/Research_report_internet_ENG.pdf.

Cowan, Sharon. 2010. "All Change or Business as Usual? Reforming the Law of Rape in Scotland." In *Rethinking Rape Law: International and Comparative Perspectives,* edited by Claire McGlynn and Vanessa Muro, 154–69. Oxford: Routledge.

Cox, Gary. 2000. "On the Effects of Legislative Rules." *Legislative Studies Quarterly* 25(2): 169–92.

Cox, Rosie. 2007. "The Au Pair Body: Sex Object, Sister or Student." *European Journal of Women's Studies* 14(3): 281–96.

Coy, Maddy, Josephine Wakeling and Maria Garner. 2011. "Selling Sex Sells: Representations of Prostitution and the Sex Industry in Sexualized Popular Culture as Symbolic Violence." *Women's Studies International Forum* 34(5): 441–48.

Crouch, Colin. 2005. *Capitalist Diversity and Change: Recombinant Governance and Institutional Entrepreneurs.* Oxford: Oxford University Press.

Cuklanz, Lisa. 1998. "The Masculine Ideal: Rape on Prime-Time Television, 1976-1978." *Critical Studies in Mass Communication* 15(4): 423–48.

Culzac, Natasha. 2014. "Thailand beach murder: Thai PM suggests 'attractive' female tourists cannot expect to be safe wearing bikinis." *The Independent,* 17 September. Accessed 17 October 2014. http://www.independent.co.uk/news/world/asia/thailand-beach-murders-thai-pm-suggests-attractive-female-tourists-cannot-expect-to-be-safe-in-bikinis-9737016.html

Cunnen, Chris. 1998. "Zero Tolerance Policing and the Experience of New York City." *Current Issues in Criminal Justice* 10: 299–313.

Cunningham, Scott and Todd Kendall. 2011. "Prostitution 2.0: The Changing Face of Sex Work." *Journal of Urban Economics* 69(3): 273–87.

Dally, Ann. 1998. "Thalidomide: Was the Tragedy Preventable?" *Lancet* 18: 1197–99.

Daly, Kathleen. 2002. "Sexual Assault and Restorative Justice." In *Restorative Justice and Family Violence,* edited by Heather Strang and John Braithwaite, 62–88. Cambridge: Cambridge University Press.

D'Amato, Anthony. 2006. "Porn Up, Rape Down." *Northwestern Public Law Research Paper* 913013.

D'Angelo, Mary. 1999. "Reconstructing 'Real Women' in Gospel Literature: The Case of Mary Magdalene." In *Women and Christian Origins,* edited by Ross Kraemer and Mary D'Angelo, 105–28. Oxford: Oxford University Press.

Danna, Daniela. 2012. "Client-Only Criminalization in the City of Stockholm: A Local Research on the Application of the 'Swedish Model" of Prostitution Policy." *Sexuality Research and Social Policy* 9(1): 80–93.

Davenport, Justin. 2009. "Blogger cleared over 'rape and murder' of Girls Aloud." *London Evening Standard,* 29 June. Accessed 15 September 2014. http://www.standard.co.uk/news/blogger-cleared-over-rape-and-murder-of-girls-aloud-6766552.html

Davies, Michael. 1998. *Textbook on Medical Law.* London: Blackstone.

Davis, Gayle and Roger Davidson. 2006. "A Fifth Freedom or Hideous Atheistic Expediency? The Medical Community and Abortion Law Reform in Scotland, c.1960-1975." *Medical History* 50(1): 29–48.

Daviter, Falk. 2007. "Policy Framing in the European Union." *Journal of European Public Policy* 14(4): 654–66.

Day and Night. 2014. "Mike Tyson stages a comeback with new cartoon comedy." *Daily Express,* 30 October. Accessed 12 November 2014. http://www.express.co.uk/news/showbiz/529543/Mike-Tyson-comeback-actor-new-cartoon-comedy

Day, Sophie. 1994. "What Counts As Rape? Physical Assault and Broken Contracts: Contrasting Views of Rape among London Sex Workers." In *Sex and Violence: Issues in Representation and Experience*, edited by Penelope Harvey and Peter Gow, 172–89. London: Routledge.

Dempsey, Michelle. 2005. "Rethinking Wolfenden: Prostitute-Use, Criminal Law and Remote Harm." *Criminal Law Review* 444: 453–54.

Denzau, Arthur, William Riker and Kenneth Shepsle. 1985. "Farquharson and Fenno: Sophisticated Voting and Home Style." *American Political Science Review* 79(4): 1117–34.

Department for Education. 2011. "Letting Children Be Children: Report of an Independent Review of the Commercialisation and Sexualisation of Childhood." London: HMSO.

Department of Health. 2011. "Abortion Statistics, England and Wales, 2010." Accessed 20 September 2014. https://www.gov.uk/government/statistics/abortion-statistics-england-and-wales-2010.

Department of Health. 2014. "Abortion Statistics, England and Wales, 2013." Accessed 9 December 2014. https://www.gov.uk/government/statistics/report-on-abortion-statistics-in-england-and-wales-for-2013

Dexter, Hedy and Steven Penrod. 1997. "Attributing Responsibility to Female Victims after Exposure to Sexually Violent Films." *Journal of Applied Psychology* 27(24): 2149–71.

DiMaggio, Paul and Walter Powell. 1991. "The Iron Cage Revisited: Institutional Isomorphism and Collective Rationality in Organizational Fields." *American Sociological Review* 48: 147–60.

Dodds, Klaus and Stuart Elden. 2008. "Thinking Ahead: David Cameron, the Henry Jackson Society and British Neo-Conservatism." *British Journal of Politics & International Relations* 10(3): 347–63.

Dodillet, Susanne. 2004. "Cultural Clash on Prostitution: Debates on Prostitution in Germany and Sweden in the 1990s." In *First Global Conference: Critical Issues in Sexuality, Salzburg, Austria.*

Doezema, Jo. 1998. "Forced to Choose: Beyond the Voluntary v. Forced Prostitution Dichotomy." In *Global Sex Workers: Rights, Resistance, and Redefinition*, edited by Kamala Kempadoo and Jo Doezema, 34–50. New York, Routledge.

Dolowitz, David and David Marsh. 1996. "Who Learns What from Whom: A Review of the Policy Transfer Literature." *Political Studies* 44(2): 343–57.

Döring, Herbert. 1995. "Time as a Scarce Resource: Government Control of the Agenda." In *Parliaments and Majority Rule in Western Europe*, edited by Herbert Döering, 223–46. New York: St. Martin's Press.

Doughty, Steve. 2005. "Most liberal abortion limit in Europe.' *Daily Mail*, 17 March. Accessed 3 April 2015. http://www.dailymail.co.uk/health/article-341702/Most-liberal-abortion-limit-Europe.html

Downs, Anthony. 1972. "Up and Down with Ecology—The 'Issue Attention Cycle.'" *Public Interest* 28 (Summer): 28–50.

Drexler, Jessica. 1996. "Governments' Role in Turning Tricks: The World's Oldest Profession in the Netherlands and United States." *Dickinson Journal of International Law* 15: 201–36.

Dunn, P. M., and G. M. Stirrat. "Capable of being born alive?." The Lancet 323, no. 8376 (1984): 553–55.

Dworkin, Andrea. 1985. "Against the Male Flood: Censorship, Pornography and Equality." *Harvard's Women's Law Journal* 8: 1–25.

Dworkin, Andrea. 1993. "Prostitution and Male Supremacy." *Michigan Journal of Gender and Law* 1: 1–12.

Easteal, Patricia. 2001. "Women in Australian Prisons: The Cycle of Abuse and Dysfunctional Environments." *Prison Journal* 81(1): 87–112.

Easton, David. 1989. "The New Revolution in Political Science." *American Political Science Review* 63(4): 1051–61.

Edwards, Catherine. 1997. "Unspeakable Professions: Public Performance and Prostitution in Ancient Rome." In *Roman Sexualities*, edited by Judith Hallett and Marilyn Skinner, 66–97. Princeton: Princeton University Press.

Edwards, Catherine. 1993. *The Politics of Immorality in Ancient Rome.* Cambridge, Cambridge University Press.

Edwards, Susan. 1997. "The Legal Regulation of Prostitution: A Human Rights Issue.' In *Rethinking Prostitution: Purchasing Sex in the 1990s,* edited by Graham Scambler and Annette Scambler, 57–82. London: Routledge.

Ekberg, Gunilla. 2004. "The Swedish Law That Prohibits the Purchase of Sexual Service: Best Practices for Prevention of Prostitution and Trafficking in Human Beings." *Violence Against Women* 10(10): 1187–1218.

Elliot, Dominic and Martina McGuinness. 2002. "Public Inquiry: Panacea or Placebo." *Journal of Contingencies and Crisis Management* 10(1): 14–25.

Elliot, Ian and Anthony Beech. 2009. "Understanding Online Child Pornography Use: Applying Sexual Offense Theory to Internet Offenders." *Aggression and Violent Behaviour* 14(3): 180–93.

Elliot, Ian, Anthony Beech and Rebecca Mandeville-Nordon. 2012. "The Psychological Profiles of Internet, Contact, and Mixed Internet/Contact Sex Offenders." *Sexual Abuse: A Journal of Research and Treatment* 25(1): 3–20.

Ellison, Graham. 2012. "The Sex Trade in Northern Ireland: The Creation of a Moral Panic." Institute of Criminology and Criminal Justice Working Paper. Accessed 16 April 2015. http://papers.ssrn.com/sol3/papers.cfm?abstract_id=2184040

Ellison, Louise and Vanessa Munroe. 2009. "Reacting to Rape: Exploring Mock Jurors' Assessments of Complainant Credibility." *Journal of Criminology* 49(2): 202–19.

Elster, Jon. 1982. "The Case for Methodological Individualism." *Theory and Society* 11(4): 453–82.

Emsley, Clive. 1991. *The English Police: A Political and Social History.* Oxford: Routledge.

Eulau, H. 1963. *The Behavourial Persuasion in Politics.* New York: Random House.

European Commission. 2014. "A Digital Single Market for Europe—Analysis and Evidence." Accessed 14 July 2015. http://ec.europa.eu/priorities/digital-single-market/docs/dsm-swd_en.pdf

Family Safe Media. 2008. "Pornography statistics." Accessed 4 April 2015. http://familysafemedia.com/pornography_statistics.html#anchor8

Fantham, Elaine. 1975. "Sex, Status, and Survival in Hellenistic Athens: A Study of Women in New Comedy". Phoenix 29 (1). Classical Association of Canada: 44–74.

Fantham, Elaine. 1983. "Sexual Comedy in Ovid's Fasti: Sources and Motivation." *Harvard Studies in Classical Philology* 87: 185–216.

Faraone, Christopher and Laura McClure. 2006. *Prostitutes and Courtesans in the Ancient World.* Wisconsin: Wisconsin Press.

Farley, Melissa. 2004. "Bad for the Body, Bad for the Heart: Prostitution Harms Women Even If Legalized or Decriminalized." *Violence Against Women* 10(10): 1087–1125.

Farley, Melissa, Ann Cotton, Jacqueline Lynne, Sybille Zumbeck, Frida Spiwak, Maria Reyes, Dinorah Alvarez and Ufuk Sezgin. 2004. "Prostitution and Trafficking in Nine Countries: An Update on Violence and Posttraumatic Stress Disorder." *Journal of Trauma and Practice* 2(3-4): 33–74.

Faúndes, A. and E. Hardy. 1997. "Illegal Abortion: Consequences for Women's Health and the Health Care System." *International Journal of Gynecology and Obstetrics* 58(1): 77–83.

Feinman, Clarice. 1994. *Women in the Criminal Justice System.* Westport: Greenwood Publishing Group.

Fenno, Richard. 1978. *Home Style: House Members in Their District.* Boston: Little, Brown.

Ferguson, Christopher and Richard Hartley. 2009. "The Pleasure Is Momentary . . . The Expense Damnable? The Influence of Pornography on Rape and Sexual Assault." *Aggression and Violent Behaviour* 14: 323–29.

Finkelhor, David and Kersti Yllo. 1985. *License to Rape: Sexual Abuse of Wives.* New York: The Free Press.

Finnie, Sarah, Robbie Foy and Jean Mather. 2006. "The Pathway to Induced Abortion: Women's Experiences and General Practitioner Attitudes." *Journal of Family Planning and Reproductive Health Care* 32: 15–18.

Flowers, Barri. 1998. *The Prostitution of Women and Girls.* North Carolina: McFarland.

Fontaine, Paul. 2011. "High Demand for Prostitutes in Iceland." *The Reykjavik Grapevine*, 5 September. Accessed 11 July 2015. http://grapevine.is/news/2011/09/05/high-demand-for-prostitutes-in-iceland/

Forbes. 2005. "The (Porn) Player." 4 July. Accessed 16 January 2015. http://www.forbes.com/free_forbes/2005/0704/124.html

Foucault, Michel. 1978. *The History of Sexuality: Volume I: An Introduction*. New York: Pantheon Books.

Francome, Colin. 1976. "How Many Illegal Abortions? A Reply to Paul Cavadino." *British Journal of Criminology* 16(4): 389–92.

Frank, David, Tara Hardringe and Kassia Wosick-Correa. 2009. "The Global Dimensions of Rape-Law Reform: A Cross-National Study of Policy Outcomes." *American Sociological Review* 74(2): 272–90.

Franklin, Mark and Christopher Wlezien. 1997. "The Responsive Public Issue Salience, Policy Change, and Preferences for European Unification." *Journal of Theoretical Politics* 9(3): 347–63.

Fudge, Colin and Susan Barrett. 1981. "Reconstructing the Field of Analysis." In *Policy and Action: Essays on the Implementation of Public Policy*, edited by Susan Barrett and Colin Fudge, 249–78. London: Methuen.

Furness, Hannah. 2012. "Prostitutes cleaned off the street ahead of the Olympics." *The Telegraph*, 2 April. Accessed 26 January 2015. http://www.telegraph.co.uk/news/uknews/law-and-order/9180739/Prostitutes-cleaned-off-the-streets-ahead-of-the-Olympics.html

Galaway, Burt and Joe Hudson. 1996. *Restorative Justice: International Perspectives*. Monsey: Criminal Justice Press.

Garrelts, Nate. 2006. *The Meaning and Culture of Grand Theft Auto: Critical Essays*. North Carolina: McFarland and Company.

Geis, Gilbert. 1978. "Lord Hale, Witches and Rape." *British Journal of Law and Society* 5(1): 26–44.

Gelles, Richard. 1977. "Power, Sex, and Violence: The Case of Marital Rape." *Family Coordinator* 26(4): 339–47.

Genschel, Phillip. 1997. "The Dynamics of Inertia: Institutional Persistence and Change in Telecommunications and Health Care." *Governance* 10(1): 43–66.

Gilligan, Thomas and Keith Krehbiel. 1990. "Organization of Informative Committees by a Rational Legislature." *American Journal of Political Science* 34(2): 531–64.

Glasier, Anna. 1993. 'The Organisation of Abortion Service." *Current Obstetrics and Gynaecology* 3(1): 23–27.

Gleeson, Kate. 2007. "Persuading Parliament: Abortion Laws Reform in the UK." *Australasian Parliamentary Review* 22(2): 23–42.

Glifoye, Timothy. 1999. "Prostitutes in History: From Parables of Pornography to Metaphors of Modernity." *American Historical Review* 104(1): 117–41.

Glover, Jonathan. 1990. *Causing Death and Saving Lives*. London: Penguin Book.

Goldsmith, Michael. 2003. "Variable Geometry, Multilevel Governance: European Integration and Subnational Government in the New Millennium." In *The Politics of Europeanization*, edited by Kevin Featherstone and Claudio Radaelli. Oxford: Oxford University Press.

Goodall, Richard. 1995. *Comfort of Sin: Prostitutes and Prostitution in the 1990s*. Kent: Renaissance Books.

Gorman, Michael. 1998. *Abortion and the Early Church: Christian, Jewish, and Pagan Attitudes in the Greco-Roman World*. Oregon: Wipf and Stock Publishers.

Gould, Arthur. 2001. "The Criminalisation of Buying Sex: the Politics of Prostitution in Sweden." *Journal of Social Policy* 30(3): 437–56.

Gravett, Sandie. 2004. "Reading 'Rape' in the Hebrew Bible: A Consideration of the Language." *Journal of the Study of the Old Testament* 28(3): 279–99.

Grear, A. 2004. "The Curate, a Cleft Palate and Ideological Closure in the Abortion Act 1967–Time to Reconsider the Relationship between Doctors and the Abortion Decision." *Web Journal of Current Legal Issues* 4. Accessed 10 August 2010. http://webjcli.ncl.ac.uk/2004/issue4/rtf/grear4.rtf

Greer, Scott L. 2006. "Uninvited Europeanization: Neofunctionalism and the EU in Health Policy." *Journal of European Public Policy* 13(1): 134–52.

Greer, Steven. 2006. *The European Convention on Human Rights: Achievements, Problems and Prospects.* Cambridge: Cambridge University Press.

Gregory, Jeanne and Sue Lees. 1996. "Attrition in Rape and Sexual Assault Cases." *British Journal of Criminology* 36(1): 1–17.

Gresswell, David and Clive Hollin. 1994. "Multiple Murder: A Review." *British Journal of Criminology* 34(1): 1–14.

Grice, Andrew. 2014. "Nick Clegg backs face-sitting protesters over UK porn ban." 15 December, *The Independent.* Accessed 6 March 2015 http://www.independent.co.uk/news/uk/politics/nick-clegg-backs-facesitting-protesters-over-uk-porn-ban-9925991.html

Gubar, Susan. 1987. "Representing Pornography: Feminism, Criticism, and Depictions of Female Violation." *Critical Inquiry* 13(4): 712–41.

Guild, Elspeth. 1996. *The Developing Immigration and Asylum Policies of the European Union: Adopted Conventions, Resolutions, Recommendations, Decisions and Conclusions.* The Hague: Kluwer Law International.

Haas, Ernst. 1958. *The Uniting of Europe: Political, Economic and Social Forces, 1950-1957.* London: Stevens & Sons.

Hale, Matthew. 1734. *Historia Placitorum Coronae.* London: Nutt and Gosling.

Hall, Peter. 1986. *Governing the Economy: The Politics of Intervention in Britain and France.* Cambridge: Polity Press.

Hall, Peter and Patrick McGinty. 1997. "Policy as the Transformation of Intentions: Producing Program from Statute." *Sociological Quarterly* 38(3): 439–67.

Hall, Peter and Rosemary Taylor. 1996. "Political Science and the Three New Institutionalisms." *Political Studies* 44(5): 936–57.

Halverscheid, Susanna and Erich Witte. 2008. "Justification of War and Terrorism: A Comparative Case Study Analyzing Ethical Positions Based on Prescriptive Attribution Theory." *Social Psychology* 39(1): 26–36.

Hamilton, Fiona, Muhad Ahmed and Billy Kenbar. 2013. "Children are 'put at risk' as prostitutes use Facebook to sell their wares." *The Times*, 30 January. Accessed 15 November 2014. http://www.thetimes.co.uk/tto/technology/internet/article3672107.ece

Hamilton, Margaret. 1978. "Opposition to the Contagious Diseases Acts, 1864-1866." *Albion: A Quarterly Journal Concerned with British Studies* 10(1): 14–27.

Hanson, A. and M. Walles. 1975. *Governing Britain.* Glasgow: Fontana.

Harcourt, Bernard. 1999. "The Collapse of the Harm Principle." *Journal of Criminal Law and Criminology* 90(1): 109–94.

Harcourt, Christine and Basil Donovan. 2005. "The Many Faces of Sex Work." *Sexually Transmitted Infections* 81(3): 201–6.

Harris, Jose. 1994. *Private Lives, Public Spirit: Britian 1870-1914.* London, Penguin Books.

Harrison, Cynthia. 1989. *On Account of Sex: The Politics of Women's Issues, 1945-1968.* California, University of California Press.

Harrison, John. 1995. "Euthanasia and the Value of Life." In *Euthanasia Examined: Ethical, Clinical and Legal Perspectives*, edited by John Keown, 6–22. Cambridge: Cambridge University Press.

Harrison, Paul and David Wilson. 2008. *Hunting Evil: Inside the Ipswich Serial Murder.* London: Sphere.

Hart, Herbert. 1963. *Law, Liberty and Morality.* Oxford: Oxford University Press.

Hartmann, Uwe. 2009. "Sigmund Freud and His Impact on Our Understanding of Male Sexual Dysfunction." *Journal of Sexual Medicine* 6(8): 232–39.

HC Deb 21 June 1990 vol. 174, col. 1199.

HC Deb 22 October 2008 c327.

Hejduk, Julia. 2011. "Epic Rapes in the Fasti." *Classical Philology* 106(1): 20–31.

Held, David and Adrian Leftwich. 1984. "A Discipline of Politics?" In *What Is Politics: The Activity and Its Study,* edited by Adrian Leftwich. Oxford: Basil Blackwell.

Henkin, Louis, Gerald Neuman, Diane Orentlicher and David Leebron. 1999. *Human Rights.* New York: Foundation Press.

Her Majesty's Inspectorate of Constabulary. 2014a. "Crime Recording: Making the Victim Count." Accessed 12 July 2014. https://www.justiceinspectorates.gov.uk/hmic/wp-content/uploads/crime-recording-making-the-victim-count.pdf

Her Majesty's Inspectorate of Constabulary. 2014b. "Crime Recording: A Matter of Fact. An Interim Report of the Inspection of Crime Data Integrity in Police Forces in England and Wales." Accessed 5 February 2015. https://www.justiceinspectorates.gov.uk/hmic/wp-content/uploads/2014/05/crime-data-integrity-interim-report.pdf

Herbert, Steve. 1998. "Police Culture Reconsidered." *Criminology* 36(2): 343–70.

Hibbing, John. 1988. "Legislative Institutionalization with Illustrations from the British House of Commons." *American Journal of Political Science* 32(3): 681–712.

Hibbing, John and David Marsh. 1987. "Accounting for the Voting Patterns of British MPs on Free Votes." *Legislative Studies Quarterly* 12(2): 375–97.

Hilliard, Christopher. 2013. "'Is It a Book That You Would Even Wish Your Wife or Your Servants to Read?' Obscenity Law and the Politics of Reading in Modern England." *American Historical Review* 11(3): 653–78.

Hindell, Keith and Madeleine Simms. 1968. "How the Abortion Lobby Worked." *Political Quarterly* 39(3): 269–82.

Hindmoor, Andrew. 2009. "Explaining Networks through Mechanisms: Vaccination, Priming and the 2001 Foot and Mouth Disease Crisis." *Political Studies* 57(1): 75–94.

Hirschman, Elizabeth and Barbara Stern. 1994. "Women as Commodities: Prostitution as Depicted in the Blue Angel, *Pretty Baby*, and *Pretty Woman*." *Advances in Consumer Research* 21: 576–81.

Hobbes, T. and C. MacPherson, ed. 1982. *Leviathan*. London: Penguin Books.

Hoff, Joan. 1989. "Why Is There No History of Pornography." In *For Adult Users Only: The Dilemma of Violent Pornography*, edited by Susan Gubar and Joan Hoff, 17–46. Bloomington: Indiana University Press.

Högberg, Ulf and Ingemar Joelsson. 1985. "The Decline in Maternal Mortality in Sweden, 1931-1980." *Acta Obstetrica et Gynaecologica Scandinavica* 64(7): 583–92.

Holehouse, Matthew. 2015. "Council chiefs who ignore child abuse will be jailed." *The Telegraph*, 3 February. Accessed 12 June 2015. http://www.telegraph.co.uk/news/uknews/law-and-order/11445791/Council-chiefs-who-ignore-child-abuse-will-be-jailed.html

Holmes, Melisa, Heidi Resnick, Dean Kilpatrick and Connie Best. 1996. "Rape-Related Pregnancy: Estimates and Descriptive Characteristics from a National Sample of Women." *American Journal of Obstetrics and Gynaecology* 175(2): 320–25.

Holy Bible: New Revised Standard Anglicized Version. 2001. Oxford: Oxford University Press.

Home Office. 2000. *Setting the Boundaries: Reforming the Law on Sex Offences*. London: HMSO.

Home Office. 2001. *Circular 27/2001—Criminal Justice and Police Act 2001 Section 46 and 47: Advertisements Relating to Prostitution*. London, HMSO.

Home Office. 2004. *Paying the Price: A Consultation Paper on Prostitution*. London: HMSO.

Home Office. 2005. *Consultation: On the Possession of Extreme Pornographic Material*. London: HMSO.

Home Office. 2008. *Tackling the Demand for Prostitution: A Review*. London: HMSO.

Home Office. 2011. *A Review of Effective Practice in Responding to Prostitution*. London: HMSO.

Home Affairs Committee. 2009. *The Macpherson Report—Ten Years On*. London: HMSO.

Hood, Christopher. 2011. *The Blame Game: Spin, Bureaucracy, and Self-Preservation in Government*. Princeton: Princeton University Press.

Horgan, Goretti. 2006. "Devolution, Direct Rule and Neo-Liberal Reconstruction in Northern Ireland." *Critical Social Policy* 26(3): 656–68.

House of Lords. 2014. Communication Committee—First Report: Social Media and Criminal Offences. http://www.publications.parliament.uk/pa/ld201415/ldselect/ldcomuni/37/3702.htm

Howell, Phillip. 2000. "A Private Contagious Diseases Act: Prostitution and Public Space in Victorian Cambridge." *Journal of Historical Geography* 26(3): 376–402.

Howitt, Dennis 1995. "Pornography and the Paedophile: Is It Criminogenic." *British Journal of Medical Psychology* 68(1): 15–27.

Htun, Mala, and S. Laurel Weldon. 2010. "When Do Governments Promote Women's Rights? A Framework for the Comparative Analysis of Sex Equality Policy." *Perspectives on Politics* 8(1): 207–16.

Hubbard, Phil. 1998. "Sexuality, Immorality and the City: Red-Light Districts and the Marginalisation of Female Street Prostitutes." *Gender, Place and Culture: A Journal of Feminist Geography* 5(1): 55–76.

Hubbard, Phil. 2002. "Maintaining Family Values? Cleansing the Streets of Sex Advertising." *Area* 34(4): 353–60.

Huber, Evelyne and John Stephens. 2001. *Development and Crisis of the Welfare State.* Chicago: University of Chicago Press.

Huffington Post. 2014. "Jennifer Lawrence Naked Pictures: Ricky Gervais Takes Comfort from 'Porridge' after Twitter Backlash to his Comments." Accessed 26 April 2015. http://www.huffingtonpost.co.uk/2014/09/02/naked-pictures-jennifer-lawrence-ricky-gervais-twitter-backlash_n_5751058.html

Immergut, Ellen. 1990. "Institutions, Veto Points, and Policy Results: A Comparative Analysis of Health Care." *Journal of Public Policy* 10(4): 319-416.

Immergut, Ellen. 1998. "The Theoretical Core of the New Institutionalisms." *Politics and Society* 26: 5–34.

Ingram, Paul and Karen Clay. 2000. "The Choice-Within-Constraints New Institutionalism and Implications for Sociology," *Annual Review of Sociology* 26: 525–46.

IPCC. 2006. Stockwell Two. http://webarchive.nationalarchives.gov.uk/20100908152737/http://www.ipcc.gov.uk/ipcc_stockwell_2.pdf.

Iyengar, Sharad. 2005. "Introducing Medical Abortion within the Primary Health System: Comparison with Other Health Interventions and Commodities." *Reproductive Health Matters* 13(26): 13–19.

Jackson, Emily. 2013. "The Legality of Abortion for Fetal Sex" in BPAS (ed.) *British Pregnancy Advisory Service Britain's Abortion Law: What It Says, and Why.* http://www.reproductivereview.org/images/uploads/Britains_abortion_law.pdf

Jackson, Gregory, Actors and Institutions. *Oxford Handbook of Comparative Institutional Analysis*, Glenn Morgan, John Campbell, Colin Crouch, Ove Pedersen, Peer H. Christensen, Richard Whitley, eds., Oxford: Oxford University Press, 2010.

Jacoby, William. 2000. "Issue Framing and Public Opinion on Government Spending." *American Journal of Political Science* 44(4): 750–67.

Jakobsson, Niklas and Andreas Kotsadam. 2013. "The Law and Economics of International Sex Slavery: Prostitution Laws and Trafficking for Sexual Exploitation." *European Journal of Law and Economics* 35(1): 87–107.

Janis, Mark, Richard Kay and Anthony Wilfred Bradley. 2008. *European Human Rights Law: Text and Materials.* Oxford: Oxford University Press.

Jewel, Malcolm and Samuel Patterson. 1977. *The Legislative Process in the United States.* New York: Random House.

Johnson, James, Lee Jackson, Leslie Gatto and Amy Nowak. 1995. "Differential Male and Female Responses to Inadmissible Sexual History Information Regarding a Rape Victim." *Basic and Applied Social Psychology* 16(4): 503 –13.

Johnson, Phillip. 2010. "Crossbow Cannibal: No one is safe from the menace of pure evil." *The Telegraph* , 22 December. Accessed 22 June 2015. http://www.telegraph.co.uk/comment/columnists/philipjohnston/8219700/Crossbow-Cannibal-No-one-is-safe-from-the-menace-of-pure-evil.html

Jones, Cathaleene and Elliot Aronson. 1973. "Attribution of Fault to a Rape Victim as a Function of Respectability of the Victim." *Journal of Personality and Social Psychology* 26(3): 415–19.

Jordan, Jan. 2011. "Here We Go Round the Review-Go-Round: Rape Investigation and Prosecution—Are Things Getting Worse Not Better?" *Journal of Sexual Aggression: An International, Interdisciplinary Forum for Research, Theory and Practice* 17(3): 234–49.

Kalven, Harry. 1960. "The Metaphysics of the Law of Obscenity." *The Supreme Court Review* 1960, 1–45.

Kantola, Johanna and Judith Squires. 2004. "Discourses Surrounding Prostitution Policies in the UK." *European Journal of Women's Studies* 11(1): 77–101.

Kapardis, Andreas and Maria Krambia-Karpardis. 2004. "Enhancing Fraud Prevention and Detection by Profiling Fraud Offenders." *Criminal Behaviour and Health* 14(3): 189–201.

Katznelson, Ira and Barry Weingast. 2005. *Preferences and Situations: Points of Intersection Between Historical and Rational Choice Institutionalism*. New York: Russell Sage.

Kay, Joyce. 2008. "It Wasn't Just Emily Davison! Sport, Suffrage and Society in Edwardian Britain." *International Journal of the History of Sport* 25(10): 1338– 54.

Keating, Heather, Sally Cunningham, Tracey Elliot and Mark Walters. 2014. Eighth Edition. *Clarkson and Keating: Criminal Law: Text and Materials*. London: Sweet and Maxwell.

Kelley, Karol. 1994. "A Modern Cinderella." *Journal of American Culture* 17(1): 87–92.

Kelly, Liz, Jo Lovett and Linda Regan. 2005. "Gap or a Chasm? Attrition in Reported Rape Cases." *Home Office Research Study* 293.

Kennedy, Ian and Andrew Grubb. 2000. *Medical Law*. London: Butterworths.

Keown, John. 1988. *Abortion, Doctors and the Law: Some Aspects of the Legal Regulation of Abortion in England from 1803 to 1982*. Cambridge: Cambridge University Press.

Keown, John. 2006. "Back to the Future of Abortion Law: Roe's Rejection of America's History and Traditions." *Issues in Law and Medicine* 22(3): 3–38.

King, Gary, Robert Keohane and Sidney Verba. 1994. *Designing Social Inquiry: Scientific Inference in Qualitative Research*. Princeton: Princeton University Press.

Kingdon, John. 1995. *Agenda, Alternatives and Public Policies*. Longman: New York.

Kingdon, John W., and James A. Thurber. 1984. *Agendas, Alternatives, and Public Policies*, Vol. 45. Boston: Little, Brown.

Kowal, Donna. 2000. "One Cause, Two Paths: Militant vs. Adjustive Strategies in the British and American's Women's Suffrage Movements." *Communication Quarterly* 48(3): 240–55.

Krahé, Barbra. 1991. "Police Officers' Definitions of Rape: A Prototype Study." *Journal of Community and Applied Social Psychology* 1: 223–44.

Krasner, Stephen. 1988. "Sovereignty: An Institutional Perspective." *Comparative Political Studies* 21: 66–94.

Kraut, Richard. 2002. *Aristotle Political Philosophy*. Oxford: Oxford University Press.

Krook, Mona Lena and Fiona Mackay, eds. 2010. *Gender, Politics and Institutions: Towards a Feminist Institutionalism*. Basingstoke: Palgrave MacMillan.

Kubler, Daniel. 2001. "Understanding Policy Change with the Advocacy Coalition Framework: An Application to Swiss Drug Policy." *Journal of European Public Policy* 8(4): 623–41.

Kulczyski, Andrzej. 2003. "Demographic Research and Abortion Policy: Limits to the Use of Statistics." In *The Sociocultural and Political Aspects of Abortion: Global Perspectives,* edited by Alaka Malwade Basu, 65–78. Westport: Praeger.

Kutchinsky, Berl. 1991. "Pornography and Rape: Theory and Practice? Evidence from Crime Data in Four Countries Where Pornography Is Easily Available." *International Journal of Law and Psychiatry* 14(1-2): 47–64.

Lanktree, Graham. 2015. "EU Law That Could Make UK Internet Porn Filter Illegal Is Heading for a Vote." *International Business Times*, 13 July. Accessed 14 July 2015. http://www.ibtimes.co.uk/eu-law-that-could-make-uk-porn-filters-illegal-heading-vote-1510673

Lape, Susan. 2001. "Democratic Ideology and The Poetics of Rape in Menandrian Comedy." *Classical Antiquity* 20(1): 79–119.

Law Society Gazette. 2013. "CPS under Fire for Failures in Two Serious Cases." http://www.lawgazette.co.uk/news/cps-under-fire-for-failures-in-two-serious-cases/71491.fullarticle

Layden, Mary Anne. Undated. "Pornography and Violence: A New Look at Research." University of Pennsylvania. http://www.socialcostsofpornography.com/Layden_Pornography_and_Violence.pdf

Lea, Susan, Ursula Lanvers and Steve Shaw. 2003. "Attrition in Rape Cases. Developing a Profile and Identifying Relevant Factors." *British Journal of Criminology* 43(3): 583–99.

Lea, Susan. 2007. "A Discursive Investigation into Victim Responsibility in Rape." *Feminism and Psychology* 17(4): 495–514.

Lee, Ellie, ed. 1998. *Abortion Law and Politics Today*. Basingstoke: Palgrave Macmillan.

Lee, Robert and Derek Morgan. 2001. *Human Fertilisation and Embryology: Regulating the Reproductive Revolution*. London: Blackstone Press.

Levi, E. 1973. "The Collective Morality of a Maturing Society." *Washington and Lee Law Review* 30(3): 399–421.

Levine, Phillipa. 1994. "Venereal Disease, Prostitution, and the Politics of Empire: The Case of British India." *Journal of the History of Sexuality* 4(4): 579–602.

Levy, Jay. 2014. *Criminalising the Purchase of Sex: Lessons from Sweden*. London: Routledge.

Lewis, Jane and Mary Campbell. 2007. "UK Work/Family Balance Policies and Gender Equality, 1997-2005." *Social Politics* 14(1): 4–30.

Lieb, Roxanne. 2000. "Social Policy and Sexual Offenders: Contrasting United States and European Policies." *European Journal on Criminal Policy and Research* 8(4): 423–40.

Lila, Marisol, Enrique Gracia and Sergio Murgui. 2013. "Psychological Adjustment and Victim-Blaming among Intimate Partner Violence Offenders: The Role of Social Support and Stressful Life Events." *European Journal of Psychology Applied to Legal Context* 5(2): 147–53.

Lilford, R. and D. Braunholtz. 1996. "For Debate: The Statistical Basis of Public Policy: A Paradigm Shift Is Overdue." *British Medical Journal* 313: 603–7.

Lipsky, Michael. 2010. *Street Level Bureaucracy: Dilemmas of the Individual in Public Services*. New York: Russell Sage.

Lister, Ruth. 1998. "From Equality to Social Inclusion: New Labour and the Welfare State." *Critical Social Policy* 18(55): 215–25.

Loftus, Bethan. 2008. "Dominant Culture Interrupted: Recognition, Resentment and the Politics of Change in an English Police Force." *British Journal of Criminology* 48(6): 756–77.

Long, Billy. 2012. "Freedom for Women in the Sex Work Occupation: Twenty-Three Reasons Why Prostitution Should Be Legalized in America." *International Journal of Humanities and Social Science* 2(16): 23–33.

Long, Julia. 2012. *Anti-Porn: The Resurgence of Anti-Pornography Feminism*. London: Zed Books.

Lovenduski, Joni. 1986. *Women and European Politics: Contemporary Feminism and Public Policy*. London: University of Massachusetts Press.

Lovenduski, Joni and Joyce Outshoorn. 1986. *The New Politics of Abortion*. London: Sage Publications.

Lovenduski, Joni and Vicky Randall. 1993. *Contemporary Feminist Politics: Women and Power in Britain*. Oxford: Oxford University Press.

Lovenduski, Joni and Pippa Norris. 2003. "Westminster Women: the Politics of Prescence." *Political Studies* 51(1): 84–102.

Lowndes, Vivien. 2002. "Institutionalism." In *Theory and Methods in Political Science*, edited by David Marsh and Gerry Stoker, 90–108. London: Palgrave Macmillan.

Lowndes, Vivien and Mark Roberts. 2013. *Why Institutions Matter: The New Institutionalism in Political Science*. Basingstoke: Palgrave Macmillan.

Mackay, Fiona. 2004. "Gender and Political Representation in the UK: The State of the 'Discipline.'" *British Journal of Politics and International Relations* 6(1): 99–120.

Macpherson, William. 1999. *The Stephen Lawrence Inquiry*. London: HMSO.

Mahood, Linda. 1990. "The Magdalene's Friend: Prostitution and Social Control in Glasgow, 1869-1890." *Women's Studies International Forum* 13(1-2): 49–61.

Manchester, Colin. 1988. "Lord Campbell's Act: England's First Obscenity Statute." *Journal of Legal History* 9(2): 223–41.

Manners, Ian. 2002. "Normative Power Europe: A Contradiction in Terms?" *Journal of Common Market Studies* 40: 235–58.

March, James and Johan Olsen. 1984. "The New Institutionalism: Organizational Factors in Political Life." *American Political Science Review* 78(2): 734–39.

March, James and Johan Olsen. 1989. *Rediscovering Institutions: The Organizational Basis of Politics*. New York: The Free Press.

Marcus, Steven. 1966. *The Other Victorians: A Study of Sexuality and Pornography in Mid-Nineteenth Century England*. New Jersey: Transaction Publishers.

Marneffe, Peter de. 2010. *Liberalism and Prostitution*. Oxford: Oxford University Press.
Marsden, Sam and Victoria Ward. 2013. "Tia Sharp Murder: Stuart Hazell Changes His Plea to Guilty." *The Telegraph*, 13 May. Accessed 2 January 2015. http://www.telegraph.co.uk/news/uknews/crime/10053483/Tia-Sharp-murder-Stuart-Hazell-changes-his-plea-to-guilty.html
Marsh, D., P. Gowin and M. Read. 1986. "Private Members Bills and Moral Panic: The Case of the Video Recordings Bill." *Parliamentary Affairs* 39(2): 179–96.
Marshall, Tony. 1996. "The Evolution of Restorative Justice in Britain." *European Journal on Criminal Policy and Research* 4(4): 21–43.
Marshall, William. 1988. "The Use of Sexually Explicit Stimuli by Rapists, Child Molesters, and Nonoffenders." *Journal of Sex Research* 25(2): 267–88.
March, James and Olsen, Johan. 2008. "The Logic of Appropriateness." In Moran, Michael, Martin Rein, and Robert E. Goodin, *The Oxford Handbook of Public Policy*. Oxford: Oxford University Press, 689–708.
Martin, Elaine, Casey Taft and Patricia Resick. 2007. "A Review of Marital Rape." *Aggression and Violent Behavior* 12(3): 329–47.
Martinez, Michelle and Tyler Manolovitz. 2010. "Pornography of Gaming." In *Videogame Cultures and the Future of Interactive Entertainment,* edited by Robert Fisher and Daniel Riha, 65–74. Oxford: Inter-Disciplinary Press.
Martinsen, Dorte Sindbjerg, and Karsten Vrangbaek. 2008. "The Europeanization of Health Care Governance: Implementing the Market Imperatives of Europe." *Public Administration* 86(1): 169–84.
Marx, Brian P., John P. Forsyth, Gordon G. Gallup, and Tiffany Fusé. 2008. "Tonic immobility as an evolved predator defense: Implications for sexual assault survivors." *Clinical Psychology: Science and Practice* 15, no. 1: 74–90.
Mason, Karen. 1986. "The Status of Women: Conceptual and Methodological Issues in Demographic Studies." *Sociological Forum*, 1(2): 284–300.
Mason, Kenyon and Graeme Laurie. 2002. *Law and Medical Ethics*. Lexis Nexis: London.
Masselot, Annick. 2007. "The State of Gender Equality Law in the European Union." *European Law Journal* 13(2): 152–68.
Matland, Richard. 1995. "Synthesizing the Implementation Literature: The Ambiguity-Conflict Model of Policy Implementation." *Journal of Public Administration Research and Theory* 5(2): 145–74.
Matthews, Roger. 1997. *Prostitution in London: An Audit*. Middlesex: Middlesex University.
Mayo, M. 1977. *Women in the Community*. London: Routledge.
Mazur, Amy. 2002. *Theorizing Feminist Policy*. Oxford: Oxford University Press.
McBride Stetson, Dorothy. 2001. "Women's Movements' Defence of Legal Abortion in Great Britain." In *Abortion Politics, Women's Movements and the Democratic State: A Comparative Study of State Feminism*, edited by Dorothy McBride Stetson, D, 1–16. Oxford: Oxford University Press.
McDermott, Joan and Sarah Blackstone. 2002. "Lilith in Myth, Melodrama, and Criminology." *Women and Criminal Justice* 13(1): 85–98.
McDonald, Henry. 2014. "Plans to reform Ulster prostituion laws are unworkable, says justice minister." *The Guardian*, 21 April. Accessed 5 June 2015. http://www.theguardian.com/uk-news/2014/apr/21/plans-reform-ulster-prostitution-laws-unworkable
McDonald, Myra. 1995. *Representing Women: Myths of Femininity in the Popular Media*. New York: St. Martin's Press.
McGee, Hannah, Madeline O'Higgins, Rebecca Garavan and Ronan Conroy. 2011. "Rape and Child Sexual Abuse: What Beliefs Persist about Motives, Perpetrators, and Survivors." *Journal of Interpersonal Violence* 26(17): 1157–71.
McGinn, Thomas. 1998. *Prostitution, Sexuality and the Law in Ancient Rome*. Oxford: Oxford University Press.
McHugh, Paul. 2013. *Prostitution and Victorian Social Reform*. Oxford: Routledge.
McLaughlin, Eugene and Karim Muriji. 1999. "After the Stephen Lawrence Report." *Critical Social Policy* 371–85.

McMillan, Lesley and Michelle Thomas. 2009. "Police Interviews of Rape Victims: Tensions and Contradictions." In *Rape: Challenging Contemporary Thinking*, edited by Miranda Horvath and Jennifer Brown, 255–80. Cullompton: Willan Publishing.

McNair, Brian. 2009. "Teaching Porn." *Sexualities* 12(5): 558–67.

McNair, Brian. 2013. *Porno? Chic! How Pornography Changed the World and Made It a Better Place.* London: Routledge.

McRobbie, Angela. 2004. "Notes on Postfeminism and Popular Culture: Bridget Jones and the New Gender Regime." In *All About the Girl: Culture, Power and Identity*, edited by Anita Harris, 3–14. London: Routledge.

Means, Cyril. 1971. "The Phoenix of Abortional Freedom: Is a Penumbral or Ninth-Amendment Right about to Arise from the Nineteenth-Century Legislative Ashes of a Fourteenth-Century Common-Law Liberty?" *New York Law Forum* 17(2): 162–89.

Meier, Kenneth and Jill-Nicholson-Crotty. 2006. "Gender, Representative Bureaucracy, and Law Enforcement: The Case of Sexual Assault." *Public Administration Review* 66(6): 850–60.

Meikle, James. 2014. "Mike Tyson Banned from UK over Rape Conviction." *The Guardian*, 10 December. Accessed 3 July 2014. http://www.theguardian.com/uk-news/2013/dec/10/mike-tyson-banned-uk-rape-conviction

Meredith, Charlotte. 2014. 'Twitter rape abuse victim left terrified by late night 'harrassment' at home'. *Daily Express*, 24 December. Accessed 13 April 2015. http://www.express.co.uk/news/uk/418265/EXCLUSIVE-Twitter-rape-abuse-victim-left-terrified-by-late-night-harassment-at-her-home

Meyer, John and Brian Rowan. 1977. "Institutionalizing Organizations: Formal Structures as Myth and Ceremony." *American Journal of Sociology* 83(2): 340–63.

Miller, Jody and Martin Schwartz. 1995. "Rape Myths and Violence against Street Prostitutes." *Deviant Behavior* 16(1): 1–23.

Ministry of Justice. 2010. *Providing Anonymity to Those Accused of Rape: An Assessment of Evidence.* Accessed 15 June 2015. https://www.justice.gov.uk/downloads/publications/research-and-analysis/moj-research/anonymity-rape-research-report.pdf

Ministry of Justice, Home Office and the Office for National Statistics. 2013a. *An Overview of Sexual Offending in England and Wales.* London: HMSO.

Ministry of Justice. 2013b. *Proven Re-offending Quarterly July 2010 to June 2011.* London: HMSO.

Mitchell, Kimberly, David Finkelhor and Janis Wolak. 2003. "The Exposure of Youth to Unwanted Sexual Material on the Internet: A National Survey of Risk, Impact, and Prevention." *Youth and Society* 34(3): 330–58.

Moglen, Helene. 1984. *Charlotte Bronte: The Self Conceived.* London: University of Wisconsin Press.

Montgomery, Jonathan. 1991. "Rights, Restraints and Pragmatism." *Modern Law Review* 54(4): 524–34.

Moravcsik, Andrew. 1998. *The Choice for Europe; Social Purpose and State Power from Messina to Maastricht.* Ithaca: Cornell University Press.

Morris, Allison. 1987. *Women, Crime and Criminal Justice.* London: Blackwell's.

Mosher, Donald. 1988. "Pornography Defined: Sexual Involvement Theory, Narrative Context, and Goodness-of-Fit." *Journal of Psychology and Human Sexuality* 1(1): 67–85.

Moss, David. 2004. *When All Else Fails: Government as the Ultimate Risk Manager.* Boston: Harvard University Press.

Mumsnet. 2012. "Mumsnet Rape and Sexual Assault Survey Results." Accessed 8 September 2014. http://www.mumsnet.com/campaigns/we-believe-you-campaign-survey-on-rape-and-sexual-assault.

Munro, Vanessa and Marina Della Giusta. 2008. *Demanding Sex: Critical Reflections on the Regulation of Prostitution.* Aldershot: Ashgate Publishing Limited.

Myhill, Andy and Ben Bradford. 2013. "Overcoming Cop Culture? Organizational Justice and Police Officers' Attitudes toward the Public." *Policing: An International Journal of Police Strategies & Management* 36(2): 338–56.

Nakamura, Robert and Frank Smallwood. 1980. *The Politics of Implementation.* New York: St. Martin's.

National Union of Students. 2014. Student Opinion Survey: November 2014. http://www.nus.org.uk/Global/SRE%20Research%20Nov%202014.pdf

Nead, Lynda. 1997. "Mapping the Self: Gender, Space and Modernity in Mid-Victorian London." In *Rewriting the Self: Histories from the Middle Ages to the Present,* edited by Roy Porter, 167–85. London: Routledge.

Newburn, Tim and Elizabeth-Anne Stanko. 1994. *Just Boys Doing Business? Men, Masculinities and Crime.* London: Routledge.

Newlands, Carole. 1995. *Playing with Time: Ovid and the Fasti, Volume 55.* Ithaca: Cornell University Press.

Newman, Melanie. 2014. "Revealed: Why the Police Are Failing Most Rape Victims." Accessed 29 October 2014. http://www.thebureauinvestigates.com/2014/02/28/revealed-why-the-police-are-failing-most-rape-victims/.

New York Times. 2004. "Best-Seller Lists." 5 September. Accessed 28 September 2014. http://www.nytimes.com/2004/09/05/books/bestseller/0905besthardnonfiction.html

North, Douglas. 1990. *Institutions, Institutional Change, and Economic Performance.* New York: Cambridge University Press.

Northern Ireland Department of Justice. 2014. *The Criminal Law on Abortion: Lethal Foetal Abnormality and Sexual Crime.* Belfast: Criminal Policy Branch.

Norton, Phillip. 2001. "Playing by the Rules: The Constraining Hand of Parliamentary Procedure." *Journal of Legislative Studies* 7(3): 13–33.

Nye, Robert. 2003. "The Evolution of the Concept of Medicalisation in the Late Twentieth Century." *Journal of the History of the Behavioural Sciences* 39: 115–29.

OECD Gender Initiative. 2011. "Gender equality: Education, employment, entrepreneurship." In *Women and the Economy Summit, USA 2011.*

Ofcom. 2014. "Report on Internet safety measures. Internet Service Providers: Network level filtering measures." http://stakeholders.ofcom.org.uk/binaries/internet/internet_safety_measures_2.pdf.

Office for National Statistics. 2014a. "United Kingdon National Accounts, The Blue Book." Accessed 2 January 2015. http://www.ons.gov.uk/ons/rel/naa1-rd/united-kingdom-national-accounts/the-blue-book--2014-edition/index.html

Office for National Statistics. 2014b. "Statistical Bulletin: Crime in England and Wales, Year Ending March 2014." Accessed 2 March 2015. http://www.ons.gov.uk/ons/rel/crime-stats/crime-statistics/period-ending-march-2014/stb-crime-stats.html#tab-Sexual-Offences-

Omitowoju, Rosanna. 2002. "Regulating Rape: Soap Operas and Self-Interest in the Athenian Courts." In *Rape in Antiquity: Sexual Violence in the Greek and Roman Worlds,* edited by Susan Deacy and Karen Pierce, 1–24. London: Gerald Duckworth and Co. Ltd.

O'Neill, Maggie. 2001. *Prostitution and Feminism.* Cambridge: Polity Press.

O'Neill, Maggie. 2013. *Prostitution and Feminism: Towards a Politics of Feeling.* Oxford: Blackwell.

Outshoorn, Joyce. 2004. *The Politics of Prostitution: Women's Movements, Democratic States and the Globalisation of Sex Commerce.* Cambridge: Cambridge University Press.

Padawer, Ruth. 2009. "Keeping Up with Being Kept." *New York Times,* 20 April. Accessed 4 June 2014. http://www.nytimes.com/2009/04/12/magazine/12sugardaddies-t.html?pagewanted=all

Painter, Kate and David Farrington. 1998. "Marital Violence in Great Britian and Its Relationship to Marital and Non-Marital Rape." *International Review of Victimology* 1998(5): 257–76.

Parton, Nigel. 2013. *The Politics of Child Protection: Contemporary Developments and Future Directions.* Basingstoke: Palgrave Macmillan.

Pawson, Ray. 2002. "Evidence and Policy and Naming and Shaming." *Policy Studies* 23(3): 211–30.

Payne, S. 2009. *Rape: The Victim Experience Review.* London: HMSO.

Pazol, Karen, Andreea Creanga, Kim Burley, Brenda Hayes and Denise Jamieson. 2013. "Abortion Surveillance United States, 2010." *Morbidity and Mortality Weekly Report* 62(8): 1–44.

Perry, Claire. 2012. "Independent Parliamentary Inquiry into Online Child Protection: Findings and Recommendations." Accessed 3 March 2015. http://www.claireperry.org.uk/downloads/independent-parliamentary-inquiry-into-online-child-protection.pdf

Peters, B. Guy. 1996. "Political Institutions Old and New." In *A New Handbook of Political Science*, edited by Robert and Hans-Dieter Klingemann, 205–21. Oxford: Oxford University Press.

Peters, B. Guy. 2005. *Institutional Theory in Political Science: the New Institutionalism.* London: Continuum.

Peters, B. Guy. 2011. *Institutional Theory in Political Science: The New Institutionalism.* London: Pinter.

Pidd, Helen. 2014. "Sheffield United Urged Not to Re-Sign Rapist Ched Evans." *The Guardian*, 13 August. Accessed 26 September 2015. http://www.theguardian.com/football/2014/aug/13/sheffield-united-ched-evans-rape-re-sign-prison

Pierson, Paul. 2000. "Increasing Returns, Path Dependence, and the Study of Politics." *American Political Science Review* 94(2): 251–67.

Plucknett, Theodore. 2001. *Concise History of the Common Law.* New Jersey: The Lawbook Exchange.

Pollard, Paul. 1992. "Judgements about Victims and Attackers in Depicted Rapes: A Review." *British Journal of Social Psychology* 31(4): 307–26.

Pollitt, Christopher. 2003. "Joined-Up Government: A Survey." *Political Studies Review* 1(1): 34–49.

Pope, Catherine and Nicholas Mays. 2006. *Qualitative Research in Health Care.* Oxford: Blackwell.

Potts, Malcolm, Peter Diggory and John Peel. 1977. *Abortion.* Cambridge: Cambridge University Press.

Powell, Gary. 1990. "One More Time: Do Female and Male Managers Differ?" *The Executive* 4(3): 68–75.

ProLife. 2009. "Nurses Against Early Medical Abortions." 20 April. Accessed 15 June 2015. http://prolife.org.uk/2009/04/nurses-against-early-medical-abortions/

Quayle, Ethel and Max Taylor. 2002. "Child Pornography and the Internet: Perpetuating a Cycle of Abuse." *Deviant Behaviour* 23(4): 331–61.

Radner, Hilary and Moya Luckett. 1999. *Swinging Single: Representing Sexuality in the 1960s.* Minneapolis: University of Minnesota Press.

Ramanna, Mridula. 2000. "Control and Resistance: The Working of the Contagious Diseases Acts in Bombay City". *Economic and Political Weekly* 35 (17). *Economic and Political Weekly* 1470–76.

Rasmussen, Jorgen and James McCormick. 1985. "The Influence of Ideology on British Labour MPs in Voting on EEC Issues." *Legislative Studies Quarterly* 10(2): 203–21.

Razavi, Lauren. 2014. "No spanking or bondage: Why the government's new porn laws are arbitrary and sexist." NewStatesman. Accessed 17 January 2015. http://www.newstatesman.com/politics/2014/12/government-s-new-porn-laws-are-arbitrary-and-sexist

Raymond, Janie. 2004. "Ten Reasons for Not Legalizing Prostitution and a Legal Response to the Demand for Prostitution." *Journal of Trauma Practice* 2(3-4): 315–32.

RCOG. 2011. *The Care of Women Requesting Induced Abortion: Evidence Based Clinical Guideline Number 7.* Hampshire: Hobbs The Printer.

Rees, Gethin. 2010. "'It Is Not for Me to Say Whether Consent Was Given or Not: Forensic Medical Examiners' Construction of 'Neutral Reports' in Rape Cases." *Social Legal Studies* 19(3): 371–86.

Rein, Martin and Donald Schön. 1993. "Reframing Policy Discourse." In *The Argumentative Turn in Policy Analysis and Planning*, edited by Frank Fischer and John Forester, 145–65. London: UCL Press.

Reiner, Robert. 2010. Fourth Edition. *The Politics of the Police.* Oxford: Oxford University Press.

Rex v Bourne. 1938. *Lancet* 232: 220–26.

Rich, Frank. 2001. "Naked Capitalists: There's No Business like Porn Business." *New York Times*. Accessed 16 April 2015. http://www.nytimes.com/2001/05/20/magazine/20PORN.html

Rich, Ruby. 1983. "Anti-Porn: Soft Issue, Hard World." *Feminist Review* 13(Spring): 56–67.

Richardson, Jeremy. 1996. *European Union: Power and Policy-Making*. New York: Routledge.

Riddle, John. 1992. *Contraception and Abortion from the Ancient World to the Renaissance*. Harvard: Harvard University Press.

Roberts, Michael. 1985. "Morals, Art and the Law: The Passing of the Obscene Publications Act, 1857." *Victorian Studies* 28(4): 609–29.

Roby, Pamela. 1969. "Politics and the Criminal Law: Revision of the New York State Penal Law on Prostitution." *Social Problems* 17(1): 83–109.

Rolling Stone. 2014. "30 Nearly Pornographic Mainstream Films." Accessed 16 September 2014. http://www.rollingstone.com/movies/pictures/barely-legal-30-nearly-pornographic-mainstream-films-20140318.

Rosecrance, Richard. 1998. "The European Union: A New Type of International Actor." In *Paradoxes of European Foreign Policy*, edited by Jan Zielonka, 15–24. The Hague: Kluwer Law International.

Rosenberg, Harold, John Melville and P. C. McLean. 2002. "Acceptability and Availability of Pharmacological Interventions for Substance Misuse by British NHS Treatment Services." *Addiction* 97(1): 59–65.

Rosenburg, Gerald. 2008. *The Hollow Hope: Can Court Bring about Social Change?* Chicago: University of Chicago Press.

Roszak, Theodore. 1970. *The Making of a Counter Culture: Reflections on the Technocratic Society and Its Youthful Opposition*. London: Faber.

Roynon, Tessa. 2013. *Toni Morrison and the Classical Tradition: Transforming American Culture*. Oxford: Oxford University Press.

Ruhama. 2015. "Submission to the European Commission in response to the Template for National Rapporteurs or Equivalent Mechanisms and in contribution to the upcoming report according Art. 20 of Directive 2011/36/EU by the Irish Civil Society Organisations (CSO) in the EU Anti-trafficking Platform: Doras Luimní, Immigrant Council of Ireland and Ruhama." http://www.ruhama.ie/assets/Press-Releases/Submission-to-2015-EC-re-NREM-by-Irish-CSO-members-of-the-EU-AT-Platfrom.pdf

Rumney, Philip. 2006. "False Allegations of Rape." *Cambridge Law Journal* 65(1): 125–58.

Russell, Diane. 1990. *Rape in Marriage*. Indiana: Indiana University Press.

Ryan, Rebecca M. 1995. "The Sex Right: A Legal History of the Marital Rape Exemption." *Law & Social Inquiry* 20(4): 941–1001.

Ryle, Michael. 1966. "Private Members' Bills." *Political Quarterly* 37(4): 385–93.

Sabatier, Paul. 1988. "An Advocacy Coalition Framework of Policy Change and the Role of Policy-Orientated Learning Therein." *Policy Sciences* 21(2-3): 129–68.

Sarikakis, Katharine. 2015. "Making Public Policy in the Digital Age: The Sex Industry as a Political Actor." In *The Routledge Companion to Media and Gender*, edited by Cynthia Carter, Linda Steiner and Lisa McLaughlin, 211–21. Oxford: Routledge.

Sanders, Teela. 2004. "A Continuum of Risk? The Management of Health, Physical and Emotional Risks by Female Sex Workers." *Sociology of Health and Illness* 26(5): 557–74.

Sanders, Teela. 2005. "Blinded by Morality? Prostitution Policy in the UK." *Capital and Class* 29(2): 9–15.

Sanders, Teela. 2006. "Behind the Personal Ads: The Indoor Sex Markets in Britain." In *Sex Work Now*, edited by Rosie Campbell and Maggie O'Neill, 9–115. Devon: Willan Publishing.

Sanders, Teela. 2010. "The Sex Industry, Regulation and the Internet." In *Handbook of Internet Crime*, edited by Yvonne Jewkes and Majid Yar, 302–17. Oxford: Routledge.

Saunders, Corinne. 2001. *Rape and Ravishment in the Literature on Medieval England*. Cambridge: D. S. Brewer.

Sawyer, Steven, Michael Metz, Jeffrey Hinds and Robert Brucker. 2001. "Attitudes towards Prostitution among Males: A 'Consumers' Report.'" *Current Psychology* 20(4): 363–76.

Scambler, Graham and Frederique Paoli. 2008. "Health Work, Female Sex Workers and HIV/ AIDS: Global and Local Dimensions of Stigma and Deviance As Barriers to Effective Interventions." *Social Science and Medicine* 66(8): 1848–62.

Scarman, Lord J. 1981. *The Brixton Disorders, 10th-12th April,* London: HMSO.

Schmidt, Viven. 2000. "Values and Discourse in the Politics of Adjustment." In *Welfare and Work in the Open Economy, Vol. I: From Vulnerability to Competitiveness,* edited by Fritz Scharpf and Viven Schmidt, 229–30. Oxford: Oxford University Press.

Schmidt, Vivien. 2008. "Discursive Institutionalism: The Explanatory Power of Ideas and Discourse." *Annual Review of Political Science* 11: 303–26.

Schmidt, Vivien. 2010. 'Taking Ideas and Discourse Seriously: Explaining Change through Discursive Institutionalism." *European Political Science Review* 2: 1–25.

Schwirtz, Michael. 2012. "Senate Candidate Provokes Ire with 'Legitimate Rape' Comments." *New York Times*, 19 August. Accessed 13 August 2015. http://www.nytimes.com/2012/08/ 20/us/politics/todd-akin-provokes-ire-with-legitimate-rape-comment.html

Scoular, Jane and Maggie O'Neill. 2007. "Regulating Prostitution: Social Inclusion, Responsibilization and the Politics of Prostitution Reform: Regulating Prostitution." *British Journal of Criminology* 47(5): 764–78.

Scoular, Jane and Anna Carline. 2014. "A Critical Account of a 'Creeping Neo-Abolitionism': Regulating Prostitution in England and Wales." *Criminology and Criminal Justice* 14(5): 608–26.

Scully, Diana and Joseph Marolla. 1984. "Convicted Rapists' Vocabulary of Motive: Excuses and Justifications." *Social Problems* 31(5): 530–44.

Shah, Nishant. 2015. "Sluts 'r' us: Intersections of Gender, Protocol and Agency in the Digital Age." *First Monday* 20(4).

Shaver, S. 1994. "Body Rights, Social Rights and the Liberal Welfare State." *Critical Social Policy* 13(39): 66–93.

Shelley, Louise. 2007. "Human Trafficking as a Form of Transnational Crime." In *Human Trafficking*, edited by Maggy Lee, 116–37. Devon: Willan Publishing.

Shepsle, Kenneth. 1979. "Institutional Arrangements and Equilibrium in Multidimensional Voting Models." *American Journal of Political Science* 23: 23–57.

Shepsle, Kenneth. 1989. "Studying Institutions: Some Lessons from the Rational Choice Approach." *Journal of Theoretical Politics* 1(2): 131–47.

Shepsle, Kenneth. 2006. "Rational Choice Institutionalism." In *The Oxford Handbook of Political Institutions*, edited by Rod Rhodes, Sarah Binder and Bert Rockman, 23–38. Oxford: Oxford University Press.

Shrage, Laurie. 1989. "Should Feminists Oppose Prostitution." *Ethics* 99(2): 347–61.

Shroder, Joy. 1997. "The Rape of Dinah: Luther's Interpretation of a Biblical Narrative." *Sixteenth Century Journal* 28(3): 775–91.

Sigel, Lisa, and Harry Cocks. 2001. "Governing Pleasures: Pornography and Social Change in England." Rutgers.

Simms, Madeleine. 1971. "The Abortion Act after Three Years." *Political Quarterly* 42(3): 233–52.

Singh, Anita. 2012. "Fifty Shades of Grey is bestselling book of all time." *The Telegraph*, 7 August. Accessed 12 March 2015. http://www.telegraph.co.uk/culture/books/booknews/ 9459779/50-Shades-of-Grey-is-best-selling-book-of-all-time.html

Sinozich, Sofi and Lynn Langton. 2014. "Special Report: Rape and Sexual Assault among College-Age Females, 1995-2013." *U.S. Department of Justice, Office of Justice Programs, Bureau of Justice Statistics.* Accessed 12 December 2014. http://www.bjs.gov/content/pub/ pdf/rsavcaf9513.pdf

Skocpol, Theda. 2002. *Protecting Soldiers and Mothers: The Political Origins of Social Policy in the United States.* Cambridge: Cambridge University Press.

Skolnick, Jerome. 2002. "Corruption and the Blue Code of Silence." *Police Practice and Research* 3(1): 7–19.

Sleath, Emma and Ray Bull. 2015. "A Brief Report on Rape Myth Acceptance: Differences Between Police Officers, Law Students, and Psychology Students in the United Kingdom." *Violence and Victims* 30(1): 136–47.

Smeaton, John. 2009. "Family Doctors Oppose Early Medical Abortion Which Politicians Want." 10 February. Accessed 28 April 2015. http://spuc-director.blogspot.co.uk/2009/02/family-doctors-oppose-early-medical.html

Smith, Allison. 1996. *The Victorian Nude: Sexuality, Morality, and Art.* New York, St. Martin's Press.

Smith, F. B. 1971. Ethics and disease in the later nineteenth century: The contagious diseases acts." *Historical Studies* 15:57, 118–35.

Smith, F. 1990. "The Contagious Diseases Acts Reconsidered." *Social History of Medicine* 3(2): 197–215.

Smith, James. 2006. *Ireland's Magdalen Laundries and the Nation's Architecture of Containment.* Notre Dame: University of Notre Dame Press.

Smith, David. 2014. "Oscar Pistorius jailed for five years for culpable homicide of Reeva Steenkamp." *The Guardian*, 21 October. Accessed 26 October 2014. http://www.theguardian.com/world/2014/oct/21/oscar-pistorius-jailed-five-years-culpable-homicide-reeva-steenkamp

Smith, Ronald, John Keating, Reid Hester and Herman Mitchell. 1976. "Role and Justice Considerations in the Attribution of Responsibility to a Rape Victim." *Journal of Research in Personality* 10(3): 346–57.

Sneddon, Ian and John Kremer. 1992. "Sexual Behaviour and Attitudes of University Students in Northern Ireland." *Archives of Sexual Behavior* 21(3): 295–312.

Soderlund, Gretchen. 2005. "Running from the Rescuers: New US Crusades against Sex Trafficking and the Rhetoric of Abolition." *NWSA Journal* 17(30): 64–87.

Steinmo, Sven, Kathleen Thelen, and Frank Longstreth. 1992. *Structuring Politics: Historical Institutionalism in Comparative Analysis.* Cambridge, UK: Cambridge University Press.

Stern, Baroness Vivien. 2010. *The Stern Review: A Report by Baroness Vivien Stern CBE of an Independent Review into How Rape Complaints Are Handled by Public Authorities in England and Wales.* Government Equalities Office and Home Office, London.

Stolberg, Sheryl Gay and Robert Pear. 2010. "Wary Centrists Posing Challenge in Health Care Vote." *New York Times*, 27 February. Accessed 28 February 2010. http://www.nytimes.com/2010/02/28/us/politics/28health.html.

Stone, Diane. 1999. "Learning Lessons and Transferring Policy across Time, Space and Disciplines." *Politics* 19(1): 51–59.

Stormo, Karia, Alan Land and Werner Stritzke. 1997. "Attributions about Acquaintance Rape: The Role of Alcohol and Individual Differences." *Journal of Applied Social Psychology* 27(4): 279–305.

Strøm, Kaare. 1997. "Rules, Reasons and Routines: Legislative Roles in Parliamentary Democracies." *Journal of Legislative Studies* 3(1): 155–74.

Strossen, Nadine. 2000. *Defending Pornography: Free Speech, Sex and Women's Rights.* New York: New York University Press.

Sulitzeanu-Kenan, Raanan. 2006. "If They Get It Right: An Experimental Test of the Effects of the Appointment and Reports of UK Public Inquiries." *Public Administration* 84(3): 623–53.

Sunstein, Cass. 1986. "Pornography and the First Amendment." *Duke Law Journal* 4: 589–627.

Sutherland, John. 1982. *Offensive Literature: Decensorship in Britian, 1960-1982.* London: Junction Books.

Sutton, Julia, 2014. "Prostitute Was Raped and Robbed by Luton Teenager Ali Hafeez a Court Is Told." *Luton on Sunday*, 30 June. Accessed 16 September 2015. http://www.luton-dunstable.co.uk/Prostitute-raped-robbed-Luton-teenager-Ali-Hafeez-court-told/story-21703219-detail/story.html

Svanström, Yvonne. 2004. "Criminalising the John—A Swedish Gender Model?" In *The Politics of Prostitution: Women's Movements, Democratic States and the Globalisation of Sex Commerce*, edited by Joyce Outshoorn, 225–44. Cambridge: Cambridge University Press.

Taylor Francis Group. 2014. "Routledge Journals Publishes Porn Studies." Accessed 3 September 2015 http://newsroom.taylorandfrancisgroup.com/news/press-release/routledge-journals-publishes-porn-studies#.VF9acL_0tUM

Taylor, N., and J. Joudo. 2005. "The impact of pre-recorded video and closed circuit television testimony by adult sexual assault complainants on jury decision-making: an experimental study." Research and Public Policy Series no. 68. Canberra: Australian Institute of Criminology.

Telegraph reporters. 2012. "£1000 a night 'high class' escort jailed over £120,000 tax fraud." 10 July. Accessed May 16 2015. http://www.telegraph.co.uk/finance/personalfinance/tax/9388075/1000-a-night-high-class-escort-jailed-over-120000-tax-fraud.html

Temkin, Jennifer. 2000. "Prosecuting and Defending Rape: Perspectives from the Bar." *Journal of Law and Society* 27(2): 219–48.

Temkin, Jennifer. 2002. *Rape and the Legal Process.* Oxford: Oxford University Press.

Terrill, Richard. 2012. *World Criminal Justice Systems: A Comparative Survey.* London: Routledge.

The Independent. 2010. "BANNED: Books you could have been jailed for reading." http://www.independent.co.uk/arts-entertainment/books/features/banned-books-you-could-have-been-jailed-for-reading-1876200.html

Thelen, Kathleen. 1999. "Historical institutionalism in comparative politics." *Annual Review of Political Science* 2(1): 369–404.

The Telegraph. 2015. "Karen Buckley killing: Judge suggest student 'put herself in vulnerable position' by drinking." http://www.telegraph.co.uk/news/uknews/law-and-order/11556187/Karen-Buckley-killing-Judge-suggests-student-put-herself-in-vulnerable-position-by-drinking.html

Thistlethwaite, Susan. 1993. "You May Enjoy the Spoil of Your Enemies: Rape as a Biblical Metaphor for War." *Semeia* 61: 59–75.

Thompson, Hazel. 2013. "Prostitution: Why Swedes believe they got it right." 11 December, *The Guardian.* Accessed 15 December 2014. http://www.theguardian.com/global-development/2013/dec/11/prostitution-sweden-model-reform-men-pay-sex

Trinks, Stephan. 2013. "Sheela-na-gig Again: The Birth of a New Style from the Spirit of Pornography." In *Pornographic Art and the Aesthetics of Pornography*, edited by Hans Maes, 163–182. Basingstoke: Palgrave Macmillan.

Tropp, Laura. 2006. "'Faking a Sonogram': Representations of Motherhood on *Sex and the City*." *Journal of Popular Culture* 39(5): 861–77.

Tseblis, George. 1990. *Nested Games: rational Choice in Comparative Politics.* California, California University Press.

Tsebelis, George. 2002. *Veto Payers: How Political Institutions Work.* Princeton: Princeton University Press.

Tsutsumi, Atsuro, Takashi Izutsu, Amod Poudyal, Seika Kato and Eiji Marui. 2008. "Mental Health of Female Survivors of Human Trafficking in Nepal." *Social Science and Medicine* 66(8): 1841–47.

Tumanov, Vladimir. 2011. "Mary Versus Eve: Paternal Uncertainty and the Christian View of Women." *Neophilologus* 95: 507–21.

UK Network of Sex Work Projects. 2007. "Good Practice Guidance: Ugly Mugs and Dodgy Punters." Accessed 16 April 2015. http://www.uknswp.org/wp-content/uploads/GPG1.pdf

Under Siege Project. 2013. "Poynter: CNN's Steubenville coverage called too sympathetic to teens found guilty." Accessed 10 February 2015. http://www.womenundersiegeproject.org/blog/entry/poynter-cnns-steubenville-coverage-called-too-sympathetic-to-teens-found-gu

United Nations. 2015. "Resources for Speakers on Global Issues: Ending Violence Against Women and Girls." 6 June. Accessed 18 October 2015: http://www.un.org/en/globalissues/briefingpapers/endviol/index.shtml

United Nations Division for the Advancement of Women. 2009. *Violence Against Women: Handbook and Supplement for Legislation.* New York: United Nations.

United Nations Office on Drugs and Crime. 2014. *Global Report on Trafficking in Persons.* New York: United Nations.

Urquhart, D. and A. Templeton. 1990. "The Use of Mifepristone Prior to Prostaglandin-Induced Mid-Trimester Abortion." *Human Reproduction* 5(7): 883–86.

U.S. Department of State. 2014. Trafficking in Persons Report. http://www.state.gov/documents/organization/226844.pdf

Van den Hoek, Anneke, Fu Yuliand, Nicole Duckers, Chen Zhiheng, Feng Jiangting, Zhang Lina and Zhang Xiuxing. 2001. "High Prevalence of Syphilis and Other Sexually Transmitted Diseases among Sex Workers in China: Potential for Fast Spread Of HIV." *AIDS* 15(6): 753–59.

Vaughan-Williams, Nick. 2007. "The shooting of Jean Charles de Menezes: New border politics?" *Alternatives: Global, Local, Political* 32(2): 177–95.

Venkatesh, Sudhir. 2011. "How Tech Tools Transformed New York's Sex Trade." Accessed 5 May 2015. http://www.wired.com/2011/01/ff_sextrade/all/

Visher, Christy. 1987. "Juror Decision Making: The Importance of Evidence." *Law and Human Behavior* 11(1): 1–17.

Von Wahl, Angelika. 2008. "From Family to Reconciliation Policy: How the Grand Coalition Reforms the German Welfare State." *German Politics and Society* 26(3): 25–49.

Waddington, Peter. 1999. "Police (Canteen) Sub-Culture. An Appreciation." *British Journal of Criminology* 39(2): 287–309.

Walker, Kirsty. 2010. "Tories In 'Dodgy' Statistics Row over False Claims of Soaring Teenage Pregnancies." *Mail Online*, 15 February. Accessed 1 July 2015. http://www.dailymail.co.uk/news/article-1251045/Tories-row-teenage-pregnancy-figure-error.html

Walkowitz, Judith and Daniel Walkowitz. 1973. "'We Are Not Beasts of the Field': Prostitution and the Poor in Plymouth and Southampton Under the Contagious Diseases Acts." *Feminist Studies* 1(3/4): 73–106.

Walkowitz, Judith. 1980. *Prostitution and Victorian Society: Women, Class and the State.* Cambridge: Cambridge University Press.

Ward, Helen, Sophie Day and Jonathan Weber. 1999. "Risky Business: Health and Safety in the Sex Industry over a 9 Year Period." *Sexually Transmitted Infections* 75(5): 340–43.

Warden, John. 1990. "Abortion and Conscience." *British Medical Journal* 301: 1103.

Warhurst, John. 2008. "Conscience Voting in the Australian Federal Parliament." *Australian Journal of Politics and History* 54(4): 579–96.

Weingourt, Rita. 1990. "Wife Rape in a Sample of Psychiatric Patients." *Journal of Nursing Scholarship* 22(3): 144–47.

Weiss, Robert and Charles Samenow. 2010. "Smart Phones, Social Networking, Sexting and Problematic Sexual Behaviors—A Call for Research." *Sexual Addiction and Compulsivity* 17(4): 241–46.

Weitzer, Ronald. 1999. "Prostitution Control in America: Rethinking Public Policy." *Crime, Law and Social Change* 32(1): 83–102.

Weitzer, Ronald. 2010. "The Movement to Criminalize Sex Work in the United States." *Journal of Law and Society* 37:1: 61–84.

Weitzer, Ronald. 2011. "Sex Trafficking and the Sex Industry: The Need for Evidence-Based Theory and Legislation." *Journal of Criminal Law and Criminology* 1337–69.

Weitzer, Ronald. 2012. *Legalizing Prostitution: From Illicit Vice to Lawful Business.* New York: New York University Press.

West, Jackie. 2000. "Prostitution: Collectives and the Politics of Regulation." *Gender, Work and Organization* 7(2): 106–18.

West, Jackie and Terry Austin. 2005. "Markets and Politics: Public and Private Relations in the Case of Prostitution." *Sociological Review* 53(s2): 136–48.

Whatley, M. 1993. "For Better or Worse: The Case of Marital Rape." *Violence and Victims* 8(1): 29–39.

Whatley, Mark. 2005. "The Effect of Participant Sex, Victim Dress, and Traditional Attitudes on Casual Judgments for Marital Rape Victims." *Journal of Family Violence* 20(3): 191–200.

Whelehan, Patricia. 2001. *An Anthropological Perspective on Prostitution: The World's Oldest Profession.* London: Edwin Mellon Press.

Williams, Brandon. 1987. "Legislation and Parliament." *Statute Law Review* 8(3): 138–41.

Winter, Søeren. 1985. "Implementation Barriers." *Politica* 17(4): 467–87.

Winter, Søeren. 1986. "How Policy-Making Affects Implementation: The Decentralization of the Danish Disablement Pension Administration." *Scandinavian Political Studies* 9(4): 361–85.

Wlezien, Christopher. 1996. "Dynamics of Representation: The Case of US Spending on Defence." *British Journal of Political Science* 26(1): 81–103.

Wolff, Larry. 1996. "'The Boys Are Pickpockets, and the Girl Is a Prostitute': Gender and Juvenile Criminality in Early Victorian England from Oliver Twist to London Labour." *New Literary History* 27(2): 227–49.

Woodhouse, Diana. 1995. "Matrix Churchill: A Case Study of Judicial Inquiries." *Parliamentary Affairs* 48(1): 24–39.

World Health Organisation. 2014. "Consolidated guidelines on HIV prevention, diagnosis, treatment and care for key populations." http://www.who.int/hiv/pub/guidelines/keypopulations/en/

Wozniak, Danielle. 1997. "Foster Mothers in Contemporary America: Objectification, Commodification, Sexualization." *Women's History Review* 6(3): 357–66.

Young-Powell, Abby. 2014. "Oxford Student Union Removes Editor Who Said Alleged Rape Victim Lied." *The Guardian*, 25 September. Accessed 14 December 2014. http://www. theguardian.com/education/2014/sep/25/oxford-editor-removed-after-blaming-rape-victim

Zehr, Howard and Harry Mika. 2003. "Fundamental Concepts of Restorative Justice." In *Restorative Justice: Critical Issues*, edited by Eugene McLaughlin, Ross Fergusson, Gordon Hughes and Louise Westmarland, 40–43. London: Sage.

Zillmann, Dolf and Jennings Bryant. 1982. "Pornography and Sexual Callousness, and the Trivialization of Rape." *Journal of Communication* 32(4): 10–21.

Index

162, 164, 166, 171; rights, 18, 35, 88;
  bodily autonomy, 24; health, 88
Women's Under Siege Project, 97
world's oldest profession, 63, 73
World War II, 35

Yorkshire Ripper, 83
Youth Justice and Criminal Evidence Act
  1999, 96, 100

zero-tolerance, 63, 79